HERE ARE JUST SOME OF THE ADVANTAGES YOU SHOULD KNOW ABOUT NO-LOAD MUTUAL FUNDS . . .

*DIVERSIFICATION—With the ups and downs of the stock market, it's not wise for anyone to corner his or her investments in single stocks. A mutual fund pools many investors' contributions and thereby spreads their risk.

*NO-LOAD—As the investment climate changes, it is easy and inexpensive to *switch* your investment because there are *no transaction costs.* In many cases it simply means placing a toll-free phone call.

*GOOD, PROFESSIONAL MANAGEMENT—Your hard-earned money is invested by people who know what they're doing, and you can choose from a *wide range of funds* that vary from the conservative to the very aggressive (but potentially high growth).

*TAX BENEFITS—New tax shelters for everyone: IRAs and salary-reduction programs give you unprecedented opportunities to shelter your investment earnings from taxes—*and take a deduction off your taxes as well.*

FIND OUT ALL YOU NEED TO KNOW IN
WILLIAM E. DONOGHUE'S
NO-LOAD MUTUAL FUND GUIDE

"*Newsday* calls him the money market guru; Louis Rukeyser of 'Wall Street Week' calls him 'a man unburdened by false modesty'; and the Federal Reserve calls him every Thursday."
—A recent introduction of Donoghue to the New York Society of Security Analysts

"The Maharishi of the mutual funds."
—ABC Talkradio

QUANTITY PURCHASES

William E. Donoghue's

NO-LOAD MUTUAL FUND GUIDE

How to Take Advantage of the Investment Opportunities of the Eighties

WILLIAM E. DONOGHUE
with THOMAS TILLING

BANTAM BOOKS
TORONTO · NEW YORK · LONDON · SYDNEY

This low-priced Bantam Book
has been completely reset in a type face
designed for easy reading, and was printed
from new plates. It contains the complete
text of the original hard-cover edition.
NOT ONE WORD HAS BEEN OMITTED.

WILLIAM E. DONOGHUE'S NO-LOAD MUTUAL FUND GUIDE

A Bantam Book / published by arrangement with
Harper & Row, Publishers, Inc.

PRINTING HISTORY

Harper & Row edition published March 1983
7 printings through May 1983

A Selection of Book-of-the-Month Club, March 1983
Fortune Book Club Dual Main Selection, March 1983
Macmillan Book Club Selection, July 1983

This book is sold with the understanding that neither the
Author nor the Publisher is engaged in rendering legal or
accounting services. Questions relevant to the practice of law
or accounting should be addressed to a member of those
professions.

The Author and Publisher specifically disclaim any liability,
loss, or risk, personal or otherwise, which is incurred as a
consequence, directly or indirectly, of the use and application
of any of the contents of this work.

Bantam edition / February 1984

ISBN 0-553-24166-4

Published simultaneously in the United States and Canada

PRINTED IN THE UNITED STATES OF AMERICA

O   0 9 8 7 6 5 4 3 2 1

Contents

Foreword to the 1984 Edition

Sometimes my timing amazes even me. I finished writing the first edition of this book in July 1982. The following month, on August 13, 1982 to be exact, a "double-your-money" bull market began.

While bull markets come along only once in a while, I would not be surprised if this one lasted for a few years. In fact, you can do well even during bear markets if you avoid stock market losses by investing in the money market.

The SLYC system which is described in this book has an excellent track record, at least when tested in retrospect. If you had followed the SLYC system over the past five years (from June 1978 to June 1983) and made a decision only once a month and ten times out of twelve decided to do nothing, you could have earned, on the average, 29.94% a year using the fund families we recommended. Using the SLYC system with the top performing family's funds you would have earned almost 45% average annual rate of return for the five years ending June 30, 1983—without taking substantial risks or giving up liquidity.

Combine that with a $2,000 annual contribution to your Individual Retirement Account, established with a no-load mutual fund family and not a bank, and if you could sustain that average—sorry, no guarantees—you could retire an after-tax millionaire in just 21 years.

You can do it—and this book can show you how. I'm on your side. Let me help.

Acknowledgments to the 1984 Edition

Many people assisted in the completion of the 1984 edition of this book. I would particularly like to thank the following members of The Donoghue Organization staff: Alan Lavine, research editor, and Jeffrey L. Seglin, editor-in-chief, who gathered the current data and organized the material for the updated edition. Connie Bugbee and her staff in the statistics department, Mary Hogy and Jeanne Long, did essential statistical work for the new edition. Lindsay Jones, Donoghue's MONEY FUND REPORT® editor, John Waggoner, staff editor, Tom Picton, editorial assistant, and John Morrill, student intern, also contributed to the effort. Gay Seemann of Monitored Assets Corporation in Iowa supplied valuable mutual fund data.

William E. Donoghue
President, The Donoghue Organization, Inc.
Holliston, MA 01746

Foreword

Within the past decade, three events occurred that changed my life dramatically. Two of those events altered your life and the lives of millions of American savers and investors just as radically.

The first event occurred in 1972, when Reserve Fund registered the original money market mutual fund with the Securities and Exchange Commission. Although Reserve Fund initially led a lonely life, by 1977 it had a host of fellow travelers in the financial community. And by 1981 over ten million investors had parked their money in money funds.

The second event was double-digit inflation, whose dark-side-of-the-moon shadow, disinflation, now haunts us. (This specter used to be called "deflation," but that sounded too similar to "depression" for political comfort, and so the fourth estate and Washington devised the new term "disinflation.") Whatever words you use to describe the phenomenon, costs and interest rates in recent years have been shooting up, and occasionally plunging, as never before in this country. That comfortable I-know-what-it-costs-and-how-much-my-money-will-earn world everyone used to take for granted is gone. And with it is gone the old you-can-bank-on-it investment mentality.

The third event was much more personal. I was "liberated" from my job as manager of financial information systems at a $2 billion retailing firm. My understanding boss agreed that I had more potential elsewhere. This occurrence gave me time to study the other two events more closely. Over the next few years, I became an expert in the field of short-term financial management, a fledgling financial writer, an investor in money funds, and, in 1977, the publisher of a newsletter on that subject.

How have these events changed your life? Since June 1, 1978, Savers' Liberation Day (when the banks first entered the retail, or consumer, money market business by offering the public $10,000-minimum, six-month money market certificates), over one trillion dollars in individual investors' money, fleeing inflation, has found its way into the retail money market. That's over 63 percent of America's total savings that would probably still be earning 5.5 percent or less had it not been for the first pioneer money fund which put so disturbing a bee in the financial community's bonnet.

I was the first with that story, showing how your money could be earning two, three, or even four times what it was earning in the bank, in my last book, *William E. Donoghue's Complete Money Market Guide*. Now, in this companion volume, I'm going to show you how to move forward from there, taking advantage of the changes that have occurred since that time and profiting from the new opportunities opening up in the fast-fluctuating investment world today.

In 1981, the average money fund earned its shareholders a total compounded annual return of 16.8 percent. The top money fund for the year earned its investors 18 percent. Fewer than two dozen professionally managed mutal funds investing in the stock and bond markets were able to exceed that yield. Only three of forty-four investment portfolios, managed on the advice of the nation's top financial newsletter publishers, were able to top the performance of the average money fund, and only one topped the highest-yielding money fund. For only one week during the entire year of 1981 did bank-offered six-month money market certificates (the $10,000-minimum variety) offer a yield higher than that which the average money fund offered for the year. Ninety-eight percent of the time you were better off in a money fund.

"Why then," you have every right to ask, "are you now writing a book on mutual funds?" The answer is that interest rates and the stock and bond markets are alive and

well and living on a new Wall Street. There's a new time
and place for them, just as there's still a time and place for
money funds in your investment planning. And now,
particularly, is the time for an integrated switching strategy that provides the means for you to move your money
from money funds to stock funds in order to maximize
your yields—and get it out of stock funds and back into a
money fund when that's the only safe place for it to be.
Have you ever noticed how investment advisers always
seem to be able to tell you what and when to buy, but
not what and when to sell? Selling right is every bit as
important as buying right, and I'll show you how to do
both.

*Even if you only have $100 with which to start your invest-
ment portfolio, you owe it to yourself to read this book.* If you are
one of the millions of Americans who had the guts and
intelligence to move their money into the money market,
you've taken the first step in gaining control of your
financial life and you're ready for the next.

Buy, hold, and pray, the traditional long-term strategy
of the stock market investor, is dead. It's been buried in
the shifting sands of a rapidly changing marketplace. Today you must be prepared to move intelligently and
skillfully, in and out of new investments, in a new market.

But you ask, "How can I make sense out of today's
complex financial playing field if even the professionals
can't?" The answer, contrary to what most bankers and
brokers will tell you, is that it's not *that* difficult, honestly it
isn't. And this book is going to give you a handle on the
markets, and tell you when to take hold of that handle and
when to let go of it.

My mother once said to me, "Bill, your father never
taught me how to be a widow," and it really brought home
to me how many investors were totally confused by all of
the market mumbo jumbo. Small savers (I'm one—and
I'm six feet two) need simple, easy-to-follow investment
guidance that will help them keep their savings ahead of
inflation without significant risk. They need it in language
that doesn't take a Ph.D. to understand.

So, I wrote this book, as I did my last, for my mother.
I've tried to keep the information simple, accurate, and to
the point. My objective is to teach you the skills you need
to make your money work as hard as you do. And once

you know the ropes, you'll understand why I say, "Sophisticated investing doesn't have to be complicated—just smart." You'll also notice that this book is *not* called "*The* Complete Mutual Fund Guide." You really don't need to have me tell you about a lot of useless mutual funds which have outlasted their original purpose, do you?

Today is the first day of the rest of your financial life. So let's get started on some down-to-earth planning for it.

Acknowledgments

Many authors of bestsellers never produce another. Many newsletter publishers are experts in only one subject area. Many writers prefer the solitary life, choosing to write their works unassisted. None of these descriptions fit my style.

While I am responsible for its contents and believe strongly in its advice, this book is the result of the efforts of several of my key colleagues. Coordinating our efforts with my collaborator Thomas Tilling and his creative partner and wife Susan was Jennifer K. Brown, Vice President and Managing Editor of The Donoghue Organization, Inc., without whom this project would not have been completed. Assisting her were staffers Conrad Grundlehner, editor of *Donoghue's Mutual Funds Almanac*, and Alan Lavine, research editor, along with William Crawford, Sr., a mutual funds expert.

Special mention must be made of the support and encouragement of Edward Burlingame, publisher at Harper & Row, and his able editors, Nancy Crawford (who started this project) and Sallie Coolidge (who saw it through to its conclusion).

Less direct, but equally important, has been the assistance of Connie Bugbee, my secretary; Lisa R. Sheeran, editor of *Donoghue's Moneyletter;* Barbara Akerley, editor of *Donoghue's Money Fund Report* of Holliston, MA 01746; and

Mary Coffey, whose skill as a production manager resulted in the clear and useful charts in this book.

I would also like to thank our consultants Al Krause, Carol Launer, Frances Harriman, Allen Grieve, and B. P. Fulmer, who have helped us develop and mold our corporate image and philosophy. Special thanks go to Marie Cardinal Hansen, who taught me how to carry my message "to the folks." Thank you's for assistance in researching some of the key insights in this book are due Marcia Horn of Investment Company Institute; Rich McFarland, Morris Smith, and Fred Newcomb of the No-Load Mutual Fund Association; and Victor Kramer of the Fidelity Group of mutual funds.

As you can see, quite a few people have contributed to this volume and have put their hearts and souls into providing you with the best investing advice. Now it is up to you to read, learn, and implement our investment plan for you.

—William E. Donoghue, President
The Donoghue Organization, Inc.

1

Investing for the Eighties

> We should all be concerned about
> the future because we will have to
> spend the rest of our lives there.
> —*Charles F. Kettering*

A few years ago, you were faced with a few easy financial choices for your savings. If you wanted government insurance and average interest, you put your money in the bank or in savings bonds. If you wanted to try to take advantage of industrial growth, playing for higher returns (but less safety), you bought stocks. If you were really a crapshooter at heart, maybe you even put some of your money in commodities—in which case that's most likely the last you saw of it.

Except for bonds and Treasury bills, usually the domain of the rich, these were about the only alternatives available for stashing your cash. Now, suddenly, a whole smorgasbord of investment possibilities and services is being unveiled before the individual. Many of them look inviting—but beware of colorful enticements! Some of them seem plain fare—yet are they better nourishment for your dollars? How do you choose among them?

Chances are you already have a large part of your liquid assets in a high-yielding money fund. And while a money fund provides safety for your savings, if that's the only place you're keeping your cash, chances are you're not utilizing the fund market to its fullest potential. The fact is that in today's volatile economy, money funds are only one of the keys to financial success. There are times when switching to another investment medium may be better for your money.

Put into money funds alone, your cash has been earning an average of 12 to 15 percent over the last couple of years. Coupling a switching strategy to your money fund, on the other hand, could have earned you a return of close to 20 percent over the same period of time. If the idea of earning an extra 7 percent or so on your money appeals to you, read on.

Mutual funds are the investments of the eighties—but not just one plain old mutual fund, even if it's a money fund. What I'm talking about here are the new series, or families, of mutual funds that allow you to ride the choppy waves of the market on a multihulled catamaran. These new mutual funds are a far cry indeed from the high-commission ripoffs of the sixties whose high-pressure salesmen ate caviar while they watched your cookie jar being cracked to pieces. So don't confuse the two. The new mutual funds are no-load funds, and they're a long-overdue commission-free way to invest in the stock and bond markets today.

What is a mutual fund? It's a way for many people to do collectively what they cannot do separately. It is much cheaper to hire an investment manager to manage a mutual fund for thousands of investors with a common goal than for each of us to hire a stockbroker.

The advantages are obvious: (1) Professional management, which is required by law to work for the investors' best interest (*not* for the managers, as in a bank); (2) more in-depth research and management of investment than each of us could afford; (3) more and better diversification than a small investor could afford; (4) little or no cost to buy or sell shares of the fund; and (5) most important, a third party—a bank or trust company—to hold the assets of the fund to provide necessary controls. Mutual funds are designed to serve *you*.

If you have a money fund account, you're already part-owner of a mutual fund, since a money fund is simply a highly specialized mutual fund. And just as money funds exploded in growth during 1980 and 1981 when the small investor realized he could liberate his money from his savings account and earn twice to three times as much on it elsewhere, now a lot of shrewd money is slipping quietly but quickly into no-load mutual funds. Why?

It's certainly not that the stock market has kept up with inflation. Far from it. That's exactly the reason a company like DuPont, for instance, was willing to pay some $7.5 billion to acquire Conoco—to pay, in other words, $92 a share for stock selling for $45 a share. *It was like buying fifty-cent pieces with dollar bills;* because of inflation, DuPont felt Conoco was a bargain.

Stock prices have been sitting in the doldrums for so long that many companies are selling for half, sometimes even less than half, of what their equipment and plants are worth, not to mention what their inventory, goodwill, and other accouterments should bring in the marketplace. The companies with cash are simply buying inflation-depressed assets at a bargain.

Now if you could spend tens of millions of dollars buying up companies at a fire sale, you too could make a bundle. If you don't have that kind of cash laying around, well, you can still make a bundle. You can do it through the new no-load mutual funds—provided you have the know-how to make the right choices, and provided you understand what's been happening.

That's the information this book is going to give you—the investment know-how and the understanding you need to use funds wisely. It will show you

- what you can do with mutual funds—and what they can do for you
- why they work so well—and when they don't
- how they are taxed—or not taxed
- how their dividend policies affect you
- how they can turn your ordinary gains into capital gains taxed at a much lower rate
- the best way to use them in IRAs and Keoghs
- their crucial ability to take advantage of the seemingly contradictory concepts of diversification and specialization

It will also explain the SLYC strategy for staying *safe*, staying *liquid*, earning a high *yield*, and *catastrophe-proofing* your earnings (so you can sleep at night). Whether you start with $100 or $100,000, and whether the stock market is going up *or* down, I want to help you learn to stay ahead of inflation—with something left for the golden years.

This book takes a no-bulls, no-bears, no-manure approach to investing, based on the premise that you work hard for your money and your money should work hard for you. The last thing you need to do is lose it.

I'm going to discuss frankly why mutual funds nearly ruined a good thing back in the early seventies, and why, with a brand-new philosophy, they are making a spectacular comeback. It's an enlightening story—with a future for you.

Banking, on the other hand, is today an adventure at best. There are very few good investment opportunities to recommend the use of bank products and services. For the most part you'll want to avoid them. But I'll tell you why, when, and to what extent to take advantage of opportunities that do exist in this possibly soon-to-disappear field.

With over 650 mutual funds in existence, I've tried my darnedest to sort out the ones you need. There are really only a few basic types of mutual funds suited to meeting your investment goals, and you don't need all of them all of the time. I'll focus on winners and losers—a lot of funds are both in the course of their careers. Being in the right place at the right time has much to do with making them work for you.

I'll give you an in-depth look at the relationships among the stock market, the bond market, and the money market, as well as a look at the dynamic impact of the past decade's roller-coaster interest rates on these markets. And, by the way, did you know that when the average maturity of the money funds shortens, signaling that interest rates are expected to rise, the stock market falls? Sometimes the simplest rules work best.

Everybody has a system—tea leaves, sun spots, charts, you name it. But the SLYC system is for the average investor who wants to avoid fads and fallacies, insulate his or her nest egg from "the coming bad years" (if indeed they turn out to be that bad), and earn a high but safe

Figure 1
Performance of the 12 Percent Solution
Compared with Money Funds

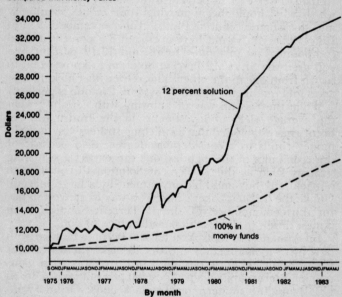

All dividends and capital gains reinvested

return. With the 12 Percent Solution, "twelve will get you twenty." Had you followed the 12 Percent Solution over the past six and three-quarters years, for instance, you would have earned an average annual compound yield of 19.1 percent (see Figure 1).

What is the SLYC 12 Percent Solution? Since you want to get the best of both the money and stock markets, the 12 Percent Solution is designed to guide you in getting the highest returns out of both (consistent with your *goals*, of course). Twelve to 13 percent is the money market rate at which you should begin moving your money cautiously into stock market mutual funds. From September 1975 to June 1983, you would have averaged 8.9 percent annual compound rate in money funds and 17.19 percent had you used the SLYC 12 Percent Solution to know when to switch from one to the other. This is even *after* making mistakes inherent in any switching system. (No one is perfect.)

While there is no way of knowing with certainty what the average yield of investments in the future will be, history has established that a switching strategy will outyield money funds to a considerable degree. And because of the economics of the eighties, one can expect a switching strategy such as the 12 Percent Solution to continue to outyield any buy-and-hold investment by a large margin. Unlike the inflated baker's dozen (a way to get you to pay for thirteen, not twelve), the 12 Percent Solution is an honest dozen that doesn't take advantage of you.

Investments are tools. You have to become familiar with how these tools function in order to make them work for you. The magic of accounting can turn short-term capital gains into long-term capital gains, those 80 percent tax-sheltered gifts from the modern marketplace gods. Ordinary income can be turned into long-term capital gains too, with the aid of a little-known loophole in the tax laws. And did you know that you can earn tax-free returns plus a capital gains bonus at the same time?

You'll benefit yourself by following the guidelines in this book for setting up your mutual fund accounts. Do it right and you can fine-tune your investment machinery to work for you. Do it wrong and the machinery will choke, sputter, and generally be a pain in the pocketbook.

Special-situation funds usually seem designed as sheet music for investors with just one tune, and I almost expect to see a designer mutual fund with Brooke Shields on the cover of the prospectus. The only thing that stands between you and your dream investment is your stockbroker's commission—and a few other considerations of practicality. These funds receive little respect from me except, of course, for the few which work, like the socially responsible Third Century Fund and the tax-free money funds.

But there are specialty tax shelters that may be realistically within your reach. A simple Clifford Trust might solve a tax problem very handily.

I tend to be suspicious of people who want me to work hard so they can get paid, which is one reason I distrust tax-shelter salesmen. But our government has generously— or carelessly—left open a few accessible, legitimate loopholes that enable us to lasso our earnings and keep most of them. It's well worth learning how to use these loopholes well—and creatively.

If you thought you liked IRA, you're going to love his younger sister SARA. She will show you how to take a graceful salary cut that will save you taxes—and cost you nothing. She's a lot more flexible and lissome than older brother IRA, and she's going to be talked about a lot. I'll be bringing IRAs and Keoghs into the conversation too, of course, in a big way.

There are a lot of people who can tell you how to get your money into your IRA, but I've added some advice on how to get your money *out* of your IRA, because if you make a false step, the IRS may confiscate half of your cache. You have to be vigilant to the end. I'll tell you how best to get out of your other investments too, when it's time to cash in on them.

I'll also have some suggestions on how to apply what you've learned from this book to your own specific investment goals, on how to sort out and weigh those goals realistically, on how to make them realizable. After all, that's what you're saving money for, isn't it?

2

The New Mutual Funds—an Idea Whose Time Has Come

> Well, the broker made money and
> the firm made money—and two
> out of three isn't bad.
> —*old Wall Street joke*

The Rise and Decline of the Traditional Mutual Fund

The big problem with making money is that it involves the risk of losing money. The Phoenician traders discovered that fact over 3,000 years ago. Putting together a trade caravan to cross the brutal deserts or building a ship to cross the raging seas wasn't exactly cheap. But the worst of the matter was that should one's caravan disappear in a sandstorm, or one's ship sink, all was lost. And what if a golden opportunity came along to ship a thousand idols to Utica just when all your money was tied up in a slow boat to Carthage?

What you really needed was more boats. But you didn't have enough money for a fleet. So there you were, sitting in the shadow of the Lebanese mountains wondering what to do. Then with sudden inspiration you realized that if you had enough money for one ship, you had enough for two half ships, or three thirds of a ship, and so on. (Actually you didn't have enough "money," since money in the form of coinage hadn't been invented yet. You were still bartering. But that's another story.) So you pooled your investments with other merchants and became part owner of several ships. Your risks were reduced, your potential profits remained as good as ever. Why? *Because you had diversified.*

The concept of pooled ownership flourished for hundreds of years in countless different societies, but mostly to the benefit of the rich. The trading fleets of continental Europe explored and looted the New World.

English ships expanded the pillage to the Far East. The wealthy profited mightily. But the average citizen didn't have the wherewithal (even after money as we know it had been invented) to own a toy ship, much less a piece of a real one.

Then in 1868 the Foreign and Colonial Government Trust of London was established. Buying stock in foreign and colonial companies, it sold its own shares to the growing ranks of middle-class investors spawned by the Industrial Revolution. Suddenly everybody—well, everybody that counted—could invest his or her savings in a diversified company, and make money just like the big capitalists. Pooled investments were what financed many of the railroads, industrial projects, and farm mortgages underlying our country's economic growth following the Civil War.

When there's money to be made, the crooks aren't far behind. Investment companies—read mutual funds—became really hot during the speculative excesses of this country's Roaring Twenties. To keep them sizzling, managers became manipulators. Deals became shady. And the house of cards came tumbling down in the financial collapse of the thirties.

Enough being enough, the government stepped in—after the fact, as usual—with a whole host of regulations such as the Federal Securities and Exchange Act of 1934 and the Federal Investment Company Act of 1940 to curtail the financial abuse of the funds. When the economy began to boom, following World War II, the investment companies flapped their clipped wings, rose from the dust—and in the period from 1946 to 1970 grew from $2 billion in assets to over $50 billion.

"Bernie the Barker" Strikes

Starting with the change in his pocket in the late fifties, Bernie Cornfeld, a former social worker from Brooklyn, New York, who once tried to help put Socialist Norman Thomas into the White House, managed over the next thirteen years to scratch together a personal fortune of $100 million.

Cornfeld was a folk hero on Wall Street. At the peak of his career, a million mutual fund clients had forked over $2 billion to him. He could do no wrong and neither could his salesmen, who lived lavishly on a fortune of commissions.

There's a classic Wall Street story about one of Cornfeld's sales trainers which sums up the aura surrounding fund marketers in those days. The trainer took a prospective salesman who was very unsure of himself to a potential customer's home for dinner. In the middle of the family meal, as the prospective salesman was launching his pitch, the old pro took off his shoe and sock and put his bare foot up on the table. While the trainee, aghast, tried to continue his pitch, the pro proceeded to pick his toenails with his fork.

After dinner the pro picked up the pieces from the trainee's sales spiel, signed the family on for the investment program, and snatched up a sizable check for the first payment. As he later explained to the shaken trainee, he merely wanted to demonstrate the fact that with enough confidence in yourself, you could get away with anything.

Cornfeld's sales pitch fitted right in with the new social consciousness of the sixties. "We're in the business," he's quoted as saying, "of literally converting the proletariat to the leisured class, painlessly and without violence. It's revolutionary and goddamn exciting." Now that was enough to make even picketing college students buy mutual funds.

Bernie Cornfeld lived in Napoleon's old Geneva villa (among other places). Champagne, movie starlets, rock and roll flowed in endless Hugh Hefner-like parties. About the only thing missing was the bunny suits. Well, it's true that Cornfeld peddled dreams of riches while Hefner catered to the flesh—but there were rumors on Wall Street that the two would merge their empires into the ultimate conglomerate, purveying sex and fortune from the same club. Back in those days, there was even talk of financial boutiques.

Things weren't what they seemed, however. And once an image cracks, it's apt to shatter. The Securities and Exchange Commission threw the first stone, claiming (though it could not prove) that some of the billions in Cornfeld funds kept overseas included Mafia money and aid from Washington to underdeveloped countries, which had somehow been diverted from feeding people to feeding banks. The SEC forbade Americans to purchase the fund's shares.

By 1969 Cornfeld's mutual fund sales were encountering resistance. Meanwhile management costs (all those flashy cars, flashy women, and just plain flash) had skyrocketed—and the stock market had begun to plummet. So a couple of high-ranking company officials borrowed some $40 million from the kitty to tide them over. Within the space of a few months the fund's stock went from $18 to $2 a share. It probably would have gone lower, but at that point the Toronto Exchange, on which the shares were listed, suspended trading.

As you can see from Figure 2, mutual fund sales, which had been booming for over two decades, went into a tailspin in 1969. Now it wasn't all Cornfeld's fault, of course. The stock market had begun its steepest decline since the crash of '29, with the month ending average of the Dow Jones going from 950.18 in April 1969 to 700.44 in May 1970, when there was talk of another depression.

What most brokers were selling at the time were extremely volatile high-beta mutual funds, which are funds that fluctuate at an exaggerated rate as compared with the price swings of the market itself. When the stock market went up, they went up even more. You couldn't lose—or could you? Well, the facts are that a lot of folks lost a lot of money. Why? Because they were not told that if the stock market were to decline, the high-beta funds would fall faster than the rest of the market. The roller coaster went up *and* down. And the sad thing was that because they had paid big fees to get into the funds, many investors were hesitant to get out until they had at least earned back the fees and "gotten even," at which point they probably would have definitely quit the game had not their salesmen kept telling them to stay in because the market was likely to

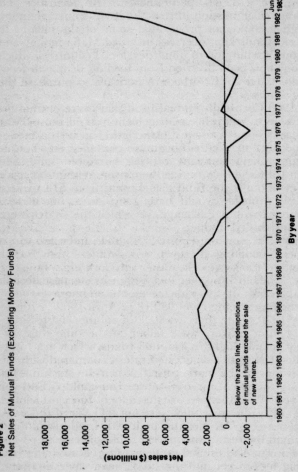

Figure 2
Net Sales of Mutual Funds (Excluding Money Funds)

Net sales ($ millions)

18,000
16,000
14,000
12,000
10,000
8,000
6,000
4,000
2,000
0
−2,000

Below the zero line, redemptions of mutual funds exceed the sale of new shares.

1960 1961 1962 1963 1964 1965 1966 1967 1968 1969 1970 1971 1972 1973 1974 1975 1976 1977 1978 1979 1980 1981 1982 1983 June

By year

Sales include reinvested dividends

Source: Investment Company Institute

turn around any time now. "You don't want to have to pay the fee *again* to get back in, do you?" was a persuasive argument, and, "Maybe tomorrow it will go up, then I'll get out," is a natural rationalization. No one, after all, wants to sell at a loss.

The Small Saver Strikes Out for Himself

I'm reminded here of the old sailor's paraphrase of the words often used by a famous president: "When the going gets tough, the tough get rowing." That's exactly what the small investor did. He paddled his way right out of Wall Street and into a new investment pool, namely, a money fund. Faced with the interest-rate explosion of the late seventies, many investors decided to simply park their money where they could earn as much interest as possible without paying those ridiculous commissions. Who wanted to play around in a stock market with less horizontal stability than a yoyo, anyway?

A few small investors did stay in the stock market. Dealing with discount brokers, they even managed to net themselves a fair deal on commissions. But they had to eat, drink, and sleep their investments in order to keep up with the slippery switchbacks of the stock market caught in the turmoil of extreme economic uncertainty.

You Can't Win If You're Not at the Table

With the Cornfeld horror tale fresh in your mind, chances are the last thing you want to do is to invest your money in anything. In fact, you probably want to stick every cent you have under the mattress. The economy being what it is, you may even want to stick your head, ostrichlike, under the mattress too. And I can't blame you. But you don't have that choice. *You must invest in order to survive.*

Saving alone was never really enough. Now, under the Economic Recovery Tax Act (ERTA) of 1981, investing instead of saving becomes crucial. Oh, I know, it wasn't meant to be that way. But read on and you'll see why it is.

"The Creeps" Are after Your Money

For most people, salaries have barely kept up with inflation, if they've even done that. And the more people make, the higher their taxes are. Bracket creep is by now a well-known bugaboo. Even the new tax law with its 1½ percent cut in 1981 tax rates, 10 percent in 1982, 19 percent in 1983, and 23 percent in 1984 isn't going to do much for most of us. It's nice to know that the top rate is going to be 50 percent. The problem is that a lot of people who used to be in the 15 percent tax bracket now find themselves in the 30 percent bracket, thanks to inflation. So if they drop back to the 25 percent bracket thanks to a tax cut, how much have they actually gained? ERTA's real break, for everyone, did not consist in what we pay in taxes on our income. Neither was it in the tax we pay on savings interest. In point of fact, under the old law we were allowed to earn $200 a year in interest tax-free. Under the new law, the 1982 limit was reduced to $100 for dividends only. For 1983, it remains the same. And, incidentally, while many people think of the earnings on their money fund as interest, it is, in fact, dividends. For tax purposes, money fund dividends are considered nonqualifying dividends. That is to say, they don't qualify for the dividend exclusion *or* the interest exclusion—or any other kind of exclusion.

No, ERTA's real break for all of us lies with capital gains—with investment, in other words. The maximum tax on capital gains has been reduced to 20 percent. So investment profits are the only way the government lets us all—regardless of age, race, sex, creed, or income—keep 80 percent or more of the money we make. If your total taxable income is $45,000, the government lets you keep almost 81 percent of your capital gains profits. If your taxable income is $20,000, you can keep 88 percent of your capital gains.

Not only that, but should one of your investments not pan out and you end up with a loss, you can deduct up to $3,000 of that loss from your other income, interest, or dividends. In this game, if you win, the government's take is much smaller than it is on any other money you earn. If you lose, the government will share your loss. And that's why you can't afford not to invest.

But Why a Mutual Fund?

When traditional mutual funds got dragged through the marketplace mud in the seventies, the crooks went off to sell empty coal mines and dry oil shelters and mutual fund managers took a good hard look at their industry. What they saw was the simple fact that the small investor had gotten wise to the outrageous commissions he'd been forced to pay. After all, with an 8½ percent or higher load charge up front, it often took a year or more for his investment to struggle back to its orginal size, never mind earn any real return, and he wasn't going to go through that again.

But sales commissions weren't really necessary to the functioning of a mutual fund. After all, commissions went straight into the pockets of those superslick salesmen. A mutual fund management company could live without them, provided it could attract money without salesmen. How could it do that? Why, with direct marketing, of course, ads and direct mail. It was when the SEC finally decided to allow the mutual funds to advertise that they were provided with the tool they needed to try and make an honest comeback.

Technically mutual funds had always been allowed to advertise—their name, address, telephone number, and other such elementary shopping information—what are called "tombstone ads." When it came to anything meatier, they had been severely restricted. Corporations are always publicizing flashy charts showing how their earnings have increased 10, 20, or even 50 percent a year for the last five years or whatever. Mutual funds until recently couldn't even print their performance figures in newspapers, and they couldn't use spans shorter than ten years in their charts.

The reasoning behind these restrictions was sound enough. You can't guarantee a mutual fund's future performance on the basis of its past record. Then again, you can't do that with a manufacturing company's profits either. Some people would even say that you can't predict anything in the future from past events, but that's going too far in the other direction. A reasonable middle ground would be to admit that past performance gives at least an indication of how fortune might smile in the future.

So customers felt, at any rate. And gradually those small investors who had fled the clutches of rapacious commission rates began thinking in terms of equity investments again. Stocks, after all, could help mitigate the effects of inflation.

And so the no-load fund came into its own. A few of these commission-free funds had existed before. But when they'd had to compete with that locustlike army of salespeople pushing the loaded funds, hardly anyone but the most sophisticated investor had paid any attention to them. Now they had a large area of the investment market more or less to themselves. Mutual fund sales took off again—not this time in the fashion of the Sizzling Sixties, however. Sales in 1982 for the old-fashioned rip-them-off-at-the-entrance mutual funds stood at $10.4 billion, those for the no-load funds at $5.4 billion. Compare these sales figures with the ones for 1960 (see Figure 3) and you can see how things have changed—for the better.

Why No-Load Funds Are the Best Deal in the Eighties

So mutual funds in the no-load mode are no longer a ripoff. Does that necessarily make them a good investment? Well, in this particular instance, yes. We have to invest, remember, to stay ahead of inflation and the tax man. So what else are we going to do? Buy straight stocks? But quite apart from the problem of putting together a diversified portfolio in today's shifting stock market, we run into the specter of commissions again.

Deciding that the little guy needed a break, the SEC arranged for fixed commissions for the buying and selling of stocks to be eliminated in 1975. In theory, increased competition would then lower transaction costs. But, as usual, the results of the SEC strategy came out backward. Oh, transaction costs were reduced, all right, but not where you or I would notice it.

An all-out price war ensued among brokerage houses, each one trying to lure business away from the others. The firms advertised much vaunted research and service as part of their enticements. However, these services were deemed by most investors to be secondary to the cost of doing business with the firms. Large-scale investors had

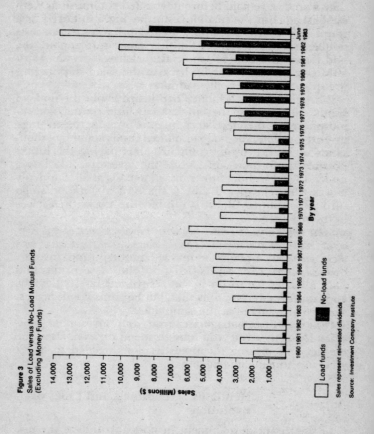

Figure 3

Sales of Load versus No-Load Mutual Funds
(Excluding Money Funds)

Sales represent reinvested dividends

Source: Investment Company Institute

their own research staffs. The small investor either didn't think much of the broker's research or did his or her buying and selling on the strength of tips and rumors. In any case, commissions did indeed plunge—to the point where now large investors often pay less than half what they would have paid before negotiated commissions were established. But the small investor buying a hundred or a couple of hundred shares watched his transaction costs double (see Table 1). As for that poor unfortunate, the odd lotter who bought ten or fifty shares (fifty shares of IBM cost almost $15,000), back in the salad days before the split, well, he'd really had it.

But by now the odd lotter had heard about the no-load funds. Here at last the buy-lots pay-little commission atmosphere of the new stock market was in the average investor's favor. The no-load mutual funds could buy thousands of shares in one company, thus paying the lowest possible transaction costs, while the investor could buy a no-load fund without any transaction costs at all. Suddenly it was a lot cheaper to buy a share of a stock portfolio through a mutual fund than to buy the stocks themselves in the marketplace.

Most small investors have two basic problems: lack of diversification and transaction costs. The no-load mutual fund solves both these problems. Because a no-load mutual fund investor owns a share of a diversified portfolio of securities and pays no sales fee to do so, he is invested safely, flexibly, and comfortably. Not only that, but he gains good, professional management at the same time.

No-load fund managers can do your investment footwork for you, saving you time to spend on evaluating the market and making the final decisions needed to direct your investments intelligently.

Hemlines, Trendlines, and Lines of Evolution

One significant development in no-load funds is the *new families of funds now evolving—stock, bond, and money funds clustered under one mutual umbrella. You can switch investment capital from one to the other of these funds quickly and without any commissions or costs* while still keeping it "all in the family."

Table 1   Transaction Cost for Small Investors Versus Large Investors Before and After the Elimination of Fixed Commissions

		Transaction Cost, Individual Round Lots					Transaction Cost, Individual Odd Lots		
Shares		Price	1975	1982	Shares		Price	1975	1982
100	@	$25	$ 48.95	$ 62.00	50	@	$10	$15.00	$27.00
200	@	30	109.29	126.00	50	@	20	22.50	36.00
300	@	40	183.81	214.00	50	@	40	37.50	55.00
400	@	50	280.68	305.00	50	@	50	44.25	62.00
		Large-Scale Institutional					*Large-Scale Institutional*		
50,000	@	$25	$6,000	—	50,000	@	$25	—	$3,000
50,000	@	30	6,500	—	50,000	@	30	—	3,250
50,000	@	40	8,000	—	50,000	@	40	—	4,000
50,000	@	50	9,500	—	50,000	@	50	—	4,750

Source: Fidelity Brokerage Service, Inc., Fidelity Management and Research Securities Industry Association.

This feature is going to play an important role in your future fortunes. For switching from stocks to bonds to the money market is going to be one of the prudent investor's most versatile tools in the struggle to safely navigate his savings through the inflationary-disinflationary tides and fluctuating interest rates ahead.

Note the bars in Figure 4. They make a nice neat arc from 1960 to 1980. Then they begin to move up again. It's part of a cycle. Almost everything goes in cycles—fashions, the weather, money. There are even arguments to show that the cycles go together. Take, for instance, the famous hemline indicator of Wall Street. When women start wearing miniskirts, as they did in the sixties, a bull market will follow, as indeed it did. Paris decreed maxiskirts and the market plunged. (What then does the recent trend toward pants mean? A depression? Perhaps.)

One thing is certain, whatever parallels one draws. The cycles are there. Being aware of them, making use of them whenever it works to do so is going to separate the survivors from the drifters on the investment seas.

So what are all these different funds among which we're going to navigate our way? Let me sort them out briefly for you. I'll be discussing them again in more detail, as they apply to our SLYC investment system for the eighties. But for now let's just figure out what the basic ones are and where they stand in the marketplace.

Growth Stock Funds—Capital Gains Is Their Game

Growth funds are variously referred to as capital gains, capital appreciation, and performance funds, among other things. In the wild and woolly go-go days of the sixties, some of the wilder ones were called, appropriately enough, go-go funds. Basically, a growth fund emphasizes the generating of capital gains rather than current income. That emphasis is not the same in all instances, however, and while any classification is bound to be somewhat arbitrary, for purposes of explanation we have divided them into three categories—performance, straight growth, and conservative growth—according to their volatility.

Performance funds must whet the appetites of mutual fund namers. Here are the most exciting names, employing terms like Vista, New Dimensions, Special Situation, Summit, Dynatech, Dynamic, and Venture. They don't tell you that a Venture may be an *Ad*venture if the stock market turns down.

The prime goal of the aggressively managed performance funds is as rapid growth of capital as possible. These are speculative funds geared to take large risks commensurate with large gains. They often invest in small companies, new companies, high-tech companies, companies with next to no earnings in relation to their share prices. Some funds even buy on margin, leveraging their investments even further.

Volatile investments such as these lead to quick fortunes and quick poverty for individuals. Funds usually fare better, since with millions of dollars to spend, they hold shares in numerous companies. If one company's stock collapses, two others may explode on the up side.

Performance funds are a good way for the sophisticated investor to participate in high-potential investments. Since risk is diversified, a sharp decline in one or two stocks in the fund's portfolio is not a catastrophe. Nevertheless you must always take the volatility of these funds into account in your investment planning. If you switch into them occasionally, they can be very profitable. Left unattended, they can cause grief if you suddenly need to cash them in.

Overall, performance funds will make great gains when the stock market is strong. However, when the market starts sliding, you'll run for the safety of a money fund, because the performance fund will do so badly that you'll wonder where all the bears came from.

Straight growth funds are plain-Jane, middle-of-the-road investment vehicles emphasizing a steady long-term increase in capital. They do not employ speculative investment techniques such as buying on margin and selling short, or selling borrowed stock in the hope of buying it back at a cheaper price later on. Their holdings are in the large, well-known corporations with good growth records such as Exxon, IBM, AT&T, and General Motors—which doesn't mean they own all these stocks at the same time. In the early eighties they moved out of automobile stocks, understandably enough, even though GM had been a traditional stalwart of the investor seeking good, safe growth.

A growth fund's prospectus will usually describe its ob-

Figure 4
Number of Persons Investing in Mutual Funds

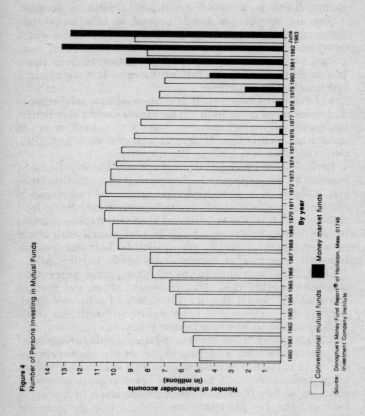

Source: Donoghue's Money Fund Report® of Holliston, Mass. 01746
Investment Company Institute

jectives in terms such as, "The fund's goal is to seek capital growth consistent with what it considers prudent risk," which translates as an investment policy of safe stocks that can be expected to increase in value over the years. These stocks usually also pay a dividend, though at less than the market rates, since a growing company needs to channel a lot of its cash flow into future development.

Because of their prudent investment policy, straight growth funds are less volatile than the performance funds. They will more closely follow overall market trends, the better funds outperforming the stock market as a whole on the up side and not losing as much on the down side. They are good investments for people with long-term goals for which they are willing to assume some risk in the hope of greater future rewards.

Slow and Steady—Is That Enough?

Conservative-growth, or growth-income, funds served a useful purpose back in the stable old days when interest rates were predictable and steady in their course. Investing in stocks with good dividend records—particularly those such as some of the utilities which increased their payout year after year—provided the investor with both capital gains and current income. Neither might be quite as large as it would have been had there existed only one objective. That, however, was both understandable and acceptable if you valued the twin goals equally. Today it is no longer acceptable.

The dividends paid out by most companies are simply no match for the high yields offered in the money market. This fact makes stocks bought in the past primarily for their dividends less desirable today. In turn, their prices are low, increasing at less than their historic rates. Overall, the growth-income funds have become laggards.

It's not that they are worthless. It's simply that better investment opportunities abound, with no greater risk involved, so what is to be gained by dealing yourself a weak hand? Remember, the object of the game is to win the largest return on your capital that can be garnered without undue risk.

Income funds are geared almost entirely toward giving you the best current yield the stock market has to offer.

Although there may be some capital gains occasionally, the focus is on providing you with spendable money on a regular basis while keeping your capital intact. Unfortunately, merely keeping capital intact today means watching it shrink at an alarming rate. Add to this the fact that money funds give you a much higher yield for current income than these ultraconservative stock funds do, and there's really no reason left at all for considering them in your investment strategy.

Bond Funds—Betting Interest Rates Will Fall

Bond funds, which promise long-term high yields and often deliver short-term capital losses when interest rates skyrocket, are labeled with names like Thrift, High Income, Fixed Income, High Yield. Municipal bond funds (not to be confused with tax-exempt money market funds) tout their federal tax-free status with adjectives such as Tax-Free, Tax-Exempt, and Municipal.

Bond funds are the even more conservative cousins of the stock market income funds. It's surprising, then, that bond funds do make sense today. As a matter of fact, not only to do they make sense, but they are essential to an effective money management plan. This paradox is brought about by the ever-changing interest rate environment.

Once the bedrock of pecuniary stability, bonds have been bloodied in the battle of inflation. Had someone on Wall Street predicted ten years ago that top-quality bonds would be selling at half their issuing price ($500 rather than $1,000) and yielding 14, 15, or even 16 percent, he probably would have been requested by his peers to have his head examined. Bonds simply did not fluctuate in price—oh, maybe they moved a point or two in a year, from 98 to 99, say, or from 100 to 101. But to suggest that they would fall in value by half, why, that was absurd.

Nevertheless, in the new reality that's precisely what they did. As fixed-interest obligations, they had to decline until their yield was equivalent to that of the money market, a phenomenon I'll cover more thoroughly later in discussing the crucial role of interest-rate fluctuation in the market value of stocks, bonds, and other equities.

Even considering their steep descent, however, long-term bonds and bond funds are for the most part no bargain, any more than a single sock on sale is. The reason for this seeming paradox is that these deep discount bonds, as they are called, would return to their issuing price—or go even higher—if the bottom were to fall out of interest rates. Now that would mean a very large capital gain indeed for the bondholder. But since such a precipitous drop in interest rates is highly unlikely, as a rule it's not a good idea to buy deep discount bonds or funds investing in them.

So who invests in bond funds at this point? SLYC investors, that's who—because it isn't impossible (nothing's impossible) for overall interest rates to return to their long-ago, 1950s level of 3 and 4 percent. Having a small part of your capital invested in bond funds—simply as disaster insurance—may make a lot of sense today. I'll be showing you why in the chapter on the SLYC system.

Money Market Mutual Funds— Investing in Money

Money funds are the easiest entities to distinguish in the mutual fund crowd. Such key phrases in their names as Liquid Income, Money Market, Cash Management, Cash Reserves, Cash Equivalent, Daily Income, Ready Assets, and Short-term emphasize the liquidity for which money funds strive.

Who invests in money funds? Everybody from bank presidents and congressmen to newlyweds and schoolchildren—people who want a parking place for their money between investments in other markets and people who want to use money funds as high-powered checking accounts.

Two specific types of money funds include government securities funds, which restrict their investments to U.S. Treasury bills and other federal agency obligations backed by the guarantee of the U.S. government, and tax-free money funds, a combination of money market investments and short-term municipal bonds and notes attractive to investors in very high tax brackets.

Investors concerned with the safety of their investments trade a few percentage points in yield for the security of being invested in government-only money funds. Recently, however, an exception to this rule occurred when, true to form, nine of the ten lower-yielding funds were government-only money funds, yet First Variable Rate Fund, also a government-only fund, earned a yield above the average for even the broadly based funds.

Money funds started in 1970 with a grand total of about $100,000 in assets. They weren't even known by the term "money funds" at the time. The first $1 million took a year to accumulate. But by early 1974 they had piled up assets of $12 million, at the end of 1974 these assets exploded into $3.5 billion, and by 1983 they reached the astounding figure of more than $220 billion.

They invest in the money market, that great amorphous international marketplace of IOUs. Governments, corporations, banks—all large entities need to borrow money on an almost constant basis. Sometimes they borrow for months or weeks, sometimes for mere days, or even quite literally hours.

The federal government is lending its money through Treasury bills and notes. The big banks borrow through jumbo certificates of deposit, Eurodollar CDs, or bankers' acceptances. Large established corporations take their loans in the form of commercial paper. What all these loans have in common is that they involve large sums of money, millions of dollars apiece, in fact. The total money market obligations outstanding at this writing amount to more than $1 trillion.

That trillion dollar loan market out there pays much higher interest rates than the bank or any other safe investment at the moment does. The only problem, before the money funds came along, was that the average individual couldn't participate in this profitable market because the minimum admission price was $100,000, and it really took $1 million to make the brokers actively interested in giving you the time of day.

There exists a rather obscure economic law first formulated by C. A. E. Goodhart, an adviser to the Bank of England, which, simply expressed, states that when the growth of a nation's money supply is effectively controlled, it inevitably leads to the development of new kinds of money that are not so strictly controlled. In plain English, if you stop people from making money one way, they'll find another way.

The other way in this case was a mutual fund investing

in high-quality IOUs, a fund investing in money, roughly indexed to inflation because it always stays a little bit ahead of the declining dollar, a fund that could earn the investor a lot more than he could glean from the tightly regulated banks or savings and loan associations—in short, a money fund.

This new repository of money has clung tenaciously to its right to existence and freedom from extraneous controls, although a strike force was organized in 1980 by the powerful American Bankers Association (ABA) lobby to attempt to unseat, or at least unsettle, it by calling on President Carter to order the Federal Reserve Board, the bank's regulatory agency, to impose reserve requirements on the money funds as part of the Credit Control Program. The restrictive attempt was abortive, the controls short-lived. During the three-month period of the onslaught, when the reserves were in force, assets grew 30 percent. Hearings held before both the House and Senate banking committees during that year and the next found the funds to be closely regulated and responsibly run. Now nearly every legislator and banker has an account at a money fund.

Money funds are not the last word in money's constant evolution. They're merely the most recent one. In time, something else will come along to maneuver you around any restrictions that arise to limit your money flow in the future. For now, however, as long as interest rates are high, the money funds are the single best place to keep your liquid cash. Here's why.

Most money funds require only a $250 to $1,000 minimum investment, the actual amount depending on the particular fund. And because the funds diversify their investments, buying the IOUs of many different companies and government agencies, they offer a higher yield with safety than an isolated individual's investment in the money market would. Although they do not have depositors' insurance per se, as banks do, their investment diversity is so great that they are fully as safe as banks. In fact, funds such as Capital Preservation Fund which invest only in U.S. government-backed obligations are probably even safer than banks.

Remember that the insurance pools for banks and savings and loans cover only a very small fraction of the total deposits. If two major banks were to go under, a not unlikely scenario in today's tumultuous financial markets, there would not be enough money in the kitty to cover every depositor.

A money fund with all its assets in government obligations may not be insured directly, but if the government were to repudiate its debts, well, it would be repudiating the dollar itself, and no amount of insurance would cover such an event. The money we currently deal in would be worthless at that point. So, short of such a disaster, the fund is as secure as the dollar itself.

Money funds, then, offer not only the high yields of the money market, commission free, and a low initial deposit requirement, but also safety. They also offer superliquidity—you can withdraw your money instantly, either by writing yourself a check or by telephoning the fund (usually through a toll-free 800 number) to wire you the money. The catch—and there has to be one, or the funds might come under banking regulations—is that the checks you write usually must be for over $500, although a few funds such as Midwest Income Trust let you write checks for as little as $250. Money fund checks are usually free. And your money keeps earning interest—or more accurately since you're a shareholder, dividends—every day until the checks actually clear. So when you pay, for instance, the IRS, which often takes weeks if not more to process checks, you keep earning for a quite a while on what technically is already the IRS's money.

But What about My Bank?

Personal finance in the past always revolved around banks. Your paycheck, your mortgage, your checking account and savings account, credit cards, car loans, even the buying and selling of stocks—all involved bank transactions. Today this is no longer the case. And with all the money draining out of their institutions as if someone had suddenly pulled the plug in the bathtub, bankers see big trouble ahead. In fact, as Lucius Arnold, Vice President of the Putnam Savings Bank of Connecticut, has put it, "They're as nervous as a bunch of long-tailed cats in a room full of rocking chairs."

Ever since the 1930s banking has been enmeshed in a

steel web of regulation. Designed to protect the industry—
and its customers—regulation also has severely curtailed
its activities. Everything had its time and place, and each
banking institution had its job cut out. Commercial banks
were allowed to take demand deposits such as the money
put into checking and savings accounts, and to make short-
term loans such as home improvement loans. The banks'
transactions were loosely overseen by the Federal Reserve
Board. Savings banks and savings and loan associations,
the so-called thrift institutions, were also allowed to take in
demand deposits in the form of passbook savings accounts—
but not checking accounts—and they could offer, as well
as short-term loans, long-term loans in the form of
mortgages, their primary means of lending money.

It was all very neat and clear-cut. Not only were the
rules spelled out, but the allowable interest each type of
institution could offer on its deposits was set by law as
well—the thrift institutions being allowed to offer a quarter of a percentage point more than the commercial banks.
Back in the days when banks were paying 2 percent
interest, this quarter of a percent differential was worth
something. At today's interest rates, about the only thing
one banking institution can proffer to lure customers away
from its competitors is a bigger toaster.

NOW the Banks Strike Back

When the money funds began to lure customers away
from the banks with their attractive interest rates and
checking privileges, the banks responded by launching the
Negotiable Order of Withdrawal, or NOW, account, a
device somewhat resembling a money fund but with three
significant differences. First of all, there is no minimum
on the size of the check you can write on a NOW account.
You can write a check for 25 cents if you want to. Second,
the amount needed to open an account and the minimum
balance required can be as low—or as high—as the bank
chooses. In some cases it's only $10, which beats all of the
money funds, but in others it's as high as $2,000. The
third difference, however, is the really telling one. The
yield on a NOW account is limited by law to $5\frac{1}{4}$ percent,
whereas at this writing my money fund account is yielding
10 percent.

It was in response to the pressure of a senior citizens' lobby that the Federal Reserve Board authorized, in June, 1978, the issuing of six-month certificates of deposit, or CDs, another small concession to bank customers. Now you no longer had to lock up your money in the bank for eight years in order to get close to money market yields. You could pull it out intact, with interest, in only six months.

The rates for the certificates were slightly lower than those of the money funds, you couldn't use them as checking accounts, and you needed a minimum of $10,000 to invest in them. On the positive side, you were assured of the initial rate of a certificate if interest rates declined, for the full six months of its term. Of course, if rates went up, as has most often been the case, you were stuck with the lower one. Nevertheless, the feature was appealing to many people because money fund rates fluctuate from week to week, following the national interest rate markets, and some people are less than comfortable with such fluctuating rates. I've always said that it doesn't make any difference how deep the water is as long as you're in a boat floating on the top—indeed, in 1981 for only one week out of the entire year were six-month certificates of deposit issued with a higher rate than the money funds averaged for the year.

In 1980 banks started down the long road of deregulation. The Depository Institutions Deregulation Committee (DIDC), created under the Depository Institutions Deregulation and Monetary Control Act of 1980, was mandated by Congress to gradually phase out, by March 31, 1986, the interest rate restrictions imposed on bank desposits by restrictive Regulation Q.

Comprised of the heads of the Treasury Department, the Federal Reserve Board, the Federal Deposit Insurance Corporation, the Federal Home Loan Bank Board, the National Credit Union Administration (whose credit unions, however, are not subject to the DIDC's rules), and the Comptroller of the Currency as a nonvoting member, the DIDC had as its objective the providing of a better footing for the commercial banks and the thrift institutions for competition with the money funds and other money market investments such as Treasury bills. But so far money is still draining out of the banks' saving coffers (see Table 2).

Table 2 Where America Saves*

Traditional Banking	1/77	1/78	1/79	1/80	1/81	1/82	6/82	1/83	6/83
Checking accounts	$ 226.6	$ 242.5	$ 252.1	$ 263.3	$ 254.1	$ 239.2	$ 231.0	$ 245.1	$ 242.1
NOW accounts	3.6	5.1	11.0	18.4	43.2	81.1	87.4	86.8	89.7
Old-style CDs	401.9	457.1	438.8	369.7	244.4	170.9	169.8	105.6	80.3
Passbook savings accounts	453.8	488.8	468.0	412.6	384.5	348.7	349.9	334.7	326.3
Subtotal	$1085.9	$1193.5	$1169.9	$1064.0	$ 926.2	$ 839.9	$ 838.1	$ 772.2	$ 738.4
The "Retail" Money Market									
Super NOW accounts	—	—	—	—	—	—	—	17.1	31.3
MMDAs	—	—	—	—	—	—	—	217.1	367.3
7-31 day CDs	—	—	—	—	—	—	—	11.7	10.2
91-day CDs	—	—	—	—	—		7.1	9.3	8.0
MMCs	—	—	107.6	290.6	425.5	454.2	463.3	389.8	337.8
SSCs	—	—	—	3.2	85.2	186.8	207.9	246.5	247.9
ASCs	—	—	—	—	—	44.3	50.5	15.3	8.5
Money market funds	3.6	4.2	12.1	49.1	85.2	186.8	207.9	209.2	177.4
IRA/Keogh Plan deposits	—	—	—	—	—	19.6	23.8	48.6	63.6
Subtotal	3.6	4.2	119.7	342.9	595.9	891.7	960.5	1164.6	1252.0

*Figures are in billions of dollars.

†All Savers' Certificate (ASC): A one-year tax-free savings certificate that pays 70 percent of the average yield on the most recent one-year Treasury bill rate.

Money Market Certificate (MMC): A six-month bank certificate of deposit with a $10,000 minimum deposit. The interest rate is tied to the six-month U.S. Treasury bill.

Small Saver's Certificate (SSC): A thirty-month bank certificate of deposit. The interest rate is tied to the thirty-month Treasury security rates. There is no set minimum deposit.

Source: Federal Reserve, Donoghue's MONEY FUND REPORT ® of Holliston, MA 01746.

Some folks have predicted the demise of money funds when the banks are finally freed of their interest-rate restrictions. But the wary are looking at the way the banks have responded to competition so far in an open market. On August 1, 1981, the interest-rate ceiling was lifted from the banks' 30-month small savers certificates (SSCs). In the months prior to August, almost all of the commercial banks and the thrifts had been offering their customers "the highest rate allowed by law," which was 12 percent, on deposits. But in August, after the ceiling was lifted, only 78 percent of the banks offered the highest market rates on the certificates. In September, only 58 percent of the banks were offering the highest rates. By October the embarrassed Fed stopped reporting the falling percentages. The moral: Keep shopping.

One successful venture of the DIDC, however, has been the creation of a four-week moving average for determining the interest rates on six-month money market certificates (MMCs). This makes the money market certificates appear more competitive with money funds during periods of declining interest rates. The allowable interest rates on the new certificates issued each week now decline more gradually than they did under the old system. Of course, this feature helps you to become poor more slowly only if you're buying new certificates regularly. Previously purchased certificates maintain the interest rate at which they were issued. A lot of investors decided this wasn't much help and continued to take their money out of their traditional savings mode, the banks.

Another important bank instrument, the MMDA (money market deposit account), went into effect in December 1982. MMDA accounts permit limited transfers every month and pay current money market rates.

There's a Hole in the Bucket, Dear Liza

In the first quarter of 1982, the thrift institutions, that is, the savings and loan associations and the savings banks, lost $2 billion because of the high interest rates they had to pay their depositors for certificates of deposit and the low return they were simultaneously receiving on old mortgages. The economic consulting firm of Townsend-Greenspan, Inc., has estimated that thrift institution losses for all of 1981 were $6 billion, and pretax losses of $10 billion are predicted for 1982 if interest rates decline even a few points. (If they continue at or near their present level or go up, which in my personal opinion is not at all unlikely, all bets are off.)

Right now nine out of ten savings and loans are in the red, according to Alan Greenspan, former chairman of the Council of Economic Advisers and presently an adviser to President Reagan. If these savings and loans were to have their balances adjusted to current values, that is, if they had to sell their old 8, 7, and even 6 percent mortgages on the open market, their total net worth would be reduced from a current $31 billion to a market deficit of $70 billion. In plain English, at today's prices these institutions are actually worth $70 billion less than nothing.

Of course, their deposits are insured by the Federal Savings and Loan Insurance Corporation (FSLIC). Unfortunately, the book value of the insurance pool is only about $5 billion. One thrift alone—say, for a hypothetical example, the West Side Federal Savings and Loan Association in New York City, with $2.5 billion in assets and in grave financial difficulties at the moment—could cost the insurance pool $700 million to rescue.

Now obviously the government wouldn't let the thrifts collapse without bailing out the depositors. No one wants to lose an election. But playing hero would leave the Treasury with a contingent liability of $65 billion, which of course would come out of your tax money. That's something nobody wants to see.

So more probably your local friendly banker simply won't be around much longer. Chances are his little bank is going to be merged out of existence. And chances are you'll find a personal loan much harder to get from the big, impersonal banks of the future. Mortgages, too, will be harder to come by if the ailing thrift institutions are absorbed by the commercial banks. Thrifts, after all, have only one major way to lend money really, and that's by isssuing mortgages. The commercial banks, on the other hand, deal in a broad spectrum of loans, most of which—those to the corporate sector, for example—are much more profitable than mortgages. So why should they bother with more mortgages? The only interest they could conceivably have in insolvent thrifts is as a ticket to interstate banking.

For decades the big banks have wanted to expand into nationwide entities. They've been forbidden to do so by laws designed to protect the consumer and prevent the banks from becoming too powerful. But chances are that these laws will now be modified to accommodate the current crisis of the savings banks. After all, politically it's much neater to pawn off the troubled institutions in a spirit of deregulation than it is to face spectacular headlines about bank failures and multibillion-dollar bail-out loans from the Treasury. By the end of the decade we may well see a couple of dozen superbanks in this country— and little else.

Meanwhile, however, in a last-ditch survival attempt to juggle increased competition, high interest rates, and deregulation all at the same time, bankers are perforce reeling off anything they can think of in the line of investment lures. Many of them, therefore, are now pushing second mortgages, either as a quick fix to financial problems or as a way of raising extra cash.

The Hari-Kari Mortgage with a Smile

At first glance, the ease with which you can now get a second mortgage might seem a positive step in personal banking. For bankers it certainly is. Second mortgages earn a higher interest rate than first mortgages do, providing a way for the banks to increase their revenues dramatically. For the consumer, on the other hand, a second mortgage may well lead to homelessness.

It's true that anyone who bought a home four or five years ago has probably seen its value increase by 50 percent or so. This extra equity is perfectly usable as collateral for a loan. But when the banks encourage individuals to hock their homes even further in order to start a business, send the kids to college, or even raise more cash to invest, then something is very wrong. This isn't free money we're talking about. You have to pay it back in order to keep your home. And if there's a real economic crunch or a decline in house values, you could be out on the street in a matter of months in some states.

California, for instance, issues second trust deeds (instead of second mortgages), on which foreclosure proceedings can be completed in as little as four months. Recently when a $200,000 house with a $100,000 first mortgage and a $20,000 second trust deed underwent foreclosure sale, the winning bid was $26,450 plus assumption of the first mortgage—barely enough, in other words, to cover the second trust deed and fees. The bank came out clean. The owners, a mere couple of payments behind on their second trust deed, ended up without a cent.

In 1981 the foreclosure rate in California was about twice that of the previous year, and it's still going up. No matter how tempting the new banking push into second mortgages may seem, stay away from them. You're not mortgaging your house. You're mortgaging your future.

You Can Fool Some of the Savers Some of the Time, But All Savers None of the Time

Everyone is complaining about paying taxes these days. So what could be more appealing than tax-free interest? Consequently, the thrift institution trade associations lobbied mightily for the All Savers bill, the as-American-as-apple-pie congressional authorization of special small-savers' certificates replete with a tax break on the first $2,000 of interest earned on them.

Unfortunately, the low-income consumer can do just as well by purchasing ordinary taxable certificates, which pay 3 to 5 percent more a year. The middle-income group is better off, and more liquid, buying tax-exempt money funds. For rich folks, the benefits are so small it isn't worth taking out the limo to go to the bank. The only ones who stand to gain are the banks and thrift institutions. With enough hype, they'll be able to convince the unwary saver that All Savers is really a great deal. The Treasury will lose several billion dollars in taxes, the saver won't come out ahead, and the thrift institutions will be buying a little time. A *New York Times* editorial sally on the subject to the effect that we should be "saving savers from 'All Savers' " was right on the mark. However, to date the banks have been able to sell only $45 billion worth of these certificates, not the $250 billion originally projected. All Savers has had all the impact of President Ford's Whip Inflation Now (WIN) buttons.

Sweep Accounts Clean Up—for the Banks

In yet another attempt to sweep every extra crumb of interest their investor's money can earn under their thread-bare rugs, the banks have invented sweep accounts. Now just what is a sweep account? Well, it's based on a relationship between a bank and a money fund. The prototype was set up at First National Bank of Springfield, Illinois. For a small fee, up to 90 basis points, or .9 percent, of the yield, and your agreement to maintain a $2,000 minimum balance in your NOW account, the bank would "sweep" any excess savings over your minimum balance into either a Dreyfus or a Fidelity money fund for you. A bank is by law prohibited from operating a money fund, but it is allowed to operate as a money fund's agent.

The First Springfield program is creatively mediocre at best. Some folks are going to like it because they like using their local bank, and they like the security of walking downtown and seeing the bank and thinking, "My money is in there." Other folks are going to realize that if future years are like 1981, such an account is going to cost them $231 a year (the difference between the average 1981 money fund yield of 16.8 percent and the 5.25 percent the bank is paying on a NOW account times the $2,000 balance) plus the 90 basis points (which would amount to $90 per year on, say, $10,000) plus any regular banking fees. That could be a very expensive "free" checking account. It is better than leaving your money in a pass-book savings account, but your cash can do better elsewhere (see Figure 5).

Sweep accounts, including the MasterCard Money Manager, a brand-new credit card money fund combination with a wide range of banking and investment services, are legitimate hybrids in the evolution of the money funds. But some banks are claiming to offer their own true money funds, and that's not right, because banks can't do that. What these so-called funds really are is retail repurchase agreements, a back-door way for a bank or a thrift to

Figure 5

A Comparison of Returns on Passbook Savings
with Returns on Alternative Investments

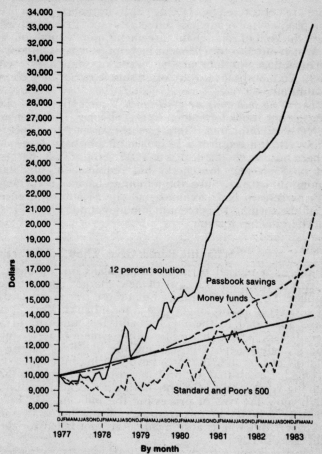

12 percent solution

Passbook savings

Money funds

Standard and Poor's 500

Money funds' dividends not reinvested

Source: Donoghue's Money Fund Report® of Holliston, Mass. 01746
Standard and Poor's 500 Composite Yield

provide a money fund-like investment. If the thrift institution or bank offering them were to fail, you would be among the last of the creditors to be paid, because since the retail repos are technically investments, not deposits, they are not covered by FDIC or FSLIC insurance. Avoid like the plague retail repurchase agreements (not to be confused with the kind of repurchase agreements money funds buy).

Watch out also for claims of high interest rates on long-term deposits of four or five years, or sometimes even eighteen months. These are often simple rather than compound interest rates.

There's no such thing as a free lunch. I can't stress this old saw enough. Look for hidden costs at all times. For instance, a NOW account that offers free checks and free everything else but requires a $2,000 minimum balance is nowhere near as good a deal as a NOW account that charges $4 or $5 a year for checks but requires only a $400 minimum balance. Sure, the minimum balance is earning 5¼ percent in both accounts, but the $1,600 difference could be earning 18 percent in a money fund. That's $164 more in savings for you.

What the Banks Give, They Take Away

If there's a myriad of new savings plans on the banks' horizons, there's also a host of new charges about to be applied. You may have noticed that those free credit cards of yesteryear are no longer free at most banks. Mortgages have appended to them points and fees unheard of a decade ago. Service charges for stop-payment orders, bank checks, safety deposit boxes, and the like have all risen sharply of late, in many cases far outpacing inflation.

One basic cost that will probably rise dramatically in the coming years is that of simply having a checking account. Right now the cost of processing the millions of checks written each day in this country is being borne by the taxpayer. But you as an individual are not billed for the full cost directly.

All that is going to change as clearing costs are passed on to the customers. Free checking may well change to a 25-cents-per-check transaction at the bank—which would alter the way many people view their checkbooks. On balance you may decide that, except for a small cash account for your little bills, you no longer need a bank.

When Merrill Lynch Talks, E. F. Hutton Listens

The banks' many new enticements will probably come to naught in the end, because the brokerage firms, seeing a good thing in money funds, have come up with an even better one in the so-called universal, or central asset, account. This is the banana split of personal money management services first conceived by Merrill Lynch.

Merrill Lynch's version, called a Cash Management Account (CMA), combines a money fund (complete with checking services), a VISA card, a stock account, and access to low-cost loans (they also offer a separate equity access account which acts as an automatic second-mortgage-like line of credit backed by the homeowner's equity in his or her house) available whenever there is a need for extra money—all detailed on one simple monthly statement. Dividend deposits, along with any other cash in your account, are automatically transferred into the money fund every week to earn high interest until you need the cash.

Dean Witter Reynolds, E.F. Hutton, and other brokerage firms have all launched variations on Merrill Lynch's CMA (see Table 3). If you'd rather have a gold card than a plain old VISA, you'll have that chance, for Shearson, bought by American Express, plans to offer services similar to those of the CMA. The Prudential-Bache merger assures that insurance in all forms will also become part of the universal account. And one or another of these super-brokers is bound to enter the first-mortgage field soon.

Merrill Lynch does require an initial deposit of $20,000, which puts the CMA out of range for many individuals. However, as the competition heats up, this minimum is sure to drop into Everyman's reach. The discount brokerage firm of Charles Schwab and Co. has just announced its own universal plan with only a $1,000 minimum, cut-rate loans on a VISA card, and even an overdraft checking feature; and Ed Jones, the broker from Missouri, will let you open an account for $5,000.

The superbrokerage accounts have almost everything to offer. Now when they offer to do my investment switching for me automatically, at a comfortable profit to me, I'll give them my allegiance. Meanwhile there's work to be done.

Table 3 Central Assets Account Table

Central Assets Account	Money Fund Names	Initial Subsequent Investments($)	Annual Fee	Checking/ Minimum	Card	Start-Up Date	Assets as of 3/3/83 ($mil)
Advest: Advest Reserve Cash Account	Parkway Cash Fund, Inc. Parkway Tax-Free Reserve Fund	$10,000*	$25	Yes/No Minimum	VISA Debit	11/81	$ 572.1 32.0
A.G. Edwards & Sons, Inc.: Total Asset Account	Centennial Money Market Trust Centennial Government Trust Centennial Tax-Exempt Trust	20,000*	$30	Yes/No Minimum	VISA Debit	11/81	151.2 37.1
Dean Witter Reynolds: Active Assets Account	Active Assets Money Trust Active Assets Government Securities Trust Active Assets Tax-Free Trust	20,000*	$30	Yes/No Minimum	VISA Debit	7/81	1,308.8 137.8 155.7
Edward D. Jones & Co.: Daily Passport Cash Trust	E.D. Jones & Co. Daily Passport Cash Trust Government Money Instruments** Tax-Free Instruments Trust	1,000/100* 5,000/1,000 5,000/1,000	NONE	Yes/No Minimum	VISA Debit	6/80	712.1 N/A N/A
E.F. Hutton: Asset Management Account	Hutton AMA Cash Fund Hutton Government Fund Municipal Cash Reserve Management	10,000 (cash) 20,000 (margin-able securities)	$50	Yes/No Minimum	American Express Gold Credit	7/82	118.4 656.7 653.0
Fidelity: Fidelity Ultra Service Account	Fidelity Daily Income Trust	10,000/500*	$36	Yes/No Minimum	MasterCard Debit	2/83	3,009.0

Fund						
John Hancock: John Hancock Cash Management Trust	5,000/25	$35	Yes/$50 Minimum	VISA Debit	2/83	541.2
Kidder Peabody: Kidder Peabody Premium Account Fund	25,000*	$75	Yes/No Minimum	VISA Debit	5/82	88.1
Merrill Lynch: Cash Management Account						
CMA Money Fund	20,000*	$50	Yes/No Minimum	VISA Debit	9/77	13,509.5
CMA Government Securities Fund						1,463.9
CMA Tax-Exempt Fund						2,825.3
Prudential-Bache: Prudential-Bache Command Account						
Command Money Fund	20,000*	$50	Yes/No Minimum	VISA Debit	2/82	447.9
Command Government Fund						N/A
Command Tax-Free Fund						N/A
Reserve: Reserve CPA Account	Reserve Cash Performance Account, Inc.	10,000/1,000*	$50-Single $70-Joint	Yes/No Minimum	MasterCard or VISA Debit	10/82	2.9
Shearson/American Express: Financial Management Account						
Shearson FMA Cash Fund	25,000*	$100	Yes/No Minimum	American Express Gold Credit	2/82	374.6
Shearson FMA Government Fund						60.9
Shearson FMA Municipal Fund						116.4
Smith Barney: Vantage℠ Account						
Vantage Money Market Cash Portfolio	20,000*	$50	Yes/No Minimum	American Express Gold Credit	1/83	N/A
Vantage Money Market Government Portfolio						

*Cash and/or securities
**Not listed on Donoghue's MONEY FUND REPORT® of Holliston, MA 01746
NA—Not available

3

A Fund for All Reasons

> Variety is the spice of life and the
> savior of capital.
>
> —*Erasmus Hoeniger*

If you as an individual buy shares in Consolidated Rocket
and Biotechnology, you stand to make a fortune if the
shares go from 15 to 50. But what if they go from 15 to 1?
It's happened more than once. Even the most respectable
companies have been known to go bankrupt or come close
to it. Remember Penn Central?

However, a few years after Penn Central went out of
the railroad business, it rose phoenix-like to become a
powerful real estate-based conglomerate, and the stock
skyrocketed. Most of the private investors had pulled out
during the disaster. Institutional investors, including mutual funds, bought in while the company was on the operating table.

Now a mutual fund that had, say, 2 percent of its stock
in Penn Central or Consolidated Rocket and Biotechnology during the plunge saw its assets shrink a bit at most. If
the fund's 98 percent invested elsewhere happened to rise
at the same time, it could even have shown a good increase in capital during the ill-fated shares' plunge.

The individual investor with 10 or perhaps even 25

percent of his savings in Consolidated Rocket probably wasn't so lucky. Lose 10 percent of your capital in one stock, and it takes an awful lot of work on the part of the rest of your portfolio to recoup that loss plus show a profit. The other stocks must chip in an 11 percent gain for you to simply break even. To cancel out a 25 percent loss, you would need a 33 percent gain in the rest of your portfolio. And that's without adding in the commission costs of getting rid of the ill-fated stock.

As for the investor with shares in both Penn Central and Consolidated Rocket and Biotechnology, who innocently thought he was buying into one safe, respectable company and one wild gamble—well, the rest of his portfolio had better be a whopper if the market happens to tumble, because if he loses 50 percent of the value of his portfolio, he must somehow gain 100 percent in order to regain his position; more than 50 percent, and the amount of gain

Table 4   The Difficult Arithmetic of Breaking Even

Amount of Stock Loss, Percent	Amount of Stock Gain Needed for You to Break Even, Percent*
5 (from 100 down to 95	5 (from 95 up to 100)
10 (from 100 down to 90)	11 (from 90 up to 100)
15 (from 100 down to 85)	17 (from 85 up to 100)
20 (from 100 down to 80)	25 (from 80 up to 100)
25 (from 100 down to 75)	33 (from 75 up to 100)
30 (from 100 down to 70)	42 (from 70 up to 100)
35 (from 100 down to 65)	53 (from 65 up to 100)
40 (from 100 down to 60)	66 (from 60 up to 100)
45 (from 100 down to 55)	81 (from 55 up to 100)
50 (from 100 down to 50)	100 (from 50 up to 100)
55 (from 100 down to 45)	122 (from 45 up to 100)
60 (from 100 down to 40)	150 (from 40 up to 100)
65 (from 100 down to 35)	185 (from 35 up to 100)
70 (from 100 down to 30)	233 (from 30 up to 100)
75 (from 100 down to 25)	300 (from 25 up to 100)
80 (from 100 down to 20)	400 (from 20 up to 100)
85 (from 100 down to 15)	566 (from 15 up to 100)
90 (from 100 down to 10)	900 (from 10 up to 100)
95 (from 100 down to 5)	1900 (from 5 up to 100)

*These figures do not include the additional commission costs of actually buying and selling stocks.

Figure 6
If You Lose a Little, You'd Better Win a Lot

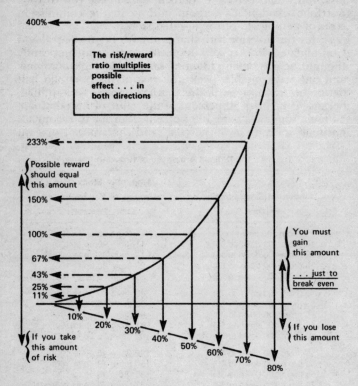

Source: Donoghue's Mutual Funds Almanac

needed to break even becomes staggering. For instance, a 65 percent loss will cost 185 percent to recoup. A loss of 75 percent takes a gain of 300 percent to remedy—and a 300 percent gain is a very big gain to hope for indeed. Look at Table 4, "The Difficult Arithmetic of Breaking Even," and Figure 6, "If You Lose a Little, You'd Better Win a Lot," and you'll see what fighting a superloss factor like this can be like.

The fact is that with less than $250,000 or so—which most of us don't have lying around to throw into the stock market—you really can't diversify enough to reduce your risks to a safe or even manageable level. You're in a feast or famine situation. If your stock shoots up and you get out at the right time, why, then you've made a killing. But if not. . . . That's the risk most of us can't afford to take. It's also the risk the modern no-load funds can help mitigate.

Mutual funds come in all sizes and shapes, and it's important to select the type of fund that's right for your goals and financial position in today's market. *Never forget that you have to be able to sleep at night while your money is floating about on the harsh seas of commerce.*

Chances are that your investment objectives will require the use of only two or three types of funds, say, a growth stock fund, a bond fund, and a money market fund. You always want to keep an eye on what else is—or becomes—available, however.

I identified the funds for you in the last chapter. Now let me see if I can't give you some guidelines for evaluating them.

First of all, a caveat. Inevitably you're going to hear talk about the bulls and bears that inhabit the stock market zoo. It's like talk about the birds and the bees. You can't get away from the basics. The market does go up and down, and it's bound to be talked about—and speculated upon. And because many times the stock market changes according to what people believe—according to their expectations of what the future will bring, in other words—bulls and bears have more say in stock market discussions than would seen proper, much less polite, at first glance.

• Bulls are of the opinion that stock prices will charge higher.

- Bears believe that stock prices will lumber down the stock market mountain.

My Advice:

- Don't be intimidated by bulls and bears.
- Don't listen to what bulls, bears, or economists say. Watch what they *do* with their money.

Volatility Cuts Both Ways

Let's talk about volatility. Let's talk about the roller coaster ride of the Nicholas Strong Fund, the best-performing no-load fund of 1971, up an eyebrow-raising 85.5 percent for that year. In 1972 the fund ranked a respectable eighteen on the list of all the funds, and it grew 28.1 percent in value per share that year. During the bear years of 1973 and 1974, the fund plunged 68.6 percent. *Now that's volatility.*

One of the founders, Strong, left the company, and the fund became just plain Nicholas Fund. Maybe that's volatility too. In any case, a strong performance from 1975 to 1981 brought the fund ahead of where it had been back in 1971. An initial $10,000 investment in the fund would have grown to about $21,327 over the past ten years. For the last five years of that period, the fund ranked twenty-nine on the list of the top fifty, and an initial $10,000 investment of five years ago would have grown to about $29,181. (See Table 5 for all the figures.)

Table 5   Performance of Nicholas Fund* During 1971–1982

Year	Gain or Loss per Share Each Year, Percent
1971	+85.5
1972	+28.1
1973	−52.7
1974	−33.5
1975	+47.9
1976	+22.7
1977	+20.5
1978	+25.6
1979	+31.0
1980	+35.6
1981	+8.6
1982	+35.6

*Formerly the Nicholas Strong Fund.

This isn't an isolated example of performance swings I'm giving you. Pennsylvania Mutual Fund lost 72 percent in the 1973–74 bear market. And remember that we're talking here about funds, which are more diversified than you could ever probably hope to be as an individual investor.

The 44 Wall Street Fund took even more of a beating in the stock market massacre of October, 1978. *This fund fell 41.5 percent in one month.*

Are you sure you want volatility?

Being a leveraged fund, 44 Wall Street Fund was permitted by its bylaws to buy shares on margin, which it did. When the market turned bullish on November 1 of that year, the fund gained an astounding 18.4 percent in one day. I'm not sure this is the largest single gain ever made by a mutual fund, but I am sure that it deserves honorable mention in the *Guinness Book of World Records.*

Performance Funds—When They're Good They're Very, Very Good, But When They're Bad . . .

Growth fund managers control the volatility of their fund's performance by controlling the fund's portfolio. An investment policy geared toward strong speculation will endorse big risks for high potential gains. The fund managers will be scouting for small companies in new fields that hint of real promise but don't yet have much in earnings to show for it. They may also invest in turn-around situations, taking a considered gamble on companies which have fallen on hard times but which because of changing market conditions, old trademarks, new products, or new management could conceivably return to their former glory —and much higher stock prices. Fund managers with high-return goals and the freedom to strive for those goals without many restrictions being imposed on them by fund policy sometimes involve their funds in arbitrage, buying stock in a company that another company is trying to buy up. With a little luck, the takeover attempt turns out to be a battle among several companies, driving the share price of the sought-after company up 50 percent or more.

Purchasing volatile stock is not the only way high-beta funds seek to improve their performance. There are times when they will sell stock short. In the well-publicized spiral into bankruptcy of Braniff, the stock fell several hundred percent in a matter of weeks. Short sellers had a field day. Of course, Braniff might have pulled itself out of its tailspin before it hit bankruptcy, in which case a lot of shorts would have lost their shirts. But that's the name of the performance game—high-risk investing with the hope of high-profit returns.

Volatility can be measured. Comparing a fund's price swings with a broader market indicator such as the Dow Jones average or the New York Stock Exchange Common Stock Index will give you its volatility coefficient. Let's take as the base for an example the NYSE Common Stock Index, which has a lot more stocks as its components than the Dow Jones average does, and is thus more representative of the market as a whole.

Suppose that in a given year a certain mutual fund gains 17 percent, while the NYSE Common Stock Index gains 10 percent. If we divide 10 into 17, we get 1.7. That's the volatility coefficient for the fund in our example. Also known as the beta coefficient, it's a number much touted among cognoscenti on the Street.

Don't worry about the math involved in arriving at the number. All you have to know in order to take the volatility temperature of the various funds is the number itself.

To read the beta thermometer, you need only remember that

- Performance funds will have a beta of 1.25 or more.
- Growth funds will have a beta of 1.0 to 1.24.
- Conservative funds will have a beta of 1.0 or less.

You can find the beta for any fund that interests you listed in Weisenberger's *Investment Companies,* a volume available at most libraries. You can also simply use the performance/growth/conservative breakdown given in the "No-Load Mutual Funds Directory" to be found in Appendix C at the back of this book. It sorts the funds for you, by their objectives, into the three beta categories. Knowing whether a fund is performance (high beta), growth (medium beta), or conservative (low beta) is really all you need to know in order to make your preliminary selection.

The primary characteristic of an aggressively managed high-beta performance fund is its volatility. And while volatility will produce the most spectacular gains during a prolonged rising market, in a falling market performance funds can be disastrous to your wealth. To regain losses sustained in a falling market may be an exceedingly difficult task, as you will recall from Table 4, "The Difficult Arithmetic of Breaking Even." And it's easier for a fund than it is for the individual investor.

So why even consider performance funds? Because they are the best way to take advantage of the spectacular growth potential of small company stocks. A study by Rolf W. Banz, professor of finance at the University of Chicago, published in the June 30, 1980, issue of *Fortune* magazine, supports Wall Street's previously undocumented feeling that the so-called secondary stocks, those of the smaller, non-blue-chip companies, often outperform the more established stocks when it comes to growth. In fact, the little companies have outperformed the big ones on a fairly regular basis ever since the crash of 1929, showing an 11.6 percent average annual rate of return compared with 8.8 percent for the big firms. The difference between a fund investing in these secondary stocks and you as an individual investing in them lies in the degree of diversification involved. A well-managed performance fund is going to have quite a number of these up-and-coming small-company stocks in its portfolio, carefully selected and researched, of course.

But—there's no getting around it—it's still going to be gambling. So what you as a potential shareholder have to determine is whether the extra growth potential of such a fund is worth the extra risk—and the extra work—that owning it would involve.

The risk should be obvious by now. The additional work might be less so. If you buy a performance fund, you'll have to watch the stock market quite carefully. And you'll have to watch the fund managers out there playing the market just as carefully, because sometimes *performance fund managers are quite willing to let the bottom fall out of their shares temporarily.*

They don't do this to be perverse. They usually stay fully invested, *even in a bear market,* in order to be sure of a fast start when the next bull phase explodes. They know that certain stocks will do well when the right time comes. Buying these stocks when their prices are falling out of bed and no one else wants them guarantees that they'll be first with the lowest prices when the market looks up again. Don't ever forget this ploy of theirs, because it's the point at which you and the managers part company if you are invested in a performance fund for a short-term goal.

You must be able to anticipate a bull market and buy the performance fund, and anticipate a bear market and sell the fund, any time you are not prepared to ride out a stock market low. You watch hard for your earnings when you invest in the high-beta equity funds.

Alternatively and more practically—unless you have some gypsy blood in your financial veins—you'll buy a performance fund for a long-term investment goal. That way you won't have to watch so hard, because if you target it ten to fifteen years away, historically a bull market lies within your range. When it comes, be it two years or ten years from now, let the performance fund go up its merry way. Then get out. Get out when? When you've made enough money on the fund to match your goal. Don't try to make a killing. Chances are you'll run into a bear.

Performance funds are for you if you want to make your money grow as fast as it can—and if you are, first, able to sustain losses, at least temporarily, without undue hardship, and second, willing to spend extra time watching both the funds and the market in general. If this sounds like more than you can handle—and probably no more than one out of every twenty-five people should put their money into performance funds—chances are your equity investment should be made in a straight-growth fund.

Growth Funds—Day by Day in Every Way . . .

The straight-growth funds, steady, stocky, slow-moving, are hardly as exciting to watch as the performance funds are. And that's the point. *For many, if not most, investors, the prudent rule is, "Watch the performance, but buy the growth."*

The investment policy of a straight-growth fund is linear. There's no buying on margin, no jumping on the band-wagon, no selling short or leveraging. Its goal is safe, gradual capital accumulation, and it keeps a steadfast eye on future development trends among the companies in, and potentially in, its portfolio. The one thing to remember, in the case of the straight-growth funds, is that even though a particular fund has performed well over the years, you should always keep your eye on the other funds of its type too. No one stays at the top forever, and you should be prepared to switch your allegiance occasionally.

The Top Ten

The present top ten no-load growth stock funds that permit telephone switching (see Table 6) would all have been profitable had you bought them a number of years ago and held onto them awhile. This is why you need a switching plan. During the inflationary burst of the late seventies, the SLYC system would have switched you out of the stock funds and into money funds at times when such a move would have increased the overall return on your investment. You would have been far better off financially today if you had consistently switched according to that plan than if you had simply let your money remain in stock funds. Today, it is truer than ever that making money on your money is not enough. You have to *maximize* your return—at the same time looking out for your financial safety.

Table 6   Top Ten No-Load Telephone Switch Funds for June 1982 to June 1983: Buy & Hold Strategy

Fund Name	Annual Rate, Percent
1. Founders Special Fund	111.25%
2. USAA Sunbelt Era	109.54
3. Stein Roe Capital Opportunities	107.32
4. Explorer	107.00
5. T. Rowe Price New Horizons	98.40
6. Columbia Growth	94.77
7. Fidelity Asset Investment Trust	91.31
8. Medical Technology Fund	87.53
9. Stein Roe Stock	86.15
10. Morgan Growth	81.34

Bond Funds—Their Loss Is Your Gain

There are some one hundred bond funds, with $1 billion or so in realized losses, at this writing. On top of that, these funds have another $2 billion in unrealized, or paper, losses.

That is to say, they are holding bonds which have gone down some $2 billion in value from their purchase price, but which have not yet been sold, so the loss shows up only in the bookkeeping. Talk about carnage!

Yet for every loser there's usually a winner, and while I would never suggest that you set out to take unfair advantage of someone, here's a losing situation that has already occurred. Taking advantage of it can't hurt anyone any more than they've already been hurt, and it can help you turn a dud into a good deal.

Among all the rules and regulations governing closed-end funds, those funds which issue a fixed number of shares that are subsequently traded in the securities market, there is a provision permitting them to carry forward capital losses for eight years in order to offset future capital gains.

A bond fund may not distribute capital losses to its shareholders directly. However, the shares sell at a discount because the losses are reflected in the per-share value.

Normally, a mutual fund must distribute 90 percent or more of its income each year to its shareholders. But a special loophole in the law allows it to use its loss carry-over to avoid that distribution. In such an event, the shareholders receive no dividends, but the price of the fund's stock increases by the amount that would have been paid out in dividends per share. If this presents a problem for any of the shareholders, they can always sell off a few shares for the money they need. However, the wise will try to hold onto their shares in a bond fund with a large loss carry-over as interest rates fall. They'll also wait to sell them until they have held them for at least a year. And they'll sell them when their price is at its highest. By doing this, they can turn earnings on which they would otherwise have paid ordinary income tax (up to the 50 percent limit) into those long-term, gifts-from-the-gods capital gains on which the maximum tax is 20 percent, thus putting at least 30 percent more money in their own pockets rather than the tax man's.

The strategy involved here assumes that interest rates will indeed fall. But both you and I know that's very likely to happen, if not in today's, then in tomorrow's highly volatile interest-rate environment. When it does happen, a bond fund is a fine thing to have in your back pocket.

From a catastrophe-proofing viewpoint, what you want to buy is the bond fund with the largest capital losses in its past, because it's the one with the potential for the largest gains, and also the best tax treatment, in a disinflationary-interest-rate market.

OPM Isn't Always Other People's Money

Now if there's one underlying common denominator to all these types of mutual funds, it's professional management. But, as I'm sure you know, there's management—and there's management. Witness the difference between Chrysler and General Motors in a collapsing car market.

So let's look a little more closely at management in mutual funds. Management is, after all, part of what you're getting for your money.

When you purchase a mutual fund, one of the things you're buying is OPM. Here I'm referring not to the classic Other People's Money, access to which is a great way to make a lot of cash—only just try to get hold of it—but rather to Other People's Management.

If you can spend two or three hours a day following the markets and the financial news, you may not need someone to help you manage your money. If you can't, it makes sense to "hire" someone else to do it, someone who makes a full-time occupation of staying abreast of the changing economic scene. You don't relinquish all personal obligations with regard to watching your nest egg by choosing this course. But you reduce geometrically the time you have to spend tending the nest.

Today a lot of professional investment advisers require you to deposit at least $200,000 with them. Then they charge a minimum of $10,000, or 5 percent, a year for their advice. It's enough to make you wonder if they're selling designer-label advice.

Investment advisers have to make a living too, of course. They don't make a bad one at that. But what the average investor needs is a McDonald's of stock market advice. Nothing fancy, just something plain and filling when the capital needs it. And that's what the mutual funds are, really, the hamburger joints of personal money management.

I don't mean this in a disparaging way at all. Frankly, I wouldn't mind owning a McDonald's franchise or two. You probably wouldn't either. The point is that just as low-priced food purveyor McDonald's high volume is responsible for its profits, so a mutual fund's large number of shareholders makes possible its low-cost investment advice. The investment adviser charging $10,000 per client may have half a dozen clients and a couple of million dollars to manage. A mutual fund manager for a fund with thousands of clients and $200 million dollars to invest will earn the same amount from the fund's ½ percent management charge, and the caliber of his advice is apt to be just as good as that of his private counterpart. There's nothing wrong with pooled advice, any more than there's anything wrong with pooled investment.

A question well asked at this point is whether professional management can do as good a job of expanding your capital base as you could on your own. If those guys are so smart, how come they're not rich? Well, a lot of them are, but that's another story.

Frankly, neither the stock market nor anything else is going to make any of us rich. If you're looking for easy affluence, there are plenty of books out there with titles like *How I Made a Million Selling Shoelaces by Mail* and *Secrets That Will Make you Wealthy* and so on. I'm sure the authors have done quite well financially. We would all like to be rich. Some of us might even make it. Most of us won't.

Most people won't even stay ahead of the money game in the coming years. Yet that's a goal within the reach of all of us. Professional management can help us reach it.

Not all professional managers perform equally well, of course, which is one reason why some mutual funds, like some investors with their own advisers, do better than others. You are always the director of your own investment plans. That's the one position you never want to relinquish to anyone else. You always have to check up on the funds, following their performance and switching where necessary.

Watching funds, however, is a lot less tedious than going cross-eyed watching several thousand separate stocks.

IBM or MBI?

Admittedly, many of the funds underperform the overall markets a lot of the time. But the good ones outperform it over the long run in a way you as an individual investor rarely could. They do this through diversification carried to a degree that would require a few million dollars for you as a single investor to match.

Sure, we've all heard the story about someone's father who bought IBM way back when and added to it every year. Nothing but IBM would do. And now the family is rich. Well, for every IBM story, there are a hundred MBI stories about someone who bought, and kept buying, Mucho Bad Investment—United Electronut, maybe, or maybe Self-Cleaning Carpet, Inc.—and how the stocks not only went down, down, down, but disappeared altogether.

Mutual funds buy MBIs as well, though when they do, they usually follow the old maxim about cutting losses and running. Also their other holdings usually compensate for the loss, so the overall portfolio still makes money.

With a mutual fund you definitely have diversity. The fund may or may not have good investment management. For even if the fund's results are excellent, there's always the chance that it may be due to sheer luck. Luck plays more of a part in market fortunes than most financial analysts would care to admit. But do you really care as long as it makes you money? Dwight D. Eisenhower is reputed to have said, "I would rather have a lucky general than a smart general in any battle. They win battles and they make me lucky." With a little bit of work, a little bit of management help, and the SLYC system, you'll have the lucky generals on your side in the battle for financial survival.

Free Advice at a No-Load Price

The less-than-a-percent management fee most no-load funds charge is really "free" in relation to what you as an individual would pay in commissions, even negotiated ones, buying a couple of hundred shares here and a couple of hundred shares there. The commission on a hundred shares of a $20 stock is $55. The commission on a hundred shares of a $50 stock is $85. There goes 1½ to 3 percent of your investment, vanishing before your very eyes. Your investment shrinks before it even begins to grow, and it shrinks again after it's grown, because you have to pay even greater commissions when you sell the stocks.

Negotiated commissions, of course, enable you to wheel and deal. Nowadays a broker charges what he thinks the market can carry. The more you buy, the better a break he'll give you on commissions.

Suppose the deal involves a block of 10,000 shares. A broker I deal with, who shall remain nameless—though when he talks, everybody listens—charges $19.70 in commission per hundred shares of $20 stock and $33.10 per hundred shares of $50 stock. Since I'm an old customer, he charges me even less, $15.76 and $26.48 respectively. If I were an old customer running a large mutual fund, he'd come close to paying *me* a commission in order to get the business.

But most of us don't buy $500,000 worth of stock at a clip. Even fewer of us can diversify our holdings at that price. When mutual funds do that for us, however, we gain management in the bargain.

We also gain convenience. A diversified private portfolio of, say, thirty stocks would spew out various-sized dividend checks over the course of a year. These might be a total of 120 checks arriving on the doorstep, depending on the stocks held and how they pay out. That represents a lot of check cashing, record keeping, and reinvesting to keep track of, not to mention a lot of stock certificates to alternately file away and ferret out if they're kept at home or at the bank rather than being left in a broker's account—something you should definitely not do, by the way, if you take the route of the lone investor.

And Some Extra Free Advice on a Loaded Subject

A brokerage firm is a third party standing between you and the company in which you are a shareholder. And any time you have a third party involved in a financial transaction, problems multiply.

Consider the recent liquidation of the once-hot Wall Street firm of John Muir and Company. Muir bit the dust in August of 1981 after a severe liquidity crisis following the price collapse of a number of new stocks it had underwritten. Like all major brokerage firms, Muir was covered by SIPC (Securities Investor Protection Corporation) insurance, good for a cool half million dollars. Still, a lot of customers had securities worth more than that in their Muir accounts. And even after they were paid, during the company's liquidation, their problems didn't stop.

In the middle of the night of January 19, 1981, W.E. Bosarge, chief executive of Texas General Resources, received a telephone call demanding that he return to the bankrupt Muir and Company all the money over $500,000 he had finally managed to collect. Otherwise the trustees, according to the *Wall Street Journal* account of his plight, were going to sue him—*for his own money*. Never mind the fact that between August and December, when Bosarge at last succeeded in unfreezing his account at Muir, his stocks had lost $1 million in value.

Account freezing is bound to affect the financial health of any investor, large or small. Had you held stock bought through John Muir and Company, and had you left the stock certificates for your shares with the company, when Muir went under in August of 1981 you would have been unable to sell those shares, buy any more, or even withdraw a nickel from your account there until the middle of December.

As it happened, the stock market did very poorly in the intervening months. The so-called protected customers fared even more poorly. And some fared far worse than others, for as of February, 1982, some 3,000 of them were still being kept in the deep freeze.

Mutual funds, it's true, are also third-party endeavors. But unlike brokers, mutual funds can't even look at your stock, much less touch it. As a matter of fact, they don't even see your money when you send it in. The law requires that the assets of a mutual fund be held by a custodian bank. Your money goes directly to this bank, which in turn holds the various shares the fund purchases in investments. Like a big safety deposit vault, it simply stores the money and holds the shares.

Your money and the fund's money are never commingled with the bank's money or deposits. Even if the bank were to go under, your investment would not be affected.

The custodian bank also issues the shares for the fund stock you buy, the certificates for which may be either kept at the bank or delivered to you. The actual transaction of your buying or selling fund shares occurs as soon as you give the instructions. But perhaps I should warn you that confirmation of the trade may take several days, and the physical stock certificates may take two or even three weeks to arrive, since for such transactions the deteriorating postal service is still used.

Interbank, fund-to-fund, and fund-to-stock-market trades—transactions comprising the actual day-to-day operation of the fund—have long since ceased to depend on the mail and are now confined to the telephone or TWX wires.

Five Dollars Buys a Lot

Sometimes it pays for you to speed up transactions. You too can use the telephone to move your money quickly. Within the new fund families, you can switch from a money fund into a stock fund when the stock market is strong, or to a bond fund if interest rates are plunging, in the space of a telephone call. Usually there is a small service charge of $5 for such a transaction, and the call is often free through a toll-free 800 number.

You will find this fast exchange feature a profitable option offered by the mutual fund families. Can you think of any other way you can buy and sell as much stock as you want as quickly as you want for $5?

How Many of Each, Please?

The beauty of mutual funds is that the good ones stay true to their colors. An aggressive growth stock fund is going to keep on investing in high-flyers. And now you know that if it reports a big loss carry-over in its prospectus, that's not necessarily an indication of poor management. A growth fund with a big hole in it has a lot of room for winners, and I for one am more interested in what new investments its management is filling up the hole with than I am in the history of the hole. A performance fund that doesn't have losers in a lousy market isn't very likely to have real winners in a good market.

Bond funds, likewise, are going to keep on holding long-term bonds. You can count on it. And you can count on their being a bad investment when interest rates are rising, a good one when rates are falling. You know that when the rates begin to fall, you can always invest in a bond fund and make money.

So how many funds do you need in the family? One of each—a money fund, a growth equity fund, and a bond fund? Several of each, to be sure you're diversified enough?

Well, while it's true that you don't want all your eggs in one basket, it's also true that you don't want them scattered about Easter-egg-hunt style. Too spread out, and at least half of them are going to be in the wrong place at the wrong time in today's market.

What you need is an orderly system for handling your nest eggs without cracking them, because what you're going to want to do is to move your eggs from one basket to another as today's and tomorrow's ever-volatile market conditions change.

That's why I'm going to talk about the SLYC system next—the strategies of investing for safe, high yields, the strategies of staying liquid but also catastrophe-proofing your savings, the strategies of switching, the strategies, in other words, that you need to invest wisely for the eighties.

4

SLYC—The Investment System for the Eighties

> Each of us has the choice—we must make money work for us or we must work for money.
>
> —*Conrad Leslie*

Can You Beat the Dart Board?

In 1967, *Forbes* magazine published a hypothetical stock market fund put together by Malcolm Forbes, James Dunn, and James Michaels, chairman, publisher, and editor, respectively, of the magazine. Each of them threw ten darts at the stock market page of the *Wall Street Journal*, and each hit represented a purchase.

This episode occurred during the heyday of the random walk theory on Wall Street. Pick a bunch of stocks at random, so the theory went, and you'd do as well as, if not better than, the overall market.

Now it so happens that there are a lot of statistical limitations to this approach. For that reason and many others, the theory has long since fallen out of favor. But the Forbes Dart Board Fund is still alive and well and published annually in the magazine. The presentation of the results on February 1, 1982, showed that since its inception the fund had gone up 239 percent, which averages out to a respectable yearly return of about 18 percent—not including dividends. I'll never forgive Forbes for that one.

But I was so intrigued by the idea back in the Sizzling Sixties that I was tempted to buy the "selected" stocks simply to see what would happen next. The list seemed to me enough to cover any contingency.

Unfortunately, I couldn't afford anything like the investment involved. Now, had the list been offered by a real live no-load mutual fund. . . .

The original dart board portfolio really did provide a good deal of diversity. Some of the stocks, like Baker International, which rose 370 percent over the fifteen-year period, were stellar performers. Others, like INCO, declining 49 percent, and Firestone Tire and Rubber, down 43 percent over the same period, left a lot to be desired. In the end, it was diversity that carried the hypothetical fund to the heights of its success. But the fact that none of the thirty darts landed on Chrysler or International Harvester, now, that was luck. What else could you possibly call it?

Founders Fund has done in real life pretty much the same thing as the Forbes Dart Board Fund has done on paper. Picking forty stocks when it was established in 1938, it has stuck with them ever since. How the stocks were originally chosen I'm not sure, but it probably wasn't with the aid of a dart board. Things like that weren't done in the thirties.

Whatever the case, Founders Fund reinvests each month's new money in the same forty stocks. Thus it has effectively eliminated the jobs of both portfolio and management.

How did the Founders Fund do without a helmsman to steer its investments through the dangerous economic shoals? Not badly, actually, though not as well as Forbes' golden darts. Compared with all other funds, it registered above-average performance for thirteen of the last sixteen five-year periods. It's been lucky. (Oh, all right, I'll let you in on the secret. It's been relying on more than luck alone. It's been using a concept called dollar cost averaging, a nifty little deal for long-term investing that allows you to turn market disasters to your benefit. Now there's a concept you'll be taking advantage of too once you've finished this book, and I'll be saying more about your personal investment strategies.)

Safety First—So You Can Count on Your Savings

To whatever degree luck plays a part in financial fortunes—and some market analysts feel its role is vastly undervalued—you certainly can't bank on it. There are simply too many risks at large in the marketplace to entrust your savings to the rule of chance. Investing in the eighties is more than enough of a gamble in and of itself. It needs the strong reins of the SLYC rules of safety. Your investments should always be evaluated for:

- *Safety* first, so you avoid unnecessary risks
- *Liquidity,* so you don't tie up your money and miss profitable opportunities
- *Yield,* so your investments earn the highest rates consistent with safety and liquidity
- *Catastrophe-proofing,* so you can sleep at night

As multimillionaire Sir Freddie Laker, that redoubtable knight of discount air fares, once put it, "You can be the richest man in the world, and be broke if you don't have cash." In November of 1981, after years of highly successful expansion, Laker Airways suddenly had to cut back spending by some $13 million, not exactly chicken feed, because what with the recession and all the competition, airline revenues were way down. And say whatever else you might about owning an airline, a liquid investment it is not. Exactly how illiquid it is came forcefully to the fore, with the sudden bankruptcy of Sir Freddie's airline. The abrupt end of Laker Airways demonstrates the highly important relationship between liquidity and safety. There are many risks in the marketplace, and one of the most telling is the likelihood of factors beyond your control unexpectedly affecting your investments. In the case of Laker Airways, the very cut-rate transatlantic fare structure Sir Freddie had initiated helped to bring him down. But the unpredicted rise in fuel costs and decline in travel due to the recession were the *coup de grâce*. This is *capital risk.*

Capital risk can come from more predictable sources, of course. If you have a hundred dollars and you put it under your mattress, you are putting this capital at very definite risk, not only from an unpredictable event such as burglary, but from what is today an established fact, <u>inflation</u>. The exact rate of inflation may not be predictable—at least the economists are in agreement on this point—but considering recent history, it would be rather absurd to assume that inflation is going to stop tomorrow.

Then there's the matter of *yield risk.* A U.S. government bond can be expected to pay interest come what may. If it doesn't, well, then chances are it's already all over on Wall Street—and every place else. So it's not worth worrying about. The interest on a Treasury bill may be worth less as you collect it because of inflation, but at least it's forthcoming. But take the ultrasafe AAA-rated bonds of United Rubber Band and Propeller Company. The company is certainly financially strong enough to stay in business. But the recession cut into its earnings severely. In fact, it cut into earnings to the point where there weren't any. Bond payments went temporarily into arrears. When you know your capital is almost completely safe, but you can't count on the yield, you have yield risk.

Yield is what you're in the market for. It's what your money earns for you, in either interest, dividends, capital appreciation, or all three. What your investment goals call for is the highest overall yield available *consistent with the risk you're willing to take.*

This System Will Self-Destruct in Ten Years

The single best investment vehicle meeting the criteria of safety, liquidity, and yield today is a money fund. Money funds have been in this position since 1979—not exactly a long time, and the reason why *for an overall financial plan you have to go beyond money funds.*

Although in times of high interest rates, money funds are still the nonpareil of investment vehicles, interest rates will fall again. The rule that what goes up must come down has never been violated yet, and it is most unlikely that we will be the first generation to witness such a miracle. But this decline will not occur overnight. Nor will it be a straight decline without ups and downs. In all likelihood new peaks will be reached many times in the eighties, followed by deep troughs during which you have to be ready to switch part of your assets into stock funds that will benefit from the declining interest rates.

Then sometime, perhaps ten years down the pike, all this will change again. It may be nine years or it may be fifteen or even twenty years until the next cyclic swing occurs. But occur it will. That's why you *always* have to *keep your financial future flexible.*

Above All, Interest Rates

In the good old days, the rich sat around clipping their bond coupons in the family bank vault. At least that was the image the media presented. In reality the rich probably had their butlers do the clipping. Either way, they bought bonds that matured in twenty, thirty, maybe forty years. Those bonds paid 2, 4, maybe 5 percent interest. Twice a year they collected the interest and devoted the next six months to spending it. It was, after all, *extra* income.

Interest rates were stable, fluctuating a percent or two over the course of a decade, and what they actually amounted to didn't really matter much. You worried about the safety of your capital and let the interest worry about itself. Stocks were bought for capital appreciation. Dividends were secondary—just a little bonus.

Today, interest rates are everything. Because of their volatility, their swift and precipitous fluctuations, they dominate every market—stocks, bonds, commodities, real estate. Today's financial world revolves around the axis of interest rates as never before. That's why economists and financial managers watch them so closely. Fund managers study them carefully when they are trying to decide which stocks to buy. In a high-interest-rate environment they will invest in areas such as the service industries not adversely affected by the high cost of borrowing. In a low-rate environment they will look for capital-intensive industries in which to invest, because they know that companies take the opportunity to refurbish and expand while the borrowing's cheap. And at all times they will look for indications of impending change in the interest-rate cycle, because it's apt to come quickly indeed these days.

For fund managers and other investment professionals, interest rates are an important indicator of which stocks to buy. *For you, the crucial importance of interest rates is in helping you to decide, not which stock or stock funds to buy, but whether to buy stocks at all.*

So we'd better talk about interest rates.

The Bond Bombshell

When interest rates go up, bonds go down. When the interest rates go down, bonds go up. This rule is as close to absolute as anything in the world of finance. Let me explain.

A bond represents an IOU for a specific amount. Usually these IOUs come in round figures of $1,000 each. Let's suppose you lend a company $1,000 by buying a bond. The company, say How Sweet It Is, Inc., agrees to pay you 12 percent a year in interest. It also agrees to pay back the full $1,000 in the year 2004.

Now suppose that a year after you buy the bond, you look in the newspaper and see a listing as follows under the bond quotations:

Name	Fixed Interest	Due Date	Current Yield	Volume	Close
How Sweet It Is, Inc.	12	04	16	10	76½

What that listing means is that while you are still getting $120 interest a year (you will always get $120 a year), if you were to sell the bond on the open market on this particular day (remember the company agreed to pay you back, but not until the year 2004), you would get only 76½, or $765. Why? Because interest rates have gone up, but the annual payout of the bond remains that constant $120.

If, a year after you buy the bond, 16 percent is the current yield, not 12 percent as the year before, then anyone can take $1,000 and earn 16 percent on it. So in order to persuade someone to buy your How Sweet It Is bond, you'd discount it enough so that whatever they put up for it would earn 16 percent. That means the bond must be marked down to $765. Twelve percent of $1,000 is $120. Sixteen percent of $765 is $120.

The bond bombshell? Over the course of the year, you've earned $120 in taxable interest but lost $235 in capital

16% of 765 = 120 = 12% of 1000

CORPORATION BONDS
Volume, $30,900,000

Bonds	Cur Yld	Vol	High	Low	Close	Net Chg.
AetnLf 8⅛07	12.	4	70	70	70	– ⅛
AlaP 9s2000	13.	9	67	67	67	+ ¼
AlaP 7⅞s02	13.	30	59	58⅞	59	+ ⅞
AlaP 7¾s02	13.	9	58	58	58	+1
AlaP 8⅞s03	14.	11	64⅞	64⅛	64⅞	+1⅜
AlaP 8¼s03	14.	14	61	61	61	+1
AlaP 10⅞05	14.	2	77	77	77	–2
AlaP 10½05	14.	13	74½	74	74½	.....
AlaP 8⅞06	14.	10	62⅞	62⅞	62⅞	+1⅛
AlaP 8¾07	14.	10	63½	63½	63½	+ ½
AlaP 9⅝08	14.	11	69	68¼	69	.....
AlaP 12⅝10	14.	14	88¾	87½	88¾	+1¼
AlaP 15¼10	15.	172	102¼	101½	101⅞	– ⅛
AlaP 17⅜11	16.	30	111	111	111	–1
AlskH 16¼99	16.	30	106½	104¾	104¾	–1¾
AlskH 18⅜01	16.	20	113	112⅛	112⅛	– ⅞
AlskH 15¼92	15.	25	103	103	103	.....
AlldC 8⅜83	8.5	45	98⅜	98 9-32	98 9-32	–3-32
AlldC zr87	..	30	54½	54¼	54½	+ ½
AlldC zr96s	..	65	20¼	19	20¼	+2¼
AlldC zr2000s	..	177	11½	11⅜	11½	– ⅛
AlsCha 12s90	16.	1	76¼	76¼	76¼	– ¾
AlsCha 16s91	17.	20	93⅛	93	93⅛	.....
AllstF 7⅞87	9.6	10	82⅛	82⅛	82⅛	– ⅞
Alcoa 9s95	12.	8	74⅝	74⅝	74⅝	.....
Alcoa 7.45s96	12.	5	63⅛	63⅛	63⅛	+ ¼
Alcoa 9.45s00	13.	50	75½	75½	75½	+2⅜
AluCa 9½95	13.	3	73⅞	73⅞	73⅞	+ ⅞
AMAX 8s86	9.9	3	81	80¾	81	+ ⅛
AMAX 8½84	9.1	5	93½	93½	93½	+ ½
Amerce 5s92	cv	4	72	71	71	–1
AForP 5s30	13.	32	40	39¾	40	+ ½
AAirl 11s88	12.	24	91	91	91	+1
AAirl 10⅞88	13.	8	86⅝	86½	86⅝	–1¼
ABrnd 5⅞92	9.3	8	63¼	63¼	63¼	–1¾
ACyan 7⅜01	12.	7	59⅜	59⅜	59⅜	+ ⅛
AExC 7.8s92	11.	5	70⅞	70⅞	70⅞	–2
AExC 8½s85	9.5	10	89¾	89¾	89¾	+ ½

($1,000 minus $765), tax-deductible only if you sell the bond and take the loss.

This is a simplified example, leaving out such factors as bond quality. Still, if you're confused, read it again. And again. Don't be embarrassed. Bonds are like one of those magic pictures where you see a goat one minute, a person the next, and then a goat again. Look at Figure 7. Just keep looking at it until you make the correlation automatically. Interest rates go up, bond prices go down. There, you've got it. Now let's go on to the simpler relationship between stocks and interest.

Figure 7
Bond Prices versus Interest Rates

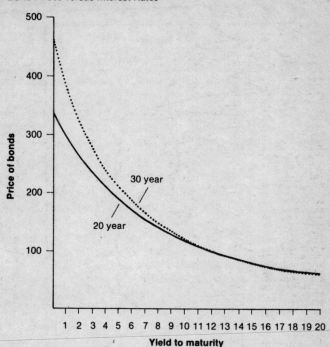

Stock Shock

When a stock company needs to borrow money—which is almost all the time these days—it is permitted to do so at slightly lower rates than you or I do. It's big, and it has influence as well as a lot of valuable assets. But one thing remains the same for the largest company and the smallest person, and that's the fact that as the general interest rates go up, so does the cost of borrowing. And if a company has to pay more for its money, the extra cost has to come out of its profits. Profits go down and the stock goes

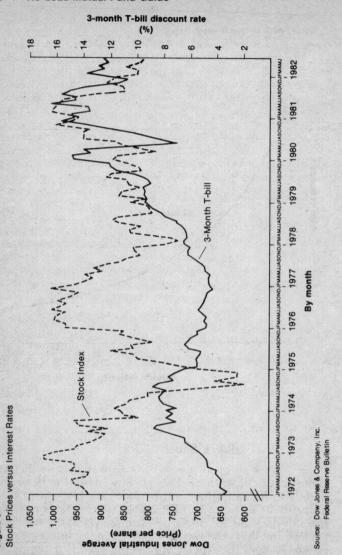

Figure 8
Stock Prices versus Interest Rates

Source: Dow Jones & Company, Inc.
Federal Reserve Bulletin

down. So here we have it again. Interest rates go up, stocks go down.

Oh, there are some exceptions. Nothing is without exception. A drug company develops a cure for cancer (more likely it is merely rumored to have discovered a cure), a solar energy company develops a way to generate electricity ten times more efficiently than by any process known heretofore, a new oil find is announced, an ambidextrous robot materializes—shares in the firms responsible will go up no matter what. The stock of a takeover candidate will do likewise. If a company's stock is trading for $22 and another company offers to buy it out for $32 a share, the stock is bound to rise.

But these are situations the average investor can't take advantage of. Either he owned the stock before the announcement—a slim chance with all the thousands of companies to choose from—or he buys after the news is released, which is when the big boys usually get out, taking the small investor's money with them. So to all intents and purposes, one can still say that when interest rates begin to climb rapidly, stock declines follow (see Figure 8).

Putting the Squeeze on Oranges

Then there's the matter of the commodity markets—copper, oats, orange juice, all the raw materials used in living. Those should be immune to the effects of interest rates, shouldn't they? After all, what's the interest rate on a truckload of bacon or a warehouseful of wheat? Plenty. Right in line with the current interest rates, as a matter of fact.

That warehouseful of wheat, or copper, or orange juice is stored until it is sold. It's usually kept in the warehouse by borrowed money. Even if it's paid for, the money tied up in the commodity could be earning lots of interest if it were in a money fund instead. So when the commodity is sold, the interest the money could have earned is tacked right onto the price. If the cash could have earned 10 percent, then the wheat is going to cost 10 percent more. Obviously the figures are somewhat simplified here. If you'd rather, you can plow through 300 pages of charts and tables in an economics text on interest rates and commodities, but you'll come up with the same general results.

There are exceptions, usually in the form of catastrophes. As I write this, it's freezing up here in New England. The month being January, this should come as no surprise to anyone familiar with the area. But it's also freezing in Florida. Now that's a nasty surprise, particularly if you happen to be an orange grower. Interest rates are going up. But you'd better believe orange juice prices are going up even faster. There's going to be a lot less of that commodity around this season—it's awfully hard to get the frozen orange into that tiny little can—so demand is going to push the price up. The volatility of interest rates is all-pervasive, but it hasn't sunk the basic economic principle of supply and demand yet.

Real Estate Has Real Problems

Real estate is most certainly affected by interest rates. Housing starts almost stopped in the high-interest environment of 1981. Even the resale value of older houses, which had been rising steadily for twenty years, began to decline.

A lot has been written lately about the fortunes made in real estate, much of the writing done by realtors, who, like stockbrokers, earn their money any time there's action. Whether the investor wins or loses is irrelevant. As long as the market is active, he gets his cut.

Now I'm not saying fortunes haven't been made in the real estate market. Over the last decade that market has probably turned more people into millionaires than the exploding high-technology companies have. But in real estate, the millionaires are not many, compared to the losers. The risk is phenomenal.

There are a lot of problems with real estate, from taxes and unpredictable tenants to insurance, not to mention all the other snafus of the business world. But the most telling problem in a volatile interest rate market is the lack of liquidity. If your money is tucked away in a money fund, you can get at it on any given day of the week. If your money is tucked away in a stock fund, you can get at it in five working days, the amount of time the SEC grants the fund before it has to pay out. If your money is tied up in real estate, it could take months for you to sell the property. With today's high interest rates it could take years.

Of course you could lower the price so greatly that you'd almost be giving the property away, in which case you'd surely find a buyer. But where's the profit in that—except for the buyer?

But enough. You get the point. In fact, all this may seem obvious to you. But surprisingly, a lot of people, even though they try to earn the best yield they can for their money, still don't take into account the all-pervasive effect of interest rates on the world of investment.

Which Interest Rate Is Which?

If it is no longer possible to invest wisely without taking interest rates into account, if you can no longer hold an investment without watching closely where those volatile interest rates are going, then exactly which interest rate or rates are you supposed to watch?

Now that's an excellent question. As I write this, there's a whole spectrum of interest rates displayed in the *Wall Street Journal* at my side, to wit:

Prime Rate	10.50%
Brokers Loan Rates	9.75%
Three Month CDs	8.49%
Federal Funds	8.63%
Treasury Bills	8.19%
Money Funds Average	8.45%
Utah P & L 16 3/8 '11	14%
U.S. Treasury 14s '11	14%
Discount Rate	8.5%
Bankers Acceptance	8.36%
Eurodollars	8.96%
S&L Passbook	5½%
U.S. Savings Bond	8.64%
MMDAs Average	8.49%

And those are but a handful of the thousands of different interest rates available on any given day. Just which one am I asking you to keep your eye on?

Well, there's the prime rate, of course. Much in the news since interest rates began swinging so wildly, it used to be an esoteric number to which only bankers paid much attention. And frankly, it's best left that way. The prime rate, although it does affect other rates, is set by the major banks and is slow to respond. Also, while it reflects the mood of the marketplace, it does so only very broadly. Large customers sometimes get rates below prime on their borrowing. Less desirable elements (from a banker's point of view) have to stick their heads in the noose for considerably more. The same or similar problems effectively eliminate from our consideration most of the other numbers listed above.

Probably the best all-around measure of interest rate moves, and the one most actively watched, is U.S. Treasury bonds. Currently the Treasury's closely watched bonds are the 14s due in the year 2011. You'll find them listed under "Treasury Issues" in the *Wall Street Journal.* You'll also often find them mentioned in that same newspaper's "Credit Markets" column, which is where the new closely watched bonds will appear when Wall Street's focus changes.

Now you may not wish to wade through these arcane columns. I wouldn't blame you for that, although I would hasten to add that the *Wall Street Journal,* while it's predominantly a business paper, is also one of the best all-around newspapers this country has to offer. But anyone with $10,000 to invest should at least scan the financial columns regularly, simply to stay abreast of the precipitous pecuniary world.

If you don't want to spend a lot of time on the bond pages trying to determine the direction of the interest rates, here's one place where you can safely let the experts do the footwork for you.

It's been said that when it comes to forecasting interest rates, there are but two kinds of economists: Those who don't know how and those who don't know that they don't know how. And there's more than a little truth in this apportionment for economics as a whole. However, there's also usually at least one well-publicized economist with a winning track record. Right now it's Henry Kaufman of Salomon Brothers. He's been right far more often than wrong for a couple of years. And if he stumbles, well, someone else will come along.

That's a bit of a tenuous proposition, you say. You don't know Mr. Kaufman and you don't want to have to rely on

Figure 9

A Comparison of the Average Maturity Index
with Interest Rates as Measured
by the Three-Month T-Bill Discount Rate

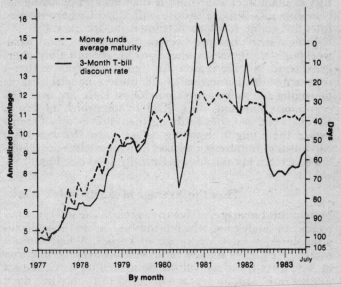

Source: (T-Bill rates) Federal Reserve Bank of Boston

scanning the news for his pronouncements. What if you miss one of them?

No, what you want is an easy-to-find once-a-week figure that will tell you without qualification which direction interest rates are heading. Well, here you're in luck. I've got just such a figure for you. And it won't cost you a cent.

Every Friday most major newspapers in this country, from *The New York Times* to the *Los Angeles Times*, carry the money fund tables prepared by my staff. These tables give the *average maturity index of the money funds.*

What's that? you may ask. Well, money funds concentrate on short-term investments maturing or becoming due in less than a hundred days. But not all of a fund's holdings mature at the same time. Hence the average maturity. Averaging all the fund's averages together gives you the average maturity index. And you could spend fifty hours a week studying the markets and probably not come up with a more precise indicator of where interest rates are going. It's dollar-weighted for accuracy.

Now this isn't because I've got the smartest, most hard-working staff in the financial world, though they are a great team. No, the reason this figure is so good is that it represents the consensus of all those financial wizards managing the money fund portfolios. Here are over 150 economists handling over $208 billion worth of assets. You can bet that they're doing their homework. One or two of them might be wrong occasionally. However, in a consensus of hundreds, mistakes iron themselves out. Nothing is perfect, but this index is awfully good (see Figure 9).

How the Average Maturity Index Works

Money fund managers have to maximize the interest their funds can safely earn, which brings us back to those fluctuating interest rates we spoke of earlier. When interest rates are rising, a money fund with an average maturity of, say, forty-five days will not do as well on its yields as a money fund with an average maturity of twenty-five days. The reason is simple enough. As the Treasury bills, certificates of deposit, and other investments a fund holds mature, the money realized from them can be reinvested by the fund. Now suppose two funds, one with an average maturity of forty-five days (let's call that one Fund A) and the other with an average of twenty-five days (Fund B), are both presently earning 10 percent. And then suppose interest rates go up to 12 percent. Fund B is going to be able to reinvest at 12 percent twenty days earlier than Fund A. So for a while Fund B will be offering its customers a 12 percent yield and Fund A will be offering only 10 percent. All other factors being equal, which fund would you put your money in?

Exactly. And that's why the fund managers keep such a tight watch on interest rates.

The basic rule of thumb here is that *the average maturity*

index moves opposite *to future interest rates*. When the index rises, interest rates can be expected to drop. When the index falls, rates will rise.

A move of one or two points of the average maturity index, say from 30 to 32, over a period of a month is not a strong indication of an interest rate shift. Money fund portfolios are large, and it normally takes weeks for a dramatic change to occur in their average maturity. So by the same token, a move of three days in the average maturity number over the course of a mere week signals a definite, significant shift. A continuous move of one or two days a week for three or four weeks running also indicates a definite, if slower, shift in interest rates.

To give you an idea of how effective this index is, I'm going to relate some events from the fall of 1981. During the months of October and November, interest rates, after almost a year at sky-high levels, declined. Wall Street was convinced the big descent had finally arrived and would continue well into the summer of 1982. Meanwhile, in just seven weeks, the average maturity index rose from 31 to a year-end high of 37. There it stopped short, refusing to go any higher. As you can see from Figure 9, this was a slow rise followed by a plateau, indicating that money fund managers, with some $180 billion worth of responsibility, felt interest rates were only going to dip a little—which is exactly what they did.

Putting the Interest Index to Work for You

Traditional measurements of an investment involved such characteristics as corporate management, corporate balance sheets, corporate asset values, projected growth, competition, market size and share, and the like. These factors are still important investment decisions. However, they are factors we small savers cannot really prudently balance out unless we make investing a full-time occupation. That's exactly why we avail ourselves of mutual funds. Their professional money managers do all this basic footwork for us. But when it comes to deciding which type of fund we should have our money in, we are once more thrown back on our own resources. Should we be invested in a money fund? A stock fund? Where else? And when?

The other decisions we can leave to professional management, but this one we must make ourselves.

Fortunately, the same volatile interest rates that have so radically changed the investment scene provide the tool we need to make fruitful and profitable decisions about that scene in the limited time most of us have available to guide our investments. For *the average maturity index gives us a handle on switching.*

The essence of switching is timing. The oldest maxim on investment profits, after all, is "Buy low, sell high." So we buy a stock fund when the market is down and sell when it's up. And the average maturity index shows us whether stocks are going up or down by showing us their inverse, the direction of interest rates. *But where's the fulcrum? That's the question. Where along the seesaw of interest rates do you buy and sell?*

Taking the Market's Temperature

Some strategists follow the Monetary Thermometer, an index composed of ten different indicators ranked from zero to $+3$. These indicators are the Federal Reserve rediscount rate, stock market margin requirements, bank reserve requirements, shifts in bank investments, cyclical banking liquidity, consolidated excess banking reserves, a basic composite equity index, debt/loan ratios, the Composite Bank Credit Barometer (original), and the Composite Bank Credit Barometer (revised).

If you've gotten through all that, don't stop reading now, you're over the worst. But how the temperature takers read the thermometer when the market really heats up, I've no idea. It seems to me the fever would be gone by the time they've diagnosed it.

Reading the Tea Leaves

Then there are the chartists, the people who calculate thirty-nine-day moving averages, two-week moving averages, five-day moving averages, just about any moving averages you can think of. They also chart cash flows, money supplies, yield ratios, and a host of other variables.

Charting is like abstract art. Anyone can see there's a picture there, but it's never the same picture for everyone.

Tracking Other Track Records

So you might try something a little less fanciful, a little more fundamental. In fundamental timing, current price/earnings ratios and dividend yields are compared with their historical levels. Then there are the monitors of odd-lot sales, the Confidence Index, short interest, secondary distribution, stock volume ratios, new offerings, and the money supply. There are also technical analysts. . . . But let me stop here. All these so-called scientific market timers have two things in common: Over the years they don't consistently work, and they usually work best for the other guy, the one who's telling you about them.

You'll Get a Kick Out of This One

The folksy, unscientific market indicators may well have the edge on their more systematic counterparts. Robert Stovall, a senior vice-president of the brokerage firm of Dean Witter Reynolds, has developed a really super Super Bowl Predictor. To quote *Business Week* on the statistics, "In the fifteen years since the first Super Bowl was played, whenever the victor was a National Football Conference team—or an old NFL team now in the American Football Conference, such as Pittsburgh or Baltimore—the stock market measured by the Standard and Poor's 500 went up. This occurred nine times. In five of the other six years that an original AFL team won, the stock market ended lower. (The only exception: 1970, when Kansas City, an original AFL team, won and the market rose—but only by 0.1 percent.)"

Well, being right fourteen out of fifteen years is certainly far above average for Wall Street prognostication. And if you happen to like football, watching the games on television certainly beats staring at a lot of graph paper.

All this is not to put down completely the concept of market timing. It's been in vogue for a couple of decades now, and it takes the credit for overthrowing the old buy, hold, and pray perspective on investing. Some market timing indicators will even work for you some of the time. They may put you ahead, in fact, if you're willing to devote a couple of days a week to them—or if you happen to subscribe to the right newsletter at the right time. But what if you're not a stock market addict? What if you don't want to spend your time charting and tracking and subscribing to a host of newsletters that may or may not be right—just when you're depending on them? What do you do then?

The 12 Percent Solution

Historically, had you owned growth mutual funds for three decades, and had you reinvested all the capital gains and dividends during those decades, your overall average return would have been 10 percent or better (see Figure 10). Now this return encompasses a long time span, remember. Some years your holdings would have been up considerably more, other years quite a bit less. You can see that on the average mutual funds investments grew only 7.8 percent from 1972 to 1981. At some point or another your return would even have been temporarily negative. Still, your total average return would have been 10 percent minimum.

What does this historical return tell us? It tells us a very simple but significant thing. It tells us that if you invest in a no-load growth mutual fund—or, better yet, if you diversify your investment into two or three top-performing funds—over the long haul you should be able to reap a return on them of somewhere in the vicinity of 10 percent *without doing anything at all.*

Of course, there are taxes to be paid, and inflation to worry about. So a 10 percent return is not enough. In fact, at that rate you'd be losing money with every passing year.

That's why you have to switch out of stock funds any time money funds offer you the opportunity of a higher return. And it's why you must switch back in again as soon as interest rates look like they're going to fall below the 10 percent historical average rate of return of the stock funds.

The basic switching strategy of the SLYC system for your medium- to long-term savings is to watch the average maturity index of the money funds and begin moving your money at the 13 percent to 12 percent level. If the return on money funds falls below 13 to 12 percent, it's time to start switching into stock funds. When money fund returns rise above 12 percent to 13 percent, then it's time to ease your savings back into money funds

Figure 10

Historical Average Annual Returns
on Growth Mutual Funds
Over the Past Three Decades, 1952-1981

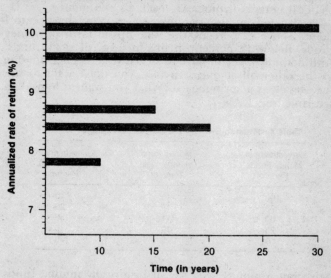

Source: Johnson's Investment Company Charts

again. *Twelve percent is the fulcrum of the interest-rate seesaw.*

Why 12 percent? Well, the 10 percent double-digit barrier has an important psychological effect. As interest rates fall toward 10 percent, the stock market begins to believe that rates will *continue* to fall and the more sensitive (high-beta) stocks begin to attract investors bidding up their prices. These are the same kind of stocks held by aggressive growth stock funds, whose prices respond and rise accordingly with the market. In short, when the stock market begins to believe its own hype about "the boom ahead," you want to take the ride up with it, and bail out quickly when it comes back to its senses, or stay in it if prosperity really does return.

But be careful. While you are in the money funds, a monthly status check is OK. When you begin to switch into the more volatile maximum capital gains or aggressive growth mutual funds, a daily status check is recommended. Don't be bashful about switching back into the money funds if the stock funds start to decline in value—you may earn less but you won't get hurt badly in a whipsaw. Good common sense should overrule any mechanical system anytime. After all, it's *your* money.

Twelve percent is not, however, a razor-sharp cutoff point. Above 12 percent, the scale tips in favor of money funds. Below 12 percent, it tips in favor of stock funds. And nothing says you have to switch your assets from one to the other all at once. In fact, you don't want to use the seesaw as a springboard. What you want is a gradual schedule (see Table 7).

Table 7   When to Switch—the Crucial Percentages

Investment in Money Funds, Percent	Money Fund Average Yield, Percent	Investment in Stock Funds, Percent
100	13	0
75	12	25
50	11	50
25	10	75
0	9	100

Now wait a minute, you say, if historically mutual funds earned roughly 10 percent, why *begin* switching into stock funds when the money fund average return is at 12 percent? Logically it would seem to make more sense to have your money entirely in money funds until the rates dropped to 10 percent. After all, 10 percent is what one should expect from the stock funds, to judge from the records. So why give up the extra 2 percent? Why not wait until the money fund return is down to 10 percent and switch then?

Well, it so happens that in the real world of investing, a gradual shift beats a sudden switch every time. It will always give you a higher rate of return on your investment, whether you're switching from a money fund to a stock fund during a period of declining interest rates or moving your savings from a stock fund to a money fund in a rising rate environment. For example, if you had invested $10,000 on October 1, 1975, when money funds first came into existence, your money would have grown to

$32,544, or at an annual compound rate of 19.1 percent, using the 12 Percent Solution (see Appendix B, especially all you math buffs).

Getting the Best of Two Possible Worlds

The essence of profitable switching is to put your money into stock funds when their return is *above* their historical average. And because your switching decisions are based on overall interest rates as measured by the money fund average maturity index, *that's exactly what you do.* Here's why.

Corporate earnings, and thus stock funds, tend to decline when interest rates are high. It costs companies a lot more to operate in a high-interest environment than it does when borrowing costs are down. So their profits are lower, which translates into lower stock prices. At times like those, the return on stock funds is below their historical average. But that doesn't matter to your money, because it's invested in money funds.

When interest rates are low, on the other hand, corporate profits tend to go up sharply, and the stock funds do too. At such times the stock funds deliver returns above their historical average. And the stock funds are precisely where your money is then.

So you're always catching the stock funds at their point of highest return. You never have to ride out the doldrums with them. As far as is humanly possible, your money is getting the best of two possible worlds when you switch by the 12 Percent Solution.

Applying the Switch

Study Figure 11. (It may take you awhile, but it's worth it.) You'll see that if you had employed the 12 Percent Solution from when we started reporting on money funds in 1975 on, then until well into 1979, you would have been fully, and continuously, invested in stock funds. At that point you would have switched a portion of your assets into a money fund—just in time to *miss* the big 1980 stock market rally. Now is that any way for a system to work!

Yes, because, at the same time, money fund yields also went through the roof. And in point of fact, the yields

Figure 11
Applying the Switch

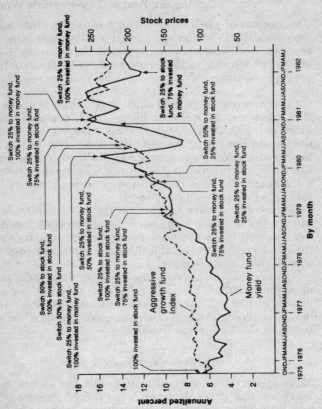

ranged from 8 to 15 percent and averaged about 12 percent in 1980. Your return in money funds during that year would have been comparable to what an individual investor could have expected in the stock market if he or she had been a good (lucky) stock picker.

Not only that, but, using the 12 Percent Solution, you would have been fully invested in money funds throughout 1981 and 1982—at least through June when we are writing this—in other words, throughout the collapse of the stock market in the autumn of that year. Had you been fully invested in a stock fund throughout both the bull and bear years, you would have enjoyed a spectacular rise in assets during 1979 and 1980, and you would have lost most of that gain in 1981. The money funds just kept earning you more and more money. Using the switching signal you also would have moved out of money funds in August 1982, when the stock market exploded, because money fund rates had broken the 10 percent barrier.

And Now a Caveat

Historically, and for the present, the 12 Percent Solution offers you the best basic investment game plan available for your money. So use it. But, of course, as I have tried to stress over and over again, *nothing in the financial world is forever.* As times change, *solutions change.* Your whole investment philosophy may have to change to suit an altered economic environment. So always remember to keep your eye on the interest-rate ball and your hand on your money fund checks—just in case you're thrown a fast curve.

A Switch in Time Instead of Nine

The 12 Percent Solution is an automatic switching system—for a very good reason. Most investors lack a certain amount of discipline. The dollar always looks greener in the other investment. And so once small savers become investors, they tend to switch their money from one investment to another more than is good for their savings. This wavering results in a common Wall Street phenomenon known as whipsawing.

Investment B looks better than the investment A you're currently holding. So you switch. But as soon as you buy investment B, it goes down, and investment A, now that you no longer own it, promptly and perversely proceeds to rise in value. As a gut reaction, you sell B and buy back A. Now return to the beginning of this paragraph and start over again—whipsawing can go on indefinitely.

Remember the difficult arithmetic of breaking even. Losses once taken are hard indeed to recoup. And whipsawing causes recurrent trading losses in your portfolio, which inevitably will erode your capital.

The SLYC system is not one that specializes in quick trades. As a SLYC investor, you will keep a regular watch on interest rates. But the actual amount of switching you do, as you can see from Figure 11, will be minimal. Future interest swings might be wild enough to cause you to switch more than three or four times a year. That rough estimate is probably on the high side, however.

One of the most difficult tactics for SLYC investors to follow may well be not doing anything a lot of the time. It's hard to sit still for long periods of time. And besides, not doing anything somehow doesn't feel very creative. Yet every time you make a trade and take a profit, you have what the IRS for some strange reason calls a "taxable event." That is to say, the IRS wants its cut. Switch less often and you pay less often. You also pay less in amount, because the capital gains tax is lower than the standard income tax. So if the do-something, do-anything urge threatens to overcome you, remember the old saying, "Never sell until you've found something better to buy." The SLYC system will help you maintain this necessary discipline, for while you may not switch often, you'll know precisely when to do it—with no leftover ifs, buts, or maybes.

An Alternative Route from 18 to 12

As rates begin to fall, investors in a high (40 percent plus) tax bracket should consider investing in intermediate-term tax-free money funds. Since these funds have longer maturities (currently over 400 days), they are likely to generate capital *gains* as well as tax-free yields in a *falling* interest-rate market. Some intermediate tax-free money funds are those offered by the Vanguard, Calvert, and Midwest (Fourth Street) groups of funds. (See Appendix C for the names of others.)

The Catastrophe Clause

Whether your savings are in the money fund phase or the stock fund phase of an interest-rate cycle, your capital is diversified. That's guaranteed by the fact that every fund has at least twenty distinct holdings. A mutual fund by law may not put more than 5 percent of its assets into any one given investment. In actuality it probably has even more holdings. Now that's almost sure safety. Nevertheless, you still have to at least contemplate the specter of latent disaster. And that's what the catastrophe-proofing clause in the SLYC system is there for.

Good arguments can be made for the probability that our economy is about to enter a period of hyperinflation. The money supply is out of control—the government in one way and another churns out far more of the stuff than the state of the economy justifies. Debt is out of control, particularly government debt, and as the inflated dollars of the future become worth less and less, the government has less and less to pay back in real dollars.

A lot of paychecks are indexed to inflation. So are pensions. So is social security. This very indexing amplifies inflation. Because these payments are indexed monthly or quarterly, each change compounds the next. Thus these unfunded liabilities grow more quickly than inflation itself does. Inflation must, then, swallow these larger pension payments, engorging itself.

And these are only a few of the indicators pointing toward hyperinflation.

Good arguments can be made for the probability that our economy is about to enter a severe recession. More and more people are beginning to talk about depression again. The gross national product is teetering on the brink of a fall. The basic industries of steel, automobiles, and farm machinery are operating far below capacity, and some of the largest producers are technically, if not yet officially, bankrupt. Trade restrictions are rising all over the world. Commodity prices are crumbling. Real estate prices are tumbling. Home construction has just about come to a halt.

These are only a few of the indicators pointing toward a depression.

Economists and statisticians alike have lost control of the

numbers they deal in—up to 15 percent of the entire gross national product of this country is now produced by the underground economy, where no one keeps statistics, much less pays taxes, putting the economists' numbers completely out of whack. If all this leaves you with the feeling that no one seems to know what's going on or what to expect, that's just fine—because the point I'm trying to make is that precisely what you buy insurance for is protection against the unknown, the unexpected. You buy fire insurance just in case your house should burn down. Most people's houses never do. But where misfortune does strike, that insurance may make all the difference between being able to continue life in a more or less normal fashion and having to start all over again from square one, something which is not always even possible. The same principle applies for any insurance policy, be it automotive, liability or life. You're buying protection from disaster, from catastrophe.

But what kind of insurance should you buy for your savings, inflation insurance or depression insurance?

You need *both*. And the only way to have both is to put 10 percent of your savings into *investments that you hope will never make you very much money*.

Deep-Discount Depression Insurance

Five percent of your capital should go into a bond fund, just in case there's a depression. You could buy bonds yourself, of course, but once again the problem of diversification arises. If there were a real depression, even some of the most solid old-line companies might have difficulty meeting their obligations. A bond fund, on the other hand, not only is diversified, but has managers whose job it is to monitor constantly the credit ratings of the fund's holdings.

For the most part, bond funds are not yet members of the great and growing no-load fraternity, though a few of them have joined the family. The Vanguard group (the new name for the old Wellington Funds, which at the peak of the load-fund boom had one of the strongest sales forces going for it) is a recent convert to investor-oriented financial goals. These and other no-load fund families dealing in bonds—Fidelity and Dreyfus, to name two—are worth looking into for the 5 percent depression segment of your catastrophe insurance. Of course, you should try to buy into the bond fund when interest rates are at their highest and bond fund shares at their lowest. *But don't try to outguess the economy and put more than the 5 percent of your portfolio reserved for depression-proofing into a bond fund.*

Another way to buy a bond fund is the closed-end route. Closed-end funds are different from all other mutual funds in that they have a fixed number of shares, which are traded on the stock exchange or over the counter—with a commission due each time they are bought or sold. (You'll be hearing more about closed-end funds in the chapter on special-situation funds.)

A third course is to buy your bond insurance through the government—either directly at a Federal Reserve bank or through your broker, since, with the exception of the Federal Reserve, the government doesn't deal directly with its citizens in financial matters except when it collects taxes and pays out for its social service programs.

No Need to Shout Fore When You're Shooting under Par

Check the bond page of the *Wall Street Journal,* and you'll see a column called "Treasury Issues—Bonds, Notes, and Bills." What you are interested in is Treasury bonds due about twenty to thirty years from now. More specifically, what you want is the one with the *lowest* interest rate for that time span. Consider, for instance, the following choices as listed in the "Treasury Issues" table on February 5, 1982.

Rate	Mat. Date	Bid	Asked	Bid Chg.	Yld.
7⅝s	2002 Feb.	56.10	56.18	−.18	13.87
12¾s	2005 Nov.	88.16	88.24	−.13	14.40
15¾s	2001 Nov.	105.12	105.20	−.4	14.86

The rate is the interest at which the bond was originally issued. In this case we have a 7⅝ percent bond, a 12¾ percent bond, and a 15¾ percent bond. They are all due within a couple of years of each other, from 2001 to 2005.

(Yes, that's only twenty years away. It's amazing how short a century is when you're dealing in long-term bonds.)

The huge differences in the interest rates at which these bonds were issued are strictly a function of when in the interest cycle they came out. The 7⅝s were sold by the government when 7⅝ percent was an acceptable rate. The 15¾s were issued a few years later, when nothing but the offer of double-digit interest would bring customers to the cashier's window.

As you will recall from earlier chapters, when interest rates go up, older bonds paying a lower interest rate fall until their payout equals the current interest rate. For instance, if you have a bond priced at 100 that pays $10 a year, it's a 10 percent bond. If a few years later the interest rates rise dramatically and the new 100 bonds are paying $20 a year, or 20 percent, then your old 100 bond falls by half, to 50 in value, because it would take two of these bonds bought at the reduced price to make you a total of $20 in interest. If they didn't fall to accommodate the new interest rates, everyone would simply buy the new bonds.

This price fluctuation as a factor of current yield is the feature that works in your favor in the eventuality of a depression. In the sample *Wall Street Journal* listing I used above, note that the 15¾ bond due in the year 2001 is selling over par. (Par is 100, or the price at which the bond is originally issued. To confuse the issue, 100 actually represents $1,000, the real denomination of the bond). The price increase is due to the fact that interest rates have dipped between the time the bond was issued and February 5, 1982, the date of the price quote. Bought at 100 when issued (and actually costing $1,000), the bond is now quoted at 105.12 bid (which means that someone is willing to pay you $1,051.20 for it).

If you look at the yield column on the far right of the table above, you'll note that the yield for each of the three sample bonds is within a percent of the yield of the other bonds, whereas in the far left-hand column the spread is over 7 percent. Don't let it worry you. Basically, it's a function of the actual due dates of the bonds, plus some other time factors, and while its whys and wherefores are too complicated to go into here, for insurance purposes it is sufficient to know that all three of these bonds are as safe as the U.S. government.

In a depression, suddenly no one wants to borrow money anymore. Actually, in some cases they'd like to borrow money, but they can't because they have no collateral. Either way, loans shrivel. And when loans shrivel, interest rates fall. Remember that banks and other financial institutions have to earn money on their money in order to stay in business. So when loans fall off, the banks begin to wheel and deal, each one trying to beat the competition to a lower rate.

If a real depression were to hit this country again, interest rates would probably drop to the 2½ or 3 percent level or even lower. That's right, 2½ or 3 percent. It's no more absurd a proposition than talking about the possibility of 15 percent mortgages way back in the ancient days of the early seventies would have been.

Now, at a prevailing interest rate of 2½ percent, say five years from now, a 7⅝ percent bond would be selling in the neighborhood of 300. That means a $560 investment now would be worth approximately $3,000 then. You'd be earning the same amount of interest as before, that is, $76.25 per bond—which wouldn't be much on $3,000. But you wouldn't be able to get anything better, because all the interest rates would have plunged. And what you're really interested in is that rise in capital from $560 to $3,000 or so. And what you're really hoping for is that it never happens. Despite the fact that with your 5 percent SLYC insurance you'd be far better off in a depression than most people would be, nothing makes a depression really pleasant.

Hyperinflation Hedging

To be effective, catastrophe-proofing must cover both economic extremes while the major portion of your money keeps playing the economic middle, keeps growing, in the hope that catastrophe will never come.

Almost everything from diamonds to real estate to fine art to mint-condition Barbie dolls in their original wrappers has been promoted as an inflation hedge. Do any of these collectibles do the job?

Real estate, as I've noted, is far too illiquid to serve the purpose. It's also subject to all kinds of tax problems in a hyperinflation situation. After the hyperinflation balloon collapsed, one might find one had come out ahead by having held real estate throughout it all. Then again, one might not. The important thing here is insurance, not speculation—something with which to buy your daily bread if inflation reaches the point where the dollar bills you'd need to buy the bread would weigh more than the loaf they purchased.

No two people are going to agree on the price of a diamond. Besides, the wholesale/retail spread of the diamond market would destroy you financially. Fine art might just turn the trick, but the prices of works of art at any given time are almost wholly dependent on fad and whim. Who knows what they would be like in the middle of chaos? As to collectibles such as Barbie dolls, Billy beer cans, and Avon bottles, well, what would they be worth to you in the middle of hyperinflation?

Which leaves probably the oldest storehouse of value in civilization, precious metals. But let me stress two points. First of all, *don't look at precious metals as an investment.* You're not playing the gold or silver market. Most of the people who have played these markets in the last few years have seen their money melt away.

What you're concerned with here is strictly insurance. You hope you'll never make money on your investment in this instance, because if you did, it would be because the world has been reduced to survival living. And being prepared for that emergency is one thing. Having to actually live through it is quite another.

Since what we're talking about is strictly an insurance investment, and since the chances of hyperinflation are about the same as those for a depression, my second caveat is this: *Don't be lured by precious metals' glitter (or by glowing sales talk) into putting more than 5 percent of your savings into this sector of your SLYC plan.*

The Midas Touch

In the matter of gold versus silver, traditionally gold has sold for sixteen times the value of silver, which means that at the moment silver is wildly underpriced. However, while history is never wrong, it has happened, after all, that things have changed in the flow of time. Historically, wam-pum was a good investment too, in colonial Massachusetts. Unfortunately, machinery evolved. The slow process of polishing the shells and drilling holes by hand was speeded up by several orders of magnitude. Wampum became valueless except as a curiosity.

Now the chances of silver becoming valueless are rather slim. Its use is widespread, far more widespread than the use of gold. Not only is it fashioned into jewelry and silverware, but it is employed in various modern electronic applications. Most important, it's the backbone of the booming photography craze. Without silver there would be no film. And so, to many, silver, especially at its current undervalued price, is a far better investment than gold.

However, this line of reasoning fails to take the future into account. First there's videotape. Bye-bye home movies. And videotape needs no silver. Add to this the fact that several Japanese camera firms are currently working on applying videotechnology to still pictures and snapshot cameras, and the fact that the high silver prices of 1980 forced even slumbering Kodak to start looking into silverless film, and you arrive at the conclusion that the commercial demand for silver could be reduced by as much as 50 percent within the present decade. Historically, silver may be underpriced in comparison with gold. Futuristically, it may well be over-valued in years to come. Strive for the Midas touch and stay with gold.

When I say stay with gold, what I'm referring to is regular cheap bullion gold coins. Krugerrand, Maple Leaf, Peso, or equivalent coins. These coins have two distinct advantages for insurance purposes. First of all, *their value is established and universally recognized.* As coins they need not be assayed the way gold bars and ingots must be. Second, they have *no numismatic value.*

Rare coins may be a good appreciation hedge. Then again, they may be worth only the gold they're made of. Do you remember how during the great silver boom of 1980 people were selling their grandmothers' sterling silver sets left and right because they were suddenly worth $30, $40, even $50 an ounce? As silverware, the sets might have been worth only $20 an ounce. Now that silver as metal is back to $8 an ounce, the silverware might still be worth $20 an ounce. Or it might be worth more, since so many sets have been melted down. Who knows? What is certain is that a collector's premium will not follow the metal's price rise during hyperinflation, except in the case of a few very special and, one might add, unpredictable items.

So stay with the basic bullion coins. Within reason, the smaller the denomination the better. Several lower-value coins would be easier to deal with than one large one if such coins ever became a medium of exchange. Remember, if hyperinflation did come, gold might well be worth $10,000, $20,000, or $50,000 an ounce. It would be pretty hard to spend a $50,000 coin for groceries—even with bread at $100 a loaf. And, by the way, if you ever have to make change for the small coins in your insurance pouch, remember that it is always possible to cut up a coin. Our slang expression, "two bits for twenty-five cents," comes from the old Spanish pieces of eight, which were cut into eighths, two bits being a quarter, whenever lower values were needed.

One Time When You *Don't* Want a Fund

You've probably noticed that hyperinflation insurance is the only facet of the SLYC system for which I have not recommended using the pooled investment structure of a fund. There are gold funds. But there are also some very good reasons for not investing in them as a hedge against hyperinflation.

For one thing, most of the gold funds involve South African mines. And South Africa is not stable enough under present circumstances to warrant any kind of investment. Even a fund investing only in U.S. gold mines is not really suitable protection against hyperinflation, for the economic and social chaos that would accompany such an event in this country would lead to an utter distrust of any kind of paper currency or storehouse of value, including the certificates issued by these gold funds. Besides, how do you collect in such a situation? And who would be doing the mining under such circumstances?

Like everything else, the fund approach to investing has its exceptions. This is one of them. *When it comes to hyperinflation insurance, stay with the real thing, and keep it close to your vest.*

The Marginal Key

Probably one of the least understood concepts in our basic income tax structure is the marginal tax rate. Yet *the marginal tax bracket, and the way it affects your money, is the first key to tax savings under any tax law, including the new one.*

Your income tax is not figured on a smooth increasing curve—earn so much, pay so much, earn a little more, pay a little more. Instead, the tax you owe on your income is determined by a series of steps, or brackets, that increase in jumps.

If your taxable income for 1982 happened to be $24,600, and you're married and filing a joint return, you would be in the 25 percent tax bracket. That is to say, Uncle Sam would rake off 25 cents on the dollar (not counting 6.3 percent for social security, and so on and so forth).

Now if you earned over $24,600, you would automatically jump into the 29 percent bracket, and Uncle Sam would take 29 cents of every dollar you earned above that amount. Over 29,900, and you're in the 33 percent bracket. And so on. Two steps forward, one step back every time.

The trick, then, is to reduce your marginal tax rate. That sometimes means it's worth squeezing your income very hard to make it a couple of hundred dollars smaller, simply in order to drop your taxes into a lower bracket. To see where you stand under the Economic Recovery Tax Act of 1981 (ERTA), take a look at Table 8, which gives the marginal tax rates for joint returns, and Table 9 showing the marginal tax rates for single returns.

Now You See It

Notice how nicely your marginal tax rate drops in 1983 and 1984, and how it's dropped even more since 1980 and 1981. Gives you a warm glow, doesn't it? At last the government's doing something about those unbearable taxes.

Now You Don't

But now look at Table 10, "What ERTA Will Really Do to Your Money," The numbers come from a cheery article in the *Wall Street Journal*, "An Introduction to Personal Tax

'Cuts,' " by Richard B. McKenzie, a professor of economics at Clemson University. Professor McKenzie's analysis shows what actually happens, assuming an average inflation of 8 percent per year, current state taxes (in this particular example the state is South Carolina), and the schedule social security taxes. *No matter what income tax bracket you're in, your average tax rate is going to be higher, and your after-tax purchasing power is going to be lower.* So what's new?

If Tax Cuts Can't Help You, Capital Gains Can

Under ERTA, the capital gains tax has been reduced to 40 percent of the ordinary income tax. Now that's not 40 percent of the money you earn as capital gains, but 40 percent of your marginal tax rate, which means that the actual maximum capital gains rate is 20 percent. Of course, that's for folks in the 50 percent tax bracket (40 percent of 50 percent is 20 percent—nobody makes things simple when it comes to taxes). But look at Tables 11 and 12, They should ease the pain.

Table 8   The Marginal Tax Rate Schedule for Married Individuals Filing Joint Returns, and for Surviving Spouses

Taxable Income		1982		1983		1984	
		Pay +	Percent on Excess*	Pay +	Percent on Excess*	Pay +	Percent on Excess*
0-$	3,400	0	0	0	0	0	0
$ 3,400-	5,500	0	12	0	11	0	11
5,500-	7,600	$ 252	14	$ 231	13	$ 231	12
7,600-	11,900	546	16	504	15	483	14
11,900-	16,000	1,234	19	1,149	17	1,085	16
16,000-	20,200	2,013	22	1,846	19	1,741	18
20,200-	24,600	2,937	25	2,644	23	2,497	22
24,600-	29,900	4,037	29	3,656	26	3,465	25
29,900-	35,200	5,574	33	5,034	30	4,790	28
35,200-	45,800	7,323	39	6,624	35	6,274	33
45,800-	60,000	11,457	44	10,334	40	9,722	38
60,000-	85,600	17,705	49	16,014	44	15,168	42
85,600-	109,400	30,249	50	27,278	48	25,920	45
109,400-	162,400	42,149	50	38,702	50	36,630	49
162,400-	215,400	68,649	50	65,202	50	62,600	50
215,400-		95,149	50	91,702	50	89,100	50

*The amount by which the taxpayer's taxable income exceeds the base of the bracket.

Table 9   The Marginal Tax Rate Schedule for Single Individuals

Taxable Income		1982 Pay +	Percent on Excess*	1983 Pay +	Percent on Excess*	1984 Pay +	Percent on Excess*
0-$	2,300	0	0	0	0	0	0
$ 2,300-	3,400	0	12	0	11	0	11
3,400-	4,400	$ 132	14	$ 121	13	$ 121	12
4,400-	6,500	272	16	251	15	241	14
6,500-	8,500	608	17	566	15	535	15
8,500-	10,800	948	19	866	17	835	16
10,800-	12,900	1,385	22	1,257	19	1,203	18
12,900-	15,000	1,847	23	1,656	21	1,581	20
15,000-	18,200	2,330	27	2,097	24	2,001	23
18,200-	23,500	3,194	31	2,865	28	2,737	26
23,500-	28,800	4,837	35	4,349	32	4,115	30
28,800-	34,100	6,692	40	6,045	36	5,705	34
34,100-	41,500	8,812	44	7,953	40	7,507	38
41,500-	55,300	12,068	50	10,913	45	10,319	42
55,300-	81,800	18,968	50	17,123	50	16,115	48
81,800-	108,300	32,218	50	30,373	50	28,835	50
108,300-		45,468	50	43,623	50	42,085	50

*The amount by which the taxpayer's taxable income exceeds the base of the bracket.

Table 10   What ERTA Will Really Do to Your Money

1980 Income	Average Tax Rate as a Percentage of Income		After-Tax Purchasing Power	
	1980	1984	1980	1984
$15,000	17.8	19.4	$12,327	$12,084
24,000	24.5	25.1	18,129	17,978
45,000	33.0	34.6	30,104	29,420

Notice that if, as in the example I used before, you are earning $24,600, and are thus in the 25 percent tax bracket, the tax you owe on any money you make through capital gains is only 11.60 percent for 1982, 10.40 percent for 1983, and 10 percent for 1984. So if you invest in a money fund or a stock fund that pays out 12 percent in dividends, you'll earn only 9 percent after taxes, whereas if you invest in a mutual fund paying 12 percent in capital gains, you'll keep over 10 percent.

Now an extra percent or two a year isn't enough to kill for. But it adds up, and under certain conditions the differential is much higher. For instance, if you have a taxable income of $35,200, putting you in the 39 percent tax bracket, and you received a 12 percent taxable return, you'd actually be earning only 7 percent. With a 12 percent capital gains return, you'd have close to a 10 percent after-tax return.

Some Returns Are Better Than Others

Earning the right kind of returns on your mutual fund investments puts more money in your pocket and less in the tax man's. So let's sort out the returns, starting with some basic definitions.

- **Return:**
  What you get back from your mutual fund investments over and above what you paid for your shares. Returns include dividend income and capital gains.
- **Ordinary Income:**
  Income from dividends and interest earned by a fund and distributed to the investors—taxable at the regular rate.
- **Capital Gains:**
  The difference between what you paid for your mutual fund shares and what you get from them when you sell your shares back to the fund. I hope the difference truly represents a gain—read profit.
- **Short-term Capital Gains:**
  Gains on investments held for a year or less—and taxed as ordinary income (up to 50 percent maximum now allowed by law).
- **Long-term Capital Gains:**
  Gains on investments held for more than a year—and taxed at the capital-gains rate (whose maximum is 20 percent). A gift from the gods of the marketplace and the IRS, long-term capital gains are 80 percent tax-free.
- **Year-End Dividends:**
  An extra payout made by a fund, usually in December. Often a misnomer, since it usually represents a distribution of capital rather than true dividend income, it is your most crucial dividend because of the fact that in most cases it represents a capital gains distribution and is thus taxable at a much lower rate than that

Table 11 The Capital Gains Tax Rate Schedule for Married Individuals Filing Joint Returns and for Surviving Spouses

Taxable Income	Capital Gains Tax, Percent		
	1982	1983	1984
0-$ 3,400	0	0	0
$ 3,400- 5,500	4.8	4.4	4.4
5,500- 7,600	5.6	5.2	4.8
7,600- 11,900	6.4	6	5.6
11,900- 16,000	7.6	6.8	6.4
16,000- 20,200	8.8	7.6	7.2
20,200- 24,600	10	9.2	8.8
24,600- 29,900	11.6	10.4	10
29,900- 35,200	13.2	12	11.2
35,200- 45,800	15.6	14	13.2
45,800- 60,000	17.6	16	15.2
60,000- 85,600	19.6	17.6	16.8
85,600- 109,400	20	19.2	18
109,400- 162,400	20	20	20
162,400- 215,400	20	20	20
215,400-	20	20	20

Table 12 The Capital Gains Tax Rate Schedule for Single Individuals

Taxable Income	Capital Gains Tax, Percent		
	1982	1983	1984
-$ 2,300	0	0	0
$ 2,300- 3,400	4.8	4.4	4.4
3,400- 4,400	5.6	5.2	4.8
4,400- 6,500	6.4	6	5.6
6,500- 8,500	6.8	6	6
8,500- 10,800	7.6	6.8	6.4
10,800- 12,900	8.8	7.6	7.2
12,900- 15,000	9.2	8.4	8
15,000- 18,200	10.8	9.6	9.2
18,200- 23,500	12.4	11.2	10.4
23,500- 28,800	14	12.8	12
28,800- 34,100	16	14.4	13.6
34,100- 41,500	17.6	16	15.2
41,500- 55,300	20	18	16.8
55,300- 81,800	20	20	19.2
81,800- 108,300	20	20	20
108,300-	20	20	20

applying to ordinary income. Your fund will specify whether or not a year-end dividend represents a capital gains distribution when it sends you your check or statement.

Mutual funds are required by law to distribute at least 90 percent of their investment income and realized capital gains for the taxable year in order to qualify for subchapter M of the Internal Revenue Code. Subchapter M allows the mutual fund (or investment company—same thing) to pass on its investment income as dividends to its shareholders in the form in which it was earned, without having to pay income taxes on it. This means that if the mutual fund earns ordinary income, it passes ordinary income on to you; if it earns tax-free income, it passes tax-free income on to you; and most important, if it earns long-term capital gains, that's what it passes on to you. So for tax purposes, keep your eye on the fund's income as well as your own.

Putting Long-Term Capital Gains to Work for You

The best way to earn long-term capital gains is in the form of capital gains distributions from your mutual fund. Your mutual fund can earn long-term capital gains by buying a stock or a bond and holding it for a year or more. Until the stock or bond is sold, its "paper" gain is carried as an unrealized profit. When the fund sells, it realizes the long-term capital gain and distributes that gain to its shareholders as a capital gains distribution.

The only thing to remember is that if you buy a mutual fund share, including unpaid dividends, for $10, and you shortly thereafter receive a capital gains distribution, of say $1 (the per-share price of your stock falling $9 after the distribution is made), you'll pay 20 cents tax on what is in fact your own original investment.

If the fund continues to increase in value, and six months later you sell at $12, you have now earned a short-term gain of $2 per share, taxable at the 50 percent maximum (or $1 after taxes) plus another $1 dividend taxable at the 20 percent maximum (or 90 cents after taxes, for a total after-tax gain of $1.80). Had the fund not paid a dividend, its price would have gone from $10 to $13, and had you sold your shares, your after-tax profit would have been $1.50 rather than $1.80 in the first example. The problem? If the per-share value decreases to, say, $8 you end up paying taxes on part of your loss unless you can use them to offset other gains. But, of course, we're trying to help you avoid losses.

One easy way to earn long-term capital gains is simply to hold your mutual fund shares for over a year and sell them at a higher price than what you paid for them. The gains are taxed at a maximum of 20 percent, leaving 80 percent of your profits tax-free.

This is an attractive opportunity. The only problem is that in today's highly volatile markets, it's increasingly difficult to find an investment to hold onto for a full year. If you can get long-term capital gains treatment—take it and run, it's a blessing. And, if you are planning to sell shares of a mutual fund that you have held for over a year, try to do so *before* the next income dividend is declared, so you can convert that last would-be dividend from ordinary income into long-term capital gains.

Beware the Taxes of December

There's one more quirk in buying mutual funds, and that's the December tax burp. Most funds make their capital gains distribution in December. Now let's say a fund is selling for $12 a share and you buy 1,000 shares with some money you've just inherited. Those shares cost you $12,000. A week later, this being December, the fund makes a capital gains distribution of $2 a share, representing the profits it has taken throughout the year. The shares now sell for $10 apiece. But you have received a $2 dividend. So you still have $12,000 (your $10,000 worth of the fund plus $2,000 in capital gains). If you are on a reinvestment plan, you now have 1,200 shares of stock, since the fund bought you another 200 shares with the dividends. You're exactly even, right? Wrong.

Because the capital gains were distributed—that is, the fund paid you—you now owe capital gains tax on $2,000. Had you waited until after the capital gains distribution had been made, you simply would have purchased 12,000 shares for $12,000, and that would have been that.

Capital gains distributions pose no particular tax problem if you are depositing only small amounts regularly, or if your deposits are made to your tax-free retirement account. But if you have a large amount of money to invest at one time, call the fund first to make sure no capital gains distribution is imminent.

Letters, We Get Letters

Speaking of calling, or writing, for that matter, by far the most common questions my newsletter readers ask have to do with the intricacies of mutual fund yields, and the way they relate to taxes. That's what gives most people the worst headaches. Here are two letters which, because the questions are so pertinent, I'd like to share with you— answers included so they won't cost you postage.

V.R., of Albuquerque, New Mexico, writes:

> I am always confused about mutual fund yields. Last year your *Mutual Funds Almanac* said my fund paid 21 percent, but I was only paid a 5 percent dividend. Is my fund cheating me or am I nuts—or are your figures wrong?

"None of the above," is the answer. You see, your fund did pay 5 percent, but its price per share increased by 16 percent over the year. However, since you did not buy on the first day of the year and sell on the last day of the year, you did not realize the 16 percent capital gain, so you only made the 5 percent dividend actually paid out. Had you been following my 12 Percent Solution, you would have sold, taken your profits, and run. As it is, your fund had declined over 15 percent in value over the past year. That means your 5 percent this year that you have to pay taxes on is really 10 percent loss and you should get some taxes back, but only if you sell your shares. Timing is everything in investment sales and purchases. Remember, buy, hold, and pray is dead!

K. S., of Brooklyn, New York writes:

> I own mutual funds; indeed they were my introduction to the stock market. One particular one that I own I will probably be selling off next year, as I plan to go to Greece and try to exist there on $400 a month. I would have sold this off a few years ago, but the income tax ramifications scared hell out of me.
>
> Now, the amount of tax is not my bugaboo; I have read and reread all the IRS publications and the pri-

vately published stuff and it simply doesn't sink in. I have always done my own taxes—with many schedules as my life became more and more complicated. I simply don't understand how you figure out the cost basis if you reinvest all the dividends and capital gains.

I manage to cope in other ways financially, but selling my mutual fund is all Greek to me.

I love to pay taxes as long as on an after-tax basis I earn more. On the other hand, I'm also afraid we'll get as much government as we seem to be paying for. But, seriously, in answer to your question, if you reinvested all of your dividends and capital gains, then you also paid taxes on them. Simply take the total value of the shares you now own, deduct your original investment and the capital gains and dividends you've already paid taxes on, and the balance is your capital gains. And no more than 20 percent of that is your tax.

The Paper Portfolio

Now when you've read this far, you may be feeling slightly overwhelmed by the complexity of it all. But investing for the eighties really isn't as difficult and involved as it might seem at the outset. My recommendation is to work out a paper portfolio first. Pretend you're making the actual investments, and keep a careful record of the results for a few months. You'll be amazed at how easily the SLYC system will come to you then. And this risk-free education won't cost you a cent. Now let's do some footwork, and set up the preliminary paperwork for your portfolio.

5

The Mechanics of Investing in No-Load Mutual Funds

> The best time to plant a tree was twenty years ago. The second best time is now.
>
> —*Anonymous*

"Which mutual fund should I invest my money in?" is probably the question I'm asked most frequently these days. And the answer isn't all that complicated, but it's not consistently the same for everyone or for every time. We'll talk some more about your personal goals and savings. But first let's finish talking about the investments to which you're going to entrust those savings.

Which fund? The first point I want to make in answer to that question is that there's no reason to invest in only one fund. In fact, the fund most suitable for, say, your IRA might not be at all suitable for a college account for the kids. In the last analysis, you'll have to weigh each fund in the balance of your own personal objectives. And you'll diversify your investment as needed to match those objectives.

But there is one statement about choosing a mutual fund that I can make categorically. Don't even consider a load fund. In the words of one disgruntled load-fund customer who has long since become anonymous, "No, no, no. Eight hundred and fifty times no."

A Last Look at Load Funds

In the back of your mind somewhere, if you're like the average investor, there's this nagging, leftover doubt—there must be some reason for buying load funds. After all, there are still a lot of them around, still charging that 8½ percent commission. Surely that must mean something. Maybe—you recite to yourself the old adage about getting what you pay for—just maybe you'd get better management for the money if you bought a load fund.

Well, according to the SEC-sponsored *Institutional Investor Study Report,* "There is no appreciable difference between the performance of funds which charge sales loads and those which do not." Another study, *Mutual Funds and Other Institutional Investors,* by Irwin Friend, et al., goes even further, concluding, "If there is a relationship between performance and sales charges, it appears to be negative. The funds with the lowest sales charges (including no-load funds) seem to perform slightly better than the other funds, but the differences are minor."

What is not minor is the fact that when you buy into a load fund, your investment takes a large step backward before it can even begin to move forward. When you deposit $10,000 in a no-load fund, that's exactly what your investment starts out with. The same investment in a load fund is instantly converted to $9,150, $850 going to the sales force. So in a load fund, you earn less on your money from the very start, and because you start with less, the compounding effect of interest on your investment just makes the difference worse. The load-fund curve *never catches up* (see Figure 12).

Now take a look at the real performance records of the load and the no-load funds (see Figure 13). In the long run, the only thing a load fund has to offer that a no-load one doesn't is a happy salesman. That's simply not worth it, even if he's your nephew.

Not Too Big, Not Too Small

Once in a while, a small growth fund is a stellar performer. But you probably want a larger one, not merely so you can readily check its quote in the newspaper, but also because its bigger size usually eliminates the chances of a single stockholder having undue influence on the fund's investments, and consequently its price, should he suddenly sell.

If such a stockholder owned, say, 10 percent of the fund, and he suddenly sold all his shares, the fund probably would not be in a cash position to pay him, and would have to sell enough of its holdings to meet its obligations to him immediately. Thus it might be forced to sell stock that could otherwise have been expected to perform quite well over the next couple of months or so. The result? The stockholder has directly influenced the fund's investment decisions. Not only that, but dumping such a quantity of stock on the market all at once could drive down its price, in turn driving down the price of the fund's shares.

Figure 12

Load Funds Mean You Earn Less from the Start

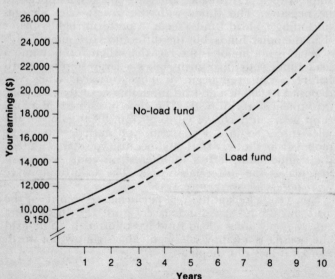

This example assumes an 8½% load on a load fund, and an annual compound rate of 10%.

Listed funds have a minimum of 2,000 shareholders. The average account being somewhere in the neighborhood of $3,500, that means total assets of around $7 million—small, but not too small. If a fund you're thinking about isn't listed in the fund tables of the business section of your newspaper, chances are it's too small for you.

You don't want too large an equity fund either. One with some $500 million in assets is about tops. Growth funds can be somewhat larger, but not by much. Performance funds should be quite a bit smaller.

Giant funds are really too large to make a meaningful profit from investing in the small, secondary companies that so often show the most promise of rapid growth. They also lose flexibility by virtue of their size, for a change in their huge holdings can actually affect the marketplace, and this works against them.

Figure 13

Performance of the Top-Ten No-Load Funds
versus the Top-Ten Load Funds

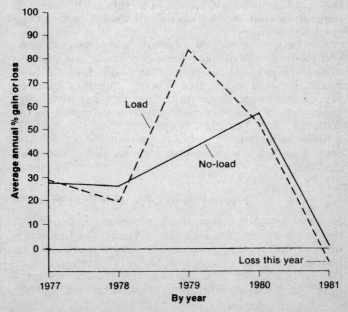

Not Too Far Out

A fund's current investments will tell you a lot about its goals, and what risks it is prepared to take to meet them. If you are striving strictly for safety, all-around diversification is a must. But if you could afford a bit of a gamble, it might interest you to know that a stock fund was placing a large percentage of its investments in one certain area, say aerospace, or communications, or heavy industry.

In checking how balanced a fund's portfolio is, don't be swayed by the number of shares it holds in a particular investment. <u>Look instead at the dollar value of each investment</u>. To give a very elementary example, if a fund has 10,000 shares in Asimov Computers, 10,000 shares in Standard Steel and Junk, and 10,000 shares in Castle on the Rhine Restaurants, Inc., it may give the appearance of being fairly balanced in its investment. However, if Castle on the Rhine Restaurants, Inc., is selling for $2 a share, Standard Steel and Junk for $6 a share, and Asimov Computers for $96 a share, then it becomes quite obvious that the fund's investment is very heavily dependent on the computer industry. So how you evaluate the fund will depend on your own feelings about the prospects of the computer industry.

Now because of your own work or field of specialization, you might feel particularly confident about one segment of the economy. If so, perhaps you will choose a fund heavily involved in this area. There's something comforting about owning shares in a fund that has investment goals akin to your own expectations with regard to the economy. And your knowledge may give you valuable insights on investment trends in that particular field. Use your knowledge with confidence—but don't lose your flexibility.

Never Fall in Love with Your Fund

However attractive certain funds may be to you personally, don't ever become too attached to them. The best funds for you this year may not be the funds you should be holding three years from now. So be prepared to switch. Of course, in order to be able to switch, you have to pick a fund—or funds—to invest in to begin with.

Picking the Winners

Your elimination process begins when you first select the best-performing no-load funds of the previous year and of the previous five years. For the funds that fall into these categories at this writing, plus the funds that are part of fund families offering free switching privileges among the member funds, see Tables 13 and 14. The performance figures for the no-load funds are updated regularly by *Donoghue's Mutual Funds Almanac,* Donoghue's MONEYLETTER, Lipper Analytical Service, the Wiesenberger Investment Companies Service annual directory, and the *Forbes* annual mutual fund performance issue (see Appendix A for further information on these sources).

Table 13   Top Ten SLYC Growth Funds Using Our Switching Strategy for the Period 6/78 to 6/83

FUND	Annual Compound Rate, Percent	What $10,000 Grew To
Stein Roe Capital Opportunities	44.82%	$ 63, 690
Stein Roe Special	38.35	50,694
Founders Special	38.15	50,318
(Vanguard) Explorer	38.06	50,151
T. Rowe Price New Horizon	35.60	45,840
Stein Roe Stock	35.09	44,986
Value Line Special Situations	35.03	44,862
T. Rowe Price New Era	33.48	42,367
Janus Fund	33.32	42,121
Columbia Fund	32.49	40,821
Average for 31 SLYC funds tracked by MONEYLETTER	29.94	37,044

Source: Donoghue's MONEYLETTER®. For listing of 31 SLYC funds tracked, send for sample issue to Box 411, Holliston, MA 01746.

In choosing growth equity funds, look for the ones in the top 10 percent in the category you're interested in—performance or growth—during strong stock market periods. Then check to see how they did during bear markets. Bear markets affect funds more radically than bull markets do, but the funds you are looking for should still be in the top 20 percent of their category even when the bears are out of the woods.

Investment services reports such as the ones I have

Table 14 Top Performing SLYC Funds Based on the Total Return Using the 12% Switching Strategy for 6/78 to 6/83

Fund/Phone Number (Objective)	Assets as of 6/83 (millions)	5-Year Annual Compound Rate	What $10,000 Grew To	Funds Available For Switching (Objective)	Restrictions
1. Stein Roe & Farnham Capital Opportunities (312) 368-7825 (Growth)	401	44.82	63,690	Stein Rowe Cash Reserves (money market); Stein Roe Bond Fund (bond); Stein Roe Tax-Exempt Bond Fund (bond); Stein Roe & Farnham (SR&F) Balanced Fund (balanced); Stein Roe Special	No switching fee; unlimited switches per year, but 30-day holding period; no limit on amount exchanged if amount meets requirement of each fund
2. Stein Roe Special	120	38.35	50,694	"	"
3. Stein Roe Stock	320	34.		"	"
4. Founders Special Fund (800) 525-2440	100	38.15	50,318	Founders Money Market, Founders Growth, Founders Income, Founders Mutual	No switching fee, unlimited switching, must meet minimum requirements of the fund
5. Explorer (Vanguard) (800)362-5030 (800) 523-7025	270	38.06	50,151	Vanguard Fixed Income High Yield/B Vanguard Fixed Income Investment/Grade B Vanguard Fixed Income GNMA/Portfolio B Vanguard Municipal High Yield/B Vanguard Municipal Long-term/B Vanguard Municipal Short-term/B	No switching fee, unlimited switches per year, minimum must meet require-ments of each fund no telephone exchange ex-cept for IRAs; will accept telegrams

				Funds offered for exchange	Switching rules
				Vanguard Municipal Money Market/B; Vanguard Money Market Trust Prime/MF; Vanguard Money Market Trust Federal 1/MF; Wellesley Income Fund/I; Wellington Fund Bal.; Windsor Fund/G	No switching fee; no more than one buy or one sell in a 90-day period; no limit on amount exchanged
6. T. Rowe Price New Horizons Fund, Inc. (800) 638-1527 (Performance)	1,675	35.60	45,840	T. Rowe Price Reserves (money fund); T. Rowe Price Tax Exempt Money Fund (money fund); T. Rowe Price New Income Fund (income); T. Rowe Price Growth Stock Fund, Inc. (growth); T. Rowe Price New ERA Fund, Inc. (growth); T. Rowe Price International Fund (international)	
7. Value Line Special Situations (800) 223-0818 (Performance)	381	35.03	44,862	Value Line Cash (money market); Value Line Income (income); Value Line Leveraged Growth (performance); Value Line Bond (bond)	No switching fee; unlimited switches per year; no limit on amount exchanged up to $50,000
8. T. Rowe Price New Era	486	33.48	42,367	(see 6 above)	
9. Janus Fund (800) 525-3713	243	33.32	42,121	Kemper Money Market	unlimited switching; $2.50 fee per $1,000; minimum requirements of the fund
10. Columbia Growth (800) 547-1037	148	32.49	40,821	Columbia Daily Income	no fees, unlimited switching; minimum requirements of the fund

mentioned will not show a fund's performance during a bear or a bull market *as such*. They will merely indicate the fund's performance quarterly and/or annually over the years. So as an adjunct to the fund figures, you'll need a Dow Jones Averages or a Standard and Poor's chart showing the overall performance of the market over the past few years. (Most investment services reports include such a chart in their reference section.) From the overall market chart, you will be able to determine readily whether the market was charging bullishly up or lumbering bearishly down during any given period.

The first step in your selection process is not foolproof. A fund's historical performance may be better than the performance it offers in the future. Nevertheless, its history is a starting point. And research has shown that *a fund which does well during a substantial rally will be likely to perform well during the next market advance*. A fund that has done better than average for two successive market advances has an even higher chance of performing well during the next advance to come.

One caveat, however: The performance of a top-ten fund, as rated on its past record, may change considerably with new investment management. Check up on it.

Switching to the Winners by the 12 Percent Rule

If you look more closely at Table 13, you'll note that over a five-year span, all of the ten top-performing no-load mutual funds were either growth or performance equity funds.

These tables demonstrate more than they started out to demonstrate. For they started out simply to show you the best-performing funds over a given period of time. But what they ended up showing you was the effectiveness of the 12 Percent Solution. For by following the 12 Percent Solution, you would have had most of your money in stock funds during those years when stock funds were the top performers, and you would have been 100 percent invested in money funds during 1981, when money funds predominated on the best-performance list.

History, even statistical history, cannot prove a future point, only a past one. Therein lies a warning we must always remember. But history teaches lessons well worth heeding. Bear the lesson of the top-ten tables in mind as you plot your investment portfolio.

There is one exceptional situation that arises if you happen to be starting an investment plan just after the stock market has declined sharply. If the 12 Percent Solution indicates that all or part of your money should be in stock funds, *in this particular instance it pays to invest in the worst of the best funds*—that is to say, in the one that has recently performed the worst among the funds selected as those best meeting your current needs. Chances are that worst-of-the-best fund has accumulated a lot of tax losses—which haven't cost you a cent, and which will amplify the upswing when it comes.

Counting—and Discounting—Returns

The returns reported by various investment services are *past* returns, returns for periods completed, not future *promised* returns. They assume either that you hold onto a fund for the specified period, reinvesting your dividends, or that you hold onto your shares but take the dividends in cash. Such reports are useful for finding out which investments might have earned you more and which fund groups perform seemingly better than others, suggesting good management. They are also good for comparing investment results.

But the reports don't tell you much about the future, about when to invest. They are also probably more wrong than right about how you will invest, for you are unlikely to invest at the beginning of any given year, you are unlikely to stay 100 percent in any given fund, and you are unlikely to remain there for the whole year.

How Much Would You Really Have Made?

Mutual fund investment returns can be, and are, figured in nearly as many ways as there are reasons for investing. For decision-making purposes, however, your true return on a stock fund investment can be calculated only by you.

The basic formula you need to do the job is a formula for a total return, in other words, a formula for all the new money your investment has generated for you—income dividends, capital gains distributions, and most important, the increase or decrease in value of your investment.

If you were to buy a share of a stock fund at $10 per share and hold it for nine months, and if during that time you were to receive 50 cents in income dividends and 75 cents in capital gains distributions, and if the per-share price were to decline to $9.90, your total return (TR) for the period would be

$$TR = \frac{\text{dividend income} + \text{capital gains distribution} - \text{per share price decline}}{\text{original price of stock}}$$

$$TR = \frac{.50 + .75 - .10}{10.00} = 11.50 \text{ percent}$$

Would that be a good return, assuming, say, bond funds or money funds earned 13 percent over the same period? To answer that question truthfully, you would have to annualize the return, to adjust it, in other words, so it would be comparable to the annualized rate of return of the bond or money funds. Your annualized rate of return (ATR) would be

$$ATR = \text{total return} \times \frac{\text{early return}}{\text{period you held it for}}$$

$$ATR = 11.5 \times \frac{12 \text{ months}}{9 \text{ months}} = 15.3 \text{ percent}$$

So the stock fund's return in this example proves to have been better than a bond or money fund's return would have been. The stock fund has earned you in nine months what a money fund or a bond fund paying 15.3 percent would have earned you over the same period of time, and so its return beats that of the bond and the money funds.

Taking the hypothetical figures out, the formula for an annualized total return would read:

$$ATR = \frac{\text{income}}{\text{dividends}} + \frac{\text{capital gains}}{\text{distribution}} + \frac{\text{change in price per share}}{} \times \frac{365}{\text{no. of days invested}}$$

Substitute actual figures from your stock fund investments, and the formula gives you a check for determining how you're doing relative to a bond fund or a money fund investment.

In real life your actual return will be complicated by irregular investments and withdrawals, reinvestment and nonreinvestment of dividends, periodic price-per-share variables—and whether or not you sell your shares. Truth is much easier to find in the rarefied realm of mathematics than it is to discover in the day-to-day atmosphere in which we live. Calculate your returns, by all means, but swallow their sums with a grain of salt.

Prospecting with Prospectuses

Start your prospecting for sound investments for your savings by making some copies of the sample worksheet shown at the end of this chapter. Look it over, so you will be prepared to detail on this sheet the information you collect from each fund you are considering. Fund addresses and telephone numbers are given at the back of this book (see Appendix C). Obviously you don't want to send away for information on all funds back there—unless you have stamps to spare and really like to see your mailbox overflowing.

Now send—or call—for prospectuses from the funds you think you might be interested in. By law you must receive a prospectus from a fund before investing in it. The law doesn't say you have to read the prospectus—which is fortunate, because these documents are written by lawyers, for lawyers, with the probable expectation that no one will read them but the proofreader at the typesetter's. And he's only looking for typographical errors, not trying to understand them. Still, there is some good information to be gleaned from a prospectus.

Ordering a prospectus serves a function in and of itself. Do so by telephone, and you can learn a lot about the company you may be dealing with in the future. For instance, can you get through reasonably quickly during business hours or are the lines occupied all the time? Continuous busy signals on several different occasions may indicate that the company is either understaffed or disorganized or both. They may also indicate that you should be taking your business elsewhere. On the other hand, of course, they may indicate simply that a fund's popularity has suddenly outpaced its facilities.

While you have someone on the line, ask a few questions about the fund's holdings, management goals, and investment requirements. How well does the staff field your questions? Are they prompt and efficient? And do they really give you the answers you're looking for?

Jot down the answers on your survey worksheet. Also jot down the date you made the call. Then note the date the prospectus arrives. There will be some variation due to the mannerisms of the post office, of course. Up in my neck of the woods, even the much-vaunted guaranteed overnight express mail has been taking five to six days in transit recently. Still, if a number of fund prospectuses arrive in more or less the same span of time and one of them doesn't show up until three weeks later, I would begin to wonder about the management of that particular fund, unless, of course, an explanation is enclosed to the effect that the prospectus has just been updated during the past week.

Size is the first thing to check for in a fund's prospectus. Any recent changes in management or in the advisory company should also be mentioned there. These policy-making entities may affect the fund's future performance considerably, so read carefully. If there's no mention of management continuity in the prospectus, as is often the case, dig through Wiesenberger again.

Questions to Ask About Switching

Every mutual fund family has its own rules for switching. So be sure you understand its exchange privileges and how to use them. You can discuss a fund family's flexibility and restrictions with its investor services representatives. Ask them:

- How often you may exchange shares of one mutual fund for shares of another
- Whether there is a fee, and if so, how much is it
- Whether or not the fund family would bend the rules if you had a good reason for switching more frequently than its policy allows

- What action the fund takes if you switch too frequently
- If they can give you any suggestions about how to simplify your switching

No Commingling, Please

A real no-no in the financial world is the commingling of accounts. What is Smith's is Smith's and what is Johnson's is Johnson's. Even if the assets of Smith and Johnson are housed in the same institution, those assets remain separate, if not in individual little safety boxes, then at least by the means of modern accounting. In the same way, your own mutual fund accounts should each keep their distinct identities.

No-load funds charge no extra fee for opening more than one account. So set up a different account for each of your goals, at least your medium- and long-term ones. Your IRA and/or Keogh accounts will obviously be separate, for by law they have to be. But let's say you are also saving for a child's education, and for a sailboat or a summer house, and for a new car, because you've decided it's foolish to keep paying exorbitant interest on a car loan that lasts longer than the vehicle itself does, so next time you want to be able to pay cash. Give each target its own account.

The most important investment to keep separate is your catastrophe-proofing pool. It should remain invested as if it were your most distant—and failproof—goal. Don't incorporate it into your IRA or Keogh plan, even though few of us seek much spending money beyond retirement and so you might be tempted to lump the two funds together as long-term emergency reserves.

You want ready access to your disaster fund, and Keoghs and IRAs are inaccessible without penalty until you reach the age of 59½. Collectibles such as gold cannot be kept in an IRA or a Keogh account in any case, therefore you wouldn't be able to deduct the gold coin part of your disaster-insurance investment from your taxes for either of these retirement accounts anyway.

So open a catastrophe-proofing account all by itself for your bond investments —and don't forget to put a gold coin or two aside every year in a bank safety deposit box or tucked away at home. The safety deposit box might seem, at first glance, the more secure of the two places to keep your coin. But if real economic chaos were to break out, chances are there would be an extended bank holiday. The government would simply order the banks temporarily closed—and perhaps indefinitely. Also remember that Roosevelt confiscated all the gold owned by individuals in this country when he took the United States off the gold standard. It happened once. It could happen again. And the government, with the proper papers, has the right to inspect the contents of your safety deposit box.

One last separate account you should have is a straight money fund account, not as part of your investment portfolio but for your regular living expenses. You'll want to put all your paycheck earnings directly into this account first, then try to consolidate as many of your bills as you can so their total will be high enough to be paid by a money fund check.

For instance, if you now have two or three credit cards, try to use only one of them, in most cases either your VISA or your MasterCard. You might even look for a supermarket that takes credit cards—they're beginning to do that now. And with the monthly grocery charge on your credit card, your bill should surely exceed the money fund's minimum check.

Bills you can't consolidate you can pay through a regular checking account, depositing a money fund check to cover the whole amount. The one thing you should never do is to write a check on one of your long-term target accounts to meet current expenses. That's one very good reason why you need separate accounts. It puts the temptation to borrow from your investments, your savings, one step further behind you.

But, you protest, doesn't keeping track of all these different accounts make life rather complicated? Well, sometimes a little more work at the outset makes things a lot easier later on. And the funds do most of that work for you, plus most of your ongoing record keeping over the years. The trick is to set up your accounts right, so they will run smoothly from the very start. If you don't, you may well involve yourself with that long and tedious twentieth-century process known as straightening out the computer. And we all know what that's like!

The Hassle-Free Guide to Setting Up a Mutual Fund Account

Nothing you do in mutual fund investing can make your life easier than setting up your account properly in the first place. So here are a few guidelines on getting the job done right.

Rule #1. *Each and every mutual fund has investor service representatives—use them.* They are part of what you're paying for through the fund's management fee, and their willingness and ability to help you is one of the criteria of an efficient, effectively managed company. If you ever get a "dud" on the phone, ask for his or her supervisor (politely, of course). I can't stress enough how many hassles a professional service representative can save you.

Rule #2. *The first mutual fund account you set up should be a money fund account, as a home base for your investments.* Be sure you apply for the check-writing and wire-redemption privileges. You never know exactly when that rainy day you're saving for will come, and you should be prepared for it well in advance.

Even if you intend to invest at the outset in another type of mutual fund, set up your home-base money fund first, then switch all but the minimum required by the money fund into the mutual fund you want. As long as you leave the necessary minimum in your money fund account, you will have a place to come home to.

Rule #3. *Be consistent.* Use the same name and mailing address for all your fund accounts, your bank of record, your signature cards, and your own files. For instance, don't use a middle initial one time and skip it another. Consistency. It will simplify the bookkeeping and paperwork for both you and the funds.

Rule #4. *When you open joint accounts, make sure that you fill out the signature cards to specify that either you or your spouse can sign.* If your spouse were to die, and all your money happened to be in your mutual fund accounts, you might find your cash tied up until the estate was probated, which in some cases can take a very long time indeed. But if you have set up your accounts so that either you or your spouse has the right to sign, all you have to do is transfer any monies needed into your money fund, then write a check or request a wire redemption for it. Possession is nine-tenths of the law, as they say.

Rule #5. *If a mutual fund does not have telephone exchange privileges, clear in advance the procedure for switching by mail.* Most funds can provide you with a form letter for the purpose. But before sending it off, check it over to be sure it's filled out properly. Here's the right sequence of events for a letter withdrawal of your assets.

1. Clear the form letter with your fund's investor service representative.
2. Ask if a guaranteed signature is required on the letter. (Most funds do require it.)
3. Make sure the signature is guaranteed by either: (a) a commercial banker, that is, a representative of a national bank, state bank, or trust company, as opposed to a savings and loan association or savings bank, (b) a stockbroker who is a member of a major exchange, or (c), if abroad, a foreign bank with a New York correspondent bank (if there is no such bank available, the United States consulate is a permissible alternative).
4. Make any appropriate provisions you may need for your systematic withdrawal (check-a-month) program.
5. Make sure you include your account numbers.
6. Sign the letter *exactly* as your name appears on the mutual fund account.
7. If the account is a joint account, and if you have set up the account so that two signatures are required, make sure your spouse signs the letter as well.

What happens if, after following the rules for making this work smoothly, suddenly you can't get through to your money fund when you need to, as when, for instance, you want to make a redemption?

If you must get in touch with your money fund and the lines are tied up, here's what you do next:

1. Try again, most likely you'll get through the next time you call.

2. If you cannot get through on the indicated number, call information for the phone number of the fund's office. The 800-555-1212 information number will locate any other 800 numbers the fund might have for you, and the (area code) 555-1212 number will locate its main office phone number. Call collect if you wish; most funds will accept your phone call.

3. If it's after hours or if you *still* can't get through, send a mailgram, telegram, telex message, or express mail letter *asking the mutual fund to call you.*

This is important, because the fund will need a record (it may be a letter with a guaranteed signature or it may be simply your voice recorded off the telephone, depending on the fund's rules) in order to make the redemption. It must know where to call if you cannot call them.

Accounting Magic—Making the Numbers Earn More for You

If you had your choice, you would earn all of your income as long-term capital gains and receive no ordinary income such as dividends and short-term capital gains. And, of course, you'd have no losses. But, since things don't always work out exactly the way we'd like them to, here are a few magic tricks to help you make the best of the investing situation as it exists.

Trick #1. *How to turn a short-term capital gain into a long-term capital gain.* Buy a performance fund which is likely to pay a capital gains dividend this year and which is likely to appreciate more value than the gain realized in the distribution. When the fund pays out its year-end dividend, your share of the distribution will be taxed at a maximum capital gains rate of 20 percent. Thus you will have earned at least part of your profit at the lowest possible tax rate.

Trick #2. *How to turn a bond fund from a loser into a real winner.* Buy a bond fund with realized capital losses, one that has stopped paying dividends, as interest rates are falling. Hold your shares for at least one year, and you'll turn what would otherwise be ordinary income into long-term capital gains. You see, if a fund has carry-forward losses, it can avoid paying quarterly dividends. The accumulation of earnings improves the tax treatment of the investor's gains, the shares rising in value over a long enough period of time for the investor to take his profit as long-term capital gains when he sells his shares.

Trick #3. *How to have tax-free income and capital gains opportunities as well.* Simply buy an intermediate-term or a long-term tax-exempt bond or money fund when interest rates are falling. You will receive dividends 100 percent free of federal income tax (although probably not competitive yields) plus long-term capital gains 80 percent tax-free on the profit when you sell the shares if you hold them for at least a year and a day. The folks who bought these funds as rates rose are the ones who got stuck for the losses.

Trick #4. *How to put mutual fund pricing to work for you.* Periodically, usually daily, a mutual fund must price its investment portfolio at its current market value, divide that value by the number of shares outstanding, and determine the price per share that new investors will have to pay to invest. Now when a fund pays a dividend, the price per share drops by the amount of the dividend because the amount has been paid out to the shareholders. As the fund accumulates income and capital gains that it has earned (but not distributed), the price per share rises. As the value of the mutual fund's investment portfolio rises or falls, so does the fund's price per share.

Filling Up Your Savings Pool

The more you can put into your investments initially, the faster they will grow. But don't wait to invest until you have a large sum put aside somewhere—in a passbook savings account or your checking account or under the mattress—places where it's not being put to work for you. Start with whatever you have, even if it's as little as $250, the minimum you usually need to open that first money fund account. (Some funds have no minimum initial investment requirement.) Then try to add to the pool regularly, in monthly installments, however small. Once you become used to the idea, I think you'll find it's no more difficult to discipline yourself to monthly deposits to your mutual fund than it is to meet your car payments.

I'd Like Five and 32/100s Shares, Please

But, you may ask, how does one go about investing, say $63 or $170 a month? Money funds present no problem, since a dollar deposited buys a dollar of the fund. Stock fund shares, on the other hand, are selling for very odd prices, like $12.31 or $9.88 apiece. The math involved in dividing the share into my $63 or $170 each month must be fantastic. Besides, since the price fluctuates daily, how do I know exactly what number of shares I can afford to buy on the day my check arrives at the fund? The answer is, you don't have to worry about it.

One of the great conveniences of equity mutual funds is that they can match the number of shares to the number of dollars you want to invest. They issue fractional shares (and buy them back when you cash in) to three digits. For instance, if a fund is selling for $9.83, your $63 would get you 6.409 shares.

The Dollar-Cost-Averaging Advantage

Making regular monthly deposits to an investment instead of investing in a lump sum works to your advantage more than you may have realized, owing to a market phenomenon known as the dollar-cost-averaging effect. If you deposit a given amount in a lump sum, you may inadvertently do so just after the stock market has risen—and when it is about to make one of its periodic descents. After all, since it's impossible to determine exactly where the market is going when, how do you decide the best time to make that deposit? You don't. By buying continuously, however, you almost always end up with an average price better than the lump-sum price.

For example, suppose you anticipate having $400 to invest over the course of a year, in quarterly installments (just to simplify the example, because it would take forever to discuss it on a monthly installment basis) of $100. And suppose a stock you're interested in buying is selling at $10 a share at some point in January. You buy, and what you get for your initial $100 investment is 10 shares. In April you have another $100 to invest in the market, and your favorite stock is selling for $7.60 a share. Your $100 this time brings you 13.157 shares. A July investment of $100 this time brings you 10.526 shares, because the stock has gone up in value again, and is selling for $9.50 a share. In October, with the share price at $11, you buy 9.01 shares with your $100. You now own 42.784 shares of your favorite stock, for which you've paid $400.

Now suppose you had invested $400 as a one-shot deal in January. It would have bought only 40 shares. Had you invested the $400 in April, you would have come out ahead because the stock market was down; you would have ended up with 52.631 shares. Investing in July, you would have been behind again, with only 42.105 shares to put into your portfolio. And investing in October, you'd have been really behind, with only 36.36 shares to show for your money.

Periodic saving not only disciplines, but it pays. And over the years it pays a lot, because all those little gains add up to a big one when you reach your goal.

THE SLYC SYSTEM WORKSHEET FOR EVALUATING YOUR INITIAL FUND CHOICES

Fund Name_____ Objective_____

      For the 12 months ending: /   /

      A. Capital Gains Distribution _____
      B. Income Dividends _____
      C. Beginning Price/Share _____
      D. Ending Price/Share _____

TOTAL RETURN:_____% **Total Return** $= \dfrac{A + B + (D - C)}{C}$

_____

Fund Family Name_____
Toll-free phone numbers: Inquiries_____
Investor Services_____

_____

Is there a money fund in this fund family? Yes____**No**____
What is the minimum check permitted? $_____
Are there any fees for checks? Yes____**Amount $**____**No**____
Are there any limitations on check usage? _____
Is wire redemption permitted? Yes____**No**____

Are there any fees? Yes___Amount $_____No___

Does this fund permit exchanges with other funds? Yes___No___
Are there exchange fees? Yes_____Amount $_____No_____
Are there limits on the frequency of switches? Yes_____
Amount $___No___
Does this fund family permit telephone switches?
Yes___No___

Does this fund's holdings match my diversification re-
quirements? Yes_____ No_____
Does the fund have an investment specialty? Yes___No_____
If so, is it one in which I have confidence? Yes___No_____

6

Special-Situation Funds and Tax Sheltering

> To speculate in Wall Street when
> you are not an insider is like buying
> cows by candlelight.
> —*Daniel Drew*

None of us want to pay any more taxes than we have to. And most of us should be paying less than we do. Yet every tax cut seems to lead to more taxation, not less. The income tax is reduced—but then the social security tax rises, and so do state and local taxes, and the real estate tax, and the sales tax. Look at the bottom line, and what we get to keep is somehow always less than we had before. The simple fact is that the overall level of taxation in this country has proceeded from the point of mere extraction to the point of extortion for almost everyone. Even so, *throwing away your money simply to avoid taxes doesn't make sense.*

The Titanic Had a Pool Too

In the throwaway category I must place almost all those speculative pooled investments in such areas as oil and gas drilling, orange groves, gold mines, timberlands, dairy cattle, and kangaroo cloning. These fields are so specialized that it's very hard for the average investor to comprehend what is being done—or not done—with his money.

And it does take money—lots of it—to enter these fields. If you have a net worth of $250,000, excluding the old homestead, and an annual income of over $100,000, an accountant might be able to make a case for "investing" in one of these tenuous deals. He would also be happy to hold your hand when the IRS called you in for an audit, as it almost certainly would.

Then there are the other potential problems that may arise. Spread out in front of me at the moment is a prospectus from a timber partnership planning to raise $10 million to purchase softwood timber properties in Georgia. Now I have a friend who knows a little about forestry. Going through the company's plans and its description of the properties, he thought it might just be possible to eke out a small overall profit on the deal. He could see no way of telling for sure, since the prospectus passes over such minor profit inhibitors as the real estate tax on several thousand acres of land. On that particular issue it comments that investors "may be subject to state and local taxes" and "such taxes may include real property taxes, income taxes, estate or inheritance taxes, or other types of taxes."

Part of this discreet verbosity is simply the gobbledygook required of a prospectus. You can't actually say that an investor may be liable for a lot of extra taxes if he tries to avoid income taxes. You have to bury a warning like that in legalese on page 38.

What such a proposed investment really means, however, is that *you're asking to make your life a lot more complicated than it already is in exchange for the bare possibility of cutting your taxes and the even more barren possibility of seeing some of your money come back with a profit.*

Above and beyond questions of capital risk and taxes, there's the matter of fees. Investors woke up a long time ago to the fact that mutual fund commissions of 8½ percent were really outrageous, and benefited no one but the salesman, right? Guess who's back.

They're getting 8 percent up front on this deal, which isn't quite as bad as 8½ percent. But looking a bit more closely at the "Estimated Use of Proceeds," that is, at how the company is going to spend the money, one also notices a 5.9 percent charge for "Organizational and Offering Expenses" (read legal fees to make sure you can't sue when you lose your shirt, plus accounting costs, plus printing expenses, plus all those fetes to celebrate the sale of a few more units to someone looking to bury his money in Georgia instead of the IRS coffers).

Last but not least, there's a footnote stating that "The General Partner will receive Acquisition Fees from the Partnership" (read they're going to get a cut on the land they sell you). It's a long footnote, so I'll spare you everything but the core. "The aggregate amount of Acquisition Fees payable to all parties will not exceed 8 percent."

Now adding 8 percent + 5.9 percent + 8 percent, I get 21.9 percent. Of course, that's only a possible 21.9 percent. But it's also a probable 21.9 percent, since when it comes to costs, they always seem to be at the high end of the range—right off the top of your investment before it even starts, in fact. Remember what just 8½ percent off the top of a mutual fund investment used to do to slow down the growth of your capital?

And, oh yes, further on, the management fees are mentioned. They're 1 percent here, 5 percent there, 15 percent elsewhere.

This timber partnership I've been describing is not an unusual speculative offering in any way. In point of fact, it's quite typical. If you really want a loss in order to pay less in taxes, then this is the route to take. You're almost *guaranteed* losses.

To Every Rule There Are Exceptions

Speculation, especially in jerry-built tax shelters, is almost the antithesis of the SLYC system of balanced holdings. And, frankly, the 12 Percent Solution—automatic, periodic, and measured—is more profitable for probably ninety-nine out of a hundred investors than regularly playing the stock market will ever be. Still, there are times when an investor may have a good reason for trying something besides the dependable plain old vanilla. One of the best of these reasons is familiarity, through your work or field of specialization, with a particular sector of the economy.

Overseas Investments the Mutual Fund Way

Suppose you're in a business that involves frequent dealings with Japan and you feel the Japanese business boom has a long way to go on the up side. You'd like to invest over there, but Japanese is all Greek to you. Well, there are several funds that specialize in Japanese stocks. G.T. Pacific Fund, for example, is invested almost entirely in Japanese securities. With an annual change in asset value of +50.9 percent in 1978, −20.3 percent in 1979, +34.0 percent in 1980, +10.3 percent in 1981, and −3.8 percent in 1982, it might be an intriguing gamble on the Bobbing Sun.

Then there's Canadian Fund for north-of-the-border aficionados, and there's Mexico Fund for the more southerly inclined. Canadian Fund, however, like many of the specialty funds, is a load fund, charging a full 8½ percent commission. And the question you always have to ask yourself about such load specialty funds is, will their specialty really outperform the overall market by enough of a margin for you to give up all that money up front?

Only you can make that decision. All I can contribute to it is a word of warning. You're probably not going to turn a more handsome profit on a load specialty fund than you would on a no-load fund unless you know something most of the world's investors don't.

Case Closed

Mexico Fund represents a different type of mutual fund, namely, the closed-end fund. Closed-end funds issue a fixed number of shares. In the case of Mexico Fund, it was 10,090,000. That's all the shares there are and ever will be unless there's a stock split.

My mentioning the possibility of a "stock split" gives you another indicator about closed-end funds. Their shares are traded just like the stock of, say, AT&T. *The price goes up and down on the basis of what people are willing to pay for the shares, not on the underlying value of the securities held, as in the case of a regular mutual fund.* The shares are quoted like stocks, with a bid and an asked price. Mexico Fund is listed on the New York Stock Exchange, as a matter of fact. You can check its price there every day. If you decide to buy it, you'll pay a commission just as you do on a stock transaction—which brings you back into the arms of that sometimes rather rapacious stockbroker again.

Nevertheless, for some traders, closed-end funds make sense. Traditionally, the shares of a closed-end fund sell at a considerable discount. For example, if the fund has company holdings worth a total of $10 million, and a million shares outstanding, the fund should be quoted at something like $9\frac{7}{8}$ bid and $10\frac{1}{8}$ asked. Yet it's much more likely to be selling for $7\frac{7}{8}$ bid and $8\frac{1}{8}$ asked, meaning that you're buying $10 worth of stock for every $8 you invest. (Of course, you would get the $10 only if the fund were liquidated, and few of these funds are.)

The reason for this strange market behavior is unclear. My own feeling is that the fund sells at a considerable discount because buyers don't think it's worth as much as it really is, and sellers have to agree—otherwise they'd have no one to sell to. This tacit agreement drives down the price.

Exactly why the buyers feel the fund is worth less than the net asset value of the stocks it holds is hard to establish, but it may be explained in part by the fact that the price of a closed-end mutual fund is determined by the market forces of supply and demand. In the case of a regular mutual fund, you know the fund is always there to buy back your shares. On any given day you can receive the net asset value of those shares listed for that day in the newspapers. In the case of a closed-end fund, on the other hand, a listing at $9\frac{7}{8}$–$10\frac{1}{8}$ doesn't necessarily tell you what your return would be if you sold. You might or might not receive 10 for it, or $9\frac{7}{8}$, or even 9. It would all depend on what someone else felt it was worth and what you are willing to settle for.

In other words, what's involved here is really a question of defining value. The risk of capital loss is also involved. And because added risk always translates into higher yield, the funds are forced down in price in the marketplace to raise the yield.

If It's Always a Bargain, Is It a Bargain?

Many people would advise buying closed-end funds because they sell at a discount, so they must be a bargain.

The problem is that they almost always sell at a discount of 5 percent to 20 or even 30 percent off their asset value (see Table 15). I've never yet found a store featuring sales 365 days a year that was a real bargain.

Table 15   A Sample Newspaper Listing of Closed-End Funds

Following is a weekly listing of unaudited net asset values of publicly traded investment fund shares, reported by the companies as of Friday's close. Also shown is the closing listed market price or a dealer-to-dealer asked price of each fund's shares, with the percentage of difference.

	N.A. Value	Stk Price	% Diff.
Diversified Common Stock Funds			
Adams Express	15.78	14¾ −	6.5
Baker Fentress	94.37	65 −	31.1
Equity Strat	b9.78	8½ −	13.1
Gen'l Amer Inv	15.71	17⅜ +	10.6
Lehman	14.38	13⅞ −	3.5
Madison	23.69	18⅝ −	21.4
Niagara Share	14.33	14½ +	1.2
Overseas Sec	5.35	5⅞ +	9.8
Source	27.33	25 −	8.5
Tri-Continental	a24.89	21 −	14.3
US & Foreign	23.89	20⅜ −	14.7
Specialized Equity and Convertible Funds			
Amer Gen Cv	24.65	24¼ −	1.6
ASA	b50.46	48 −	1.6
Bancroft Conv	20.55	19⅝ −	4.5
Castle Conv	a28.07	25¼ −	10.0
Central Sec	11.00	8¼ −	25.0
Claremont	28.06	21⅜ −	23.8
CLAS	(3.87)	7/16	
CLAS PFD	26.15	....	
Cyprus	0.32	5/16 −	2.3
Engex	11.25	7½ −	33.3
Japan Fund	9.12	8½ −	6.8
Mexico (b)	z	z	z
Nautilus	22.94	22 −	4.1
New American Fd	26.06	21¼ −	18.5
Pete & Res	26.27	26⅞ +	2.3
Prec Megal	14.75	14⅜ −	2.5

a-Ex-Dividend. b-As of Thursday's close.
z-Not available

It's true that the discount does vary, and in a spectacular bull market you might profit from this phenomenon. But you would profit in a well-chosen no-load fund as well.

Money Today, Paper Tomorrow

Besides being load funds, Mexico Fund and other international funds of its type pose yet another problem to be taken into account, and that problem is the exchange rates. Mexico devalued the peso by approximately 40 percent in 1982, which obviously clobbered Mexico Fund. The shares went from 7.24 to 5.74 each in less than two months—for a 21 percent loss to investors.

The risk of further devaluation in Mexico is considerable, and it obviously tempers Mexico Fund's growth. Why then do I even mention it?

I do so for two reasons. First of all, you're going to come across funds like this when you start looking around, and I'd like to try to answer as many of your questions as I can before you have to ask them.

Second, Mexico Fund is the only vehicle through which you can legitimately invest in Mexico. So if you really want to put your money there, you have no other choice.

This circumstance arises because *Bolsa,* Mexico's only stock exchange, cannot sell stock to non-Mexicans. The fund gets around this proviso by having the shares it purchases held in trust, the trustee being a Mexican bank controlled by Mexicans, who in turn vote the stock. Mexico Fund has no control over the stock whatsoever. It has only the right to buy, sell, and profit.

An Extra-Specialty Fund

At the other end of the international scheme is the Dreyfus Third Century Fund. Comparing G. T. Pacific Fund or Mexico Fund with Third Century reminds me of a friend of mine who set out to buy a small diesel farm tractor. He wanted to buy American, and he shopped around at International Harvester, Ford, John Deere, Allis-Chalmers—you name it, he looked at it. Finally he decided on an Allis. The engine was made in Japan, as were all the other engines, *and* the body, *and* the transmission, *and* the electrical system. *But at least the ignition key was made in the United States of America.*

Later he found out that the key was Japanese as well. The original had been lost and replaced. Well, at least he'd tried, he told himself.

Much the same story can be told about the no-load Dreyfus Third Century Fund. To quote the sales literature, "The Dreyfus Third Century Fund was established out of a conviction that investment in enterprises that do the best job in trying to improve the quality of American life would also be rewarding to the individual investor. The areas of corporate endeavor which the Fund's management considered essential were environmental protection, occupational health and safety, purity of consumer products, and equal employment opportunity."

Whether Dreyfus has the original or the replacement key I leave to you to decide. Its portfolio does, however, include a fair number of United States-based oil and mining companies with primarily overseas holdings. Other companies in its portfolio such as Dome Petroleum, Dorchester Gas, and Shell Canada are listed as "enhancing the quality of life through the development of technology, products, or services." And any way you look at it, the fund has been outperforming both the stock market and the ever-rising consumer price index.

Ifs, Maybes, and Sometimes Buts

Many once-and-never-again investors, some of whom are now returning to the stock market by way of the mutual funds, will remember the excitement of the over-the-counter market, where stocks sometimes double or collapse in less than a week. You guessed it, there's a fund called Over-the-Counter-Securities. It's done reasonably well over the years, actually, although the fact that it too is a load fund is something I hold against it. I mention it only because the over-the-counter fever seems to be making a comeback.

Medical Technology Fund specializes in health-care companies. National Aviation and Technology is the only no-load fund specializing in airlines and aerospace. If you think oil is your future, Energy Fund or Able Associates Fund is for you. And if you like to mix and match specialties, there's Fidelity Select Portfolios, which boasts four specialized portfolios: energy, precious metals and minerals, technology, and health care. You can switch back and forth among the specialized portfolios within the fund itself. It's like playing the stock market, except that you're buying a diversified group each time around instead of the stock of single company.

Why Not Buy the Market Itself?

If you really want to buy the stock market, Vanguard Index Trust is for you. The index concept of investing says, "If you can't beat 'em, join 'em." Vanguard Index Trust owns "*all* 500 stocks in the Standard & Poor Index. It is designed to match the performance of the index."

In some cases, I'm not sure it pays to beat *or* join them.

Commodities—Making Las Vegas Seem Conservative

Frankly, that's the way I feel about commodity funds. In 1978 there were only a handful of these funds around at the starting gate of the big race for the small investor's commodity money. Now almost every major brokerage firm from E. F. Hutton to Smith Barney to Merrill Lynch has one either on the drawing board or already out in the marketplace.

The big commodity companies like Heinold and Conti Commodity Services are also entering the field of funds. And why not? Reading the "Conflict of Interest" portion of their prospectuses, you find that they collect the commissions on all the trades made in the funds, besides collecting management fees. By the time you finish reading the prospectuses, you may have decided that *the only person not likely to collect baksheesh is the elevator man.* (And come to think of it, the elevators are probably self-service anyhow.) The management fees topping off the commissions typically run 5 percent of assets plus 15 percent of any appreciation. Of course, you do have the soundness of long-established specialty firms within the commodity fraternity behind your investment.

As Jay Klopfenstein, president of Norwood Securities, Inc., a tracker of commodity funds, commented in an article entitled "Low-Risk Commodity Funds" in *The New York Times*, Conti is "about as respectable a house as one can find." Of course its fund collapsed spectacularly in 1980, wiping out its investors. According to Mr. Klopfenstein, "They were simply caught on the wrong side in the silver and gold debacle." For this you need your money managed?

My own favorite among the commodity funds is one of the earliest of them all, Heinold's Pro-Com II. Offered at $1,000 per unit in 1975, it managed to shoot down to $188 per unit by early 1978. At that point Heinold fired the manager and changed the name of the fund to Recovery Fund II. The units recouped, reaching $231 towards the end of 1978. Where they are now I can't exactly tell. Heinold's latest prospectus is for its new Future Fund II, and while it gives some very profitable performance examples for other funds it's currently managing, Recovery Fund II is not among those cited to portray its investment skills. In fact Recovery Fund II is mentioned only along with several other problems grouped under the heading "Certain Litigation Concerning the General Partner."

All this doesn't totally exclude commodity funds from the consideration of some speculators. These funds are growing by leaps and bounds. Since a commodity fund is much more profitable for its managers than even the most expensive old-line load mutual fund ever was, the sales force puts a lot of effort into selling this vehicle. And the commodity funds have shown spectacular gains, often running into the hundreds of percent. They've also shown some spectacular losses—which I can't say run into the hundreds of percent, since *you can't lose more than everything*.

Now there's at least a distinct advantage commodity funds have over plain old commodity speculation. In the old kind, you can easily lose two or three times what you put up.

Besides, there's always the possibility that you might get out while the fund is way ahead—lots of luck and the post office being willing. "A limited partner," to quote the Future Fund II prospectus, "may cause any or all of his Units to be redeemed by the Partnership at their net asset value as of the first day of any month next following ten days written notice to the General Partner, commencing on the first day of the seventh full month after the partner begins trading." What could be simpler and quicker!

Taking the Tax-Exempt Route

One last category of specialized funds you might come across is the tax-exempt money funds and tax-exempt bond funds. These funds invest in various tax-free government securities issued by state and local governments as well as by federal agencies. Their dividends are exempt from federal income taxes, though not usually from state and local income taxes.

Now everyone wants to save taxes, but these tax-free funds, frankly, are for hardly anyone. The simple fact is that, for most of us, the tax-shelter benefits of an IRA or Keogh are far superior. If you're in the maximum tax bracket, you might have reason to consider these esoteric investments. But before you invest in them, double-check to make sure you'll really be gaining dollars. *Cutting off your income to cut your taxes, remember, is like cutting off your nose to spite your face.*

Are Tax-Free Funds for You?

Whether the tax-free funds are for you depends on two factors: (1) your marginal tax rate and (2) the ratio between the tax-free fund yields and the taxable fund yields.

Normally you would have to be in the 40 to 50 percent tax bracket in order to turn the tax-free funds to your advantage. (Here we're talking about a federal tax status, of course. Exemption from the state tax will depend on which state you live in.) Here are the questions to ask yourself in determining whether a tax-free fund is right for you.

Question #1. *Does your taxable income* (after deductions and exemptions) *exceed the following levels?*

	1983 Taxable Income	1984 Taxable Income
Single person	$ 55,300	$ 81,800
Married person (filing jointly)	109,000	162,400
Head of household	81,800	108,300
Married person (filing separately)	54,700	81,200

If and only if you can answer yes to the above question, you are in the 50 percent maximum tax level and you probably should invest in tax-free funds rather than taxable funds.

Question #2. *What is the ratio between the yields on the taxable funds and the yields on the tax-free funds in which you might invest?*

Now apply the following rule, using the current yields:

Formula: $1 - \dfrac{\text{Tax-free fund yield}}{\text{General-purpose fund yield}} = \text{break-even tax rate}$

Sample Application: $1 - \dfrac{7.23\%}{13.64\%} = 47\%$

Conclusion: A tax-free fund is not for you unless your tax rate is 53 percent or more.

There are some words of caution to be said at this point. First of all, tax-free funds have longer average maturities than the taxable funds have, and their total return yields are subject to a much greater degree of volatility than are those of taxable funds. For example, on March 10, 1982, the average taxable money fund had an average maturity of thirty-two days while the tax-free money funds average sixty-two days, and some of them had average maturities as long as 476 days. If interest rates were to fall, this would mean an additional opportunity for capital gains, and were rates to rise, capital losses would be more likely to increase. The best time to invest in a tax-free fund is when interest rates are falling.

Additionally, there's the quality of the respective funds' investments to consider. We find a real concern emerging over the fact that many municipalities are being encouraged to add injudiciously to their short-term debts because of the ease with which they can sell these IOUs to tax-free money funds.

Traditionally, municipalities sold long-term tax-exempt bonds, which were purchased by tax-exempt bond funds among other investors. In today's high-interest-rate environment, however, these same municipalities prefer to borrow money for the short term in the hope that rates will decline soon and they will be able to borrow the money again at cheaper rates for the long term. This phenomenon could lead to financial difficulties similar to the much-publicized troubles the cities of Cleveland and New York developed when they overextended themselves with short-term borrowing.

Describing the difficulties municipalities might encounter because of growing debts and reduced cash flow, the T. Rowe Price Tax-Exempt Money Fund recently informed its shareholders that it was upgrading its investment portfolio. This move may be only a false alarm. On the other hand, it may be an early warning signal of trouble ahead for the tax-exempts.

In either event, perhaps it's best to consider surer ways of reducing your taxes. One such way is the Clifford trust.

Children, Bless 'Em, Pay Less in Taxes

One of the most basic ways to reduce your taxes is to shift part of the tax burden onto someone else, someone in a much lower tax bracket—namely, your children. You can give them your savings, and let them pay the taxes on any interest or dividends the money earns. The only catch is that you can't give any one child more than $10,000 a year, or $20,000 a year jointly with your spouse, without becoming liable for the payment of a gift tax.

Of course, you may not exactly want to hand your twelve-year-old kid $10,000 in cash with which to buy a truckload of bubble gum and thirty lifetime comic-book subscriptions. Even as a means of reducing your taxes, that would be a pretty desperate move. Besides, what if you were to need that $10,000 later on? The solution to the problem is a Clifford trust.

Often called a short-term trust or a family trust, a *Clifford trust is an effective way to divert taxable income to your children and at the same time retain your capital.* And it's an entity to which mutual funds are ideally suited as investment vehicles.

By following the 12 Percent Solution, a $10,000 trust invested in a money fund/mutual fund switching program should earn about $1,200 a year for your child. At that rate, he or she would probably owe next to no taxes, particularly since a Clifford trust has the special tax advantage of allowing a child who is a minor to claim a $1,000 personal deduction against the trust's earnings each year while the parents may also claim an annual $1,000 personal deduction for the child as long as they are contributing 51 percent of the child's support.

Warning: If you intend to use the income from the trust to pay for expenses for your child's benefit, you may be taxed on the trust's earnings, because you have previously filed for the $1,000 deduction. Consult your accountant or tax attorney because this could be a sticky issue with the IRS.

However, you must be able to afford to put a large lump sum out of reach for at least ten years. And you must be able to afford to have the capital returned to you diminished in value by inflation.

There are several other considerations to be taken into account in setting up such a trust. First of all, it's irrevocable. And once money is put into trust, it must remain there for a minimum of ten years and a day. At that point the assets used to fund the trust revert back to you, the trust creator. These assets, incidentally, cannot be paid out to the recipient of the trust, only earnings can.

Another factor to consider is that the trust must be managed by an independent trustee. Have a friend manage your family's trust in exchange for your managing his, however, and there's no cost involved apart from the initial legal fees for setting up the trusts.

The income from a Clifford trust can be distributed any time, either as it is earned or in a lump sum when the trust terminates. The choice is up to you.

When Too Much Is Too Much

Having talked about tax-saving alternatives and their high points and pitfalls, I should perhaps return you to the starting gate with a basic caveat. As you may have noticed, I don't think banks or thrift institutions such as saving and loan associations are places where you should keep any more of your money than you have to these days. And I'm afraid banks really have gone overboard hyping their savings programs. Maybe one can't blame them. What with the consumer waking up and discovering that in today's financial environment what he thought was a bank is actually the cleaners, and he's been taken there, these institutions are becoming a bit desperate. Even so, once in a while they hit the nail on the head. One such instance was when Donald E. Carver, vice-president of the Girard Bank of Philadelphia, commented, reflecting on the new tax laws, "A generation ago, you heard stories of families being "insurance poor.' One can easily envision a generation of 'savings poor' in the 1980s."

Even a trust doesn't let you really keep your money. You're simply giving it to someone else rather than the tax man. If your main problem is how to reduce taxes *and* keep the money you need for yourself, then you'll be happy to hear from ERTA and what it's done for your future.

Time was when tax shelters were strictly the province of the wealthy. Then in the seventies, with bracket creep pushing the great middle class into higher and higher tax brackets, shelters became not only a general topic of conversation, but actually a viable proposition for just about everyone earning $30,000 or more a year. *now under the Economic Recovery Tax Act of 1981* (ERTA), *tax shelters are for everyone, no matter what they earn.*

The only question that remains about the evolution of tax shelters is, why did the government have to make a tax break so complicated? Why did the legislators have to make it seem as if they were doing you a big favor—letting you keep a little more of your earnings *if* you followed some very precise rules? Why not simply, *really* cut taxes?

But that's a separate question. And we all know the answer. Bureaucracies are incapable of simplifying themselves. Even if they mean well, somehow they can't do anything without entangling themselves in rules and red tape.

The government can't deliver a simple get-well present to the economy without asking for a receipt—in triplicate, notarized, sworn to, and approved by at least three people who don't really understand what they're doing. Nevertheless, the get-well present has been delivered, and you'd be foolish not to take advantage of it.

7

IRA, Keogh, and SARA—
Your Retirement Tax Team

> And add to these retired Leisure,
> That in trim gardens takes his
> pleasure.
>
> —*John Milton*

It Used to Be So Easy

Ten years ago, when it came to building a retirement nest egg, any number of stockbrokers, insurance salesmen, or professional money managers could lay out a simple plan for you. Give them your age, tell them you wanted to retire at age sixty-five, and they'd spend a few minutes with the adding machine plus some compound interest tables and come up with the figures. Put away x number of dollars for y number of years and you could begin drawing z number of dollars per month when you retired. Unfortunately, that z wasn't sanforized, and inflation and taxes threw it in the washer-dryer.

A retirement plan drawn up twenty years ago might have been established to yield $240 a month at retirement. Could you live on $240 a month now? Or worse yet, ten years from now? Probably not. So what else is new? you ask.

ERTA to the Rescue

Well, what's new is that when the Economic Recovery Tax Act of 1981 changed the tax brackets, it also supplied us with the means to lower our tax bracket—through an IRA plan. You've heard a lot about IRAs by now, I'm sure. Banks are trumpeting them as the greatest thing since income tax deductions themselves.

IRAs are good, it's true. But they aren't *that* great. And a bank is certainly *not* the place to keep one.

What is an IRA, really, and what choices and alternatives do you have in setting one up. What changes have been wrought by the new universal IRA law which took effect on January 1, 1982? The first change is represented by the word "universal." Now, suddenly, *everyone* could—and should—have an IRA. It was possible to have an IRA plan before, but only if your employer had no pension plan at all. The IRAs available before 1982 were also more restrictive about the amounts you could deposit annually. That's one reason why you didn't hear so much about them—they weren't the tax haven they are today.

Under the new ERTA provisions, you may open an IRA account regardless of whether you have any other form of retirement benefits, including a Keogh plan if you're self-employed. You can contribute up to $2,000 a year to your IRA. A working couple may contribute $4,000 a year between them to a joint husband-and-wife account. Where only one spouse works, the limit is $2,250, split up any way they wish between the two of them, as long as no one contributes more than $2,000 each year.

All the contributions to an IRA up to these maximum amounts are tax deductible. You subtract them from your gross income when determining your taxable income. That's what makes an IRA such a valuable tax-cutting tool. It cuts your taxes and usually lowers your marginal tax rate as well. For instance, if you earn $25,000 a year and you can deduct $2,000 from it, your marginal tax rate is reduced a full 4 percent in 1982, and 3 percent more in the following years. *The deduction is available whether you normally itemize deductions or not.*

And now, from the folks who brought you federal income taxes, one of the most helpful loopholes around. For many of us, scraping together $2,000 for our IRA is a pretty hard job, especially since we always seem to be digging for it with after-tax dollars, even though we get our refund in the spring. But this year, unlike years past, the IRS has made us a deal. We can now claim a legal exemption on our W-4 withholding certificate for an IRA that we will be setting up before we file our tax return.

The exemption is a more effective tax-saving tool in the higher tax brackets than it is in the lower brackets, but only by a small margin of difference. If you are in the 30 percent tax bracket and you claim deductions for both yourself and your IRA, the IRS will withhold $750—that's $11.79 a week—less from your paycheck in the fifteen months between January and April of the following year, the deadline for setting up your IRA as you have pledged to do.

Sounds good, doesn't it? It is. And it's legal. There's only one hitch. *You have to invest the maximum $2,000 in your IRA if you apply for the additional exemptions.* But you have fifteen months plus $750 with which to get organized.

How Much Can You Give an IRA a Year?

As we have seen, you may put up to $2,000 a year in your IRA account, and a working couple between them can deposit $4,000. In a case where only one spouse is employed, the limit for the yearly contribution is $2,250.

Under the new ERTA provisions, the $2,000 contribution is allowable even if all you make is $2,000. In other words, if a part-time job pays $2,000 a sum on which ordinarily you would have taxes due if you filed jointly with your spouse, that $2,000 can now be earned without any current federal tax obligation whatsoever if it is put into an IRA account. Of course, a working couple can turn this provision to their best advantage only if one of them has a job paying enough to cover their combined living expenses—and then some—but it may come in handy at some point in your tax careers.

Speaking of combined living expenses, what happens to a joint IRA account in the event of a divorce? This is a question becoming more and more pertinent in the modern marital scene, and the IRS has an answer ready. If a joint IRA plan has been in effect for at least five years prior to the year of the divorce, and if your ex-spouse made contributions in three out of the five years, you are limited to a $1,125 contribution annually from the lesser of your wages or taxable alimony.

How Married Folk Can Use IRAs to Shelter $6,000

If your spouse receives no employment income, $2,240 is the maximum total you can put into your IRA account. However, if you are self-employed and can pay your spouse $2,000 for working for you, he or she can open an IRA to shelter that $2,000. The two of you then have tax-sheltered $4,000. If your spouse files a separate tax return, he or she will probably not have to pay taxes on the $2,000, since the IRS allows earnings of up to $3,300 (or $5,300 including an IRA) to remain tax free. Also, don't forget, you have acquired a business tax deduction of $2,000 for the salary you've paid out. *Voilà*. You have turned a $2,250 tax shelter into a $6,000 tax shelter.

Oops, My IRA's Had a Little Too Much

Now while it's highly unlikely that anybody would put too much money in an IRA, someone might just possibly decide to try to be clever, and deposit an extra couple of hundred dollars a year into a retirement account in order to build up tax-free savings. *Don't.* There is a 6 percent penalty on contributions to an IRA in excess of the $2,000 (or $2,250 for joint IRAs with only one working spouse) maximum annual contribution. However, a timely correction clause in the law allows you to withdraw any excess contributions free of penalty if you do so before you file your tax return.

A Maximum, But No Minimum

Suppose you put $2,000 into an IRA one year and for some reason you can't do the same next year. What happens? Are you committed to putting $2,000 away every year until you retire? No. The 2,000 allowable by law is the *maximum* you can contribute in any given year. There is no minimum. If for some reason you can't add to your IRA savings pool during a future year, all that will happen is that the money already in your IRA will keep right on earning more money tax-free. If you open the IRA with just $25 when you're twenty-five years old and you add $25 a year to the account, you should have about $21,800, given 12 percent annual earnings, by the time you retire.

You can skip a year. You can contribute different amounts each year, but no more than $2,000. You can start with less than $2,000. Of course, the closer you can come to putting aside the maximum allowed by law for your tax-deferred retirement investment, the faster your savings will grow, and the lower your current taxes will be. That goes without saying. But don't be discouraged if things don't always work out according to your IRA plan.

Where to Find the Wherewithal to Fund an IRA

An IRA account must be opened with cash. You can't make a contribution to the plan by simply transferring stocks to it, unfortunately. Doing so would be a nice way to avoid paying capital gains tax on your earnings, but it's not allowed, I'm afraid.

As far as the income tax deduction goes, on the other hand, where the money for your IRA actually comes from doesn't matter, for tax purposes, as long as you have a matching amount earned as employment income from which to take the deduction. For instance, if you have $2,000 in earnings generated from a stock fund or a money fund investment, you can open up an IRA with these earnings and take a tax deduction provided you have made $2,000 in employment income during the tax year. The IRS doesn't care where you've earned the rest of the money.

Borrowing to Set Up an IRA

You cannot borrow money to invest in such tax-exempt obligations as tax-free bonds and money funds and claim the interest costs of that loan as an income tax deduction. Other interest costs—for instance, those on your credit card, car loan, or any personal loans you may have taken out—are deductible. But the IRS doesn't want you double-dipping your deductions. That's why it disallows the interest deduction on money borrowed to purchase tax-free investments. *Not so in the case of IRA and Keogh accounts,* however.

The logic behind this exception is that taxes will eventually be paid on IRAs and Keoghs when those retirement plans are cashed in. And while this is true, those taxes are due many years from now, when, because of inflation and your lower tax bracket, the amount payable will be much less than it would be now. So if you don't have the cash on hand to start your IRA with a full $2,000, it might even pay you to borrow for it—assuming your budget can take the cost of carrying the loan. You wouldn't be double-dipping, exactly, but at least you'd be getting a scoop and a half (*as long as you have the earned income over the year to match your contribution.*). You must, however, have the income to back up what you borrow. IRS rules stipulate that IRA and Keogh contributions must be from earned income.

The Starting Gate

You don't have to open your IRA account in January, nor do you have to make a yearly contribution to it at the beginning of every year. You can invest in your IRA any time up until you file your tax return for the year—on April 15 of the *following* year. For instance, you can wait until April 15, 1983, to deposit your contribution for 1982 in your IRA and still take the credit for it on your 1982 tax return. But *the earlier you make your contributions, the earlier you start earning tax-deferred income.*

The Monthly-Installment-Plan IRA

Many large companies now offer their employees a payroll-deduction plan whereby IRA contributions can be automatically deducted from their paychecks and invested in a bank, mutual fund, or brokerage firm IRA account. By law, these deposits can now be supplemented to the company's own pension plan.

But if your employer doesn't offer such a plan, there's no reason why you can't set up a similar schedule of payments yourself.

Somehow far too many people think in terms of making only one contribution a year to their IRA plan. Now it's true that you can't deposit more than $2,000 a year and still deduct the total from your gross income for tax purposes. But whether you deposit that amount—or a lesser amount, of course—in one lump sum or budget twelve or even fifty-two smaller deposits over the course of the year makes no difference at all for tax deduction purposes. And in fact, as you may recall from my discussion of dollar-cost averaging (see pages 110–111), these regular payments over the course of the year may help your investment along considerably if your IRA is in a stock fund.

In some ways it's much easier to adjust to regular, systematic monthly payments than it is to face one big payment looming on the horizon. So you might consider simply putting your IRA on your list of monthly bills to be paid. Decide how much you can contribute each month, then fill in the blanks on the checks as you pay your other bills. If a particular IRA deposit is to go to a money fund whose minimum deposit is larger than the amount of your check, make out the check anyhow. Put it in a safe place. Then next month make out another check on schedule and mail the two in together. The important thing is to get into a regularly paced savings habit.

Suppose you have $300 that you can spare to open an IRA account. And suppose that, by squeezing your budget, you an add $100 a month to the account. At 10 percent compounded, which is the historical return you are holding as your base line for long-term investments under the SLYC system, a $300 dollar down payment plus $100 a month would grow from $1,530 the first year to $7,180 the fifth year, $19,900 the tenth year, $70,750 the twentieth year, and $202,600 the thirtieth year.

For a $2,000 down payment the first year plus monthly payments of $165 thereafter (which come reasonably close to your $2,000 a year allowable IRA deduction), the cumulative amounts are even more striking (see Figure 14). If instead of 10 percent, you average a 12 percent return—as you should with the 12 Percent Solution—or an even higher percent return on your investment, your end results positively explode. So don't forget that 10 percent is

Figure 14

Building Your IRA Investment

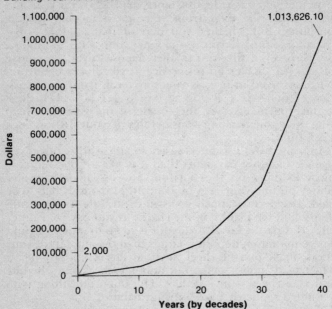

Invest $2,000 initially, and $165 at the beginning of each month thereafter. Example assumes a 10% annual compound rate on your investment.

the *minimum* you're hoping for; you may well average considerably more over the long run.

Is My IRA Locked Up?

IRAs were designed with retirement in mind. But you can withdraw money from your IRA when you reach the age of 59½ whether you're retired or not. <u>You *must* begin to withdraw by the time you're 70½</u>. And at whichever point you withdraw your money, you pay taxes on it according to your then current tax bracket.

If you take money out of your IRA before you're 59½, on the other hand, you pay not only taxes on it, at the rate currently applying to you, but a <u>10 percent tax penalty</u> as well. Disability provides the only exception to the penalty. If you are disabled, you can withdraw your IRA money at any time without penalty, but you must still pay taxes.

Now unless you're cashing in your entire IRA investment, these stipulations apply only to the amount of your IRA that you withdraw. Bear that in mind, for there may be times when paying the penalty proves to be cheaper than borrowing the money from the bank.

While early withdrawal from your IRA incurs a penalty, transferring your assets from one IRA to another or switching investments within a given IRA involves no tax consequences. This feature makes IRAs ideal vehicles for the 12 Percent Solution switching strategy of moving between money funds and growth equity funds to maximize your gains in an uncertain interest environment.

Places IRAs Shouldn't Go—and Places They Should

Because of ERTA restrictions, you will not be able to invest your IRA funds in precious metals, diamonds, or other collectibles. Municipal bonds and bond funds are already tax free, so it doesn't make much sense to tax shelter a tax shelter. Why risk losses with speculative real estate or gas partnerships, commodities or commodity funds, and options or invest in low-yielding government retirement bonds.

You can open an IRA with any mutual fund group, nonaffiliated stock fund, bond fund, or money fund, commercial bank, savings and loan association or savings bank, brokerage firm, or an insurance company that has an IRA plan. You can even use an independent trustee and manage your IRA yourself. But to do so, you'll have to deal with someone who has a plan approved by the IRS all drawn up. The legal work involved in setting up an acceptable IRA for IRS purposes is extremely complicated and expensive, which is another reason for using the already approved plans offered by mutual funds and other institutions. They simplify your life and save you a bundle.

Among these allowable alternatives, your single best choice is probably a mutual fund family, where you can direct your own investments to suit your own goals and financial temperament. The worst choice for almost anybody is a restrictive bank-sponsored retirement account with limited flexibility. Somewhere between these two, you might find a haven for your retirement savings where you personally, for reasons of your own, are more comfortable than you would be in a mutual fund group. But please, when you look over the ads, don't overlook the fine print.

You Can't Even Trust a Bank Anymore

Right now I'm looking at a bank advertisement for an IRA plan. "Save $2,000 a year. Retire on a million." That's what it tells me I can do. If at age thirty-five I begin to deposit $2,000 a year to the bank's IRA account, I'll have $654,256 by the time I'm sixty-five years old. By the time I'm seventy, I'll have $1,216,728.

The bank ad mentions that I could open an IRA account with a money fund or a stock fund instead. But money fund rates fluctuate, and who knows which way the stock market is going to go? Besides, mutual funds aren't insured by the FDIC the way bank deposits are.

I looked that bank ad over several times, wondering why somebody over there wasn't arrested for fraud before I saw the small print in the bottom corner. My millionaire status was dependent on a 12 percent per year return—guaranteed for only eighteen months. "Actual rates offered could be higher or lower. Substantial penalties for permitted premature withdrawals." There was no reference to the fact that FDIC insurance is limited to $100,000, which means that if the bank happened to go broke just when I was about to cash in my million, I might easily be $1,116,728 short of its promise.

What the footnote did make clear, however, in its own subtle way, was the fact that the bank's rates would fluctuate just as much as money fund rates (though of course they'd be consistently a little lower). Not only that, but if catastrophe struck and I really needed to pull money out—and I'd have to be really desperate before I'd consider making a move like that, because it would cost me both the IRS's 10 percent penalty and the bank's six-month interest penalty—I couldn't even do it unless the bank "permitted" me to. The same would hold true if I merely wanted to move my money into another IRA plan, something the IRS doesn't penalize at all.

The last point the bank ad failed to make reminded me of that old joke wherein an investor pulls a Rip van Winkle and falls asleep in a smoking chair at his private club after a rich lunch. Being a private club, the establishment hasn't changed much when he wakes up twenty years later. Stepping out of the familiar environs, he suddenly remembers that he'd forgotten to call his broker, so he pops into the nearest telephone booth. The broker informs him that IBM is 2,233 a share, AT&T is 1,231 a share, GM is 3,002 a share. . . . The man stands there stunned until the operator breaks into the conversation. "Please deposit $25 for the next three minutes."

If the bank continues to pay 12 percent on my IRA account, that means inflation is going to have to continue at around 10 percent annually. So my $1,216,728—assuming the bank hasn't gone under in the meantime—is going to have a purchasing power of a little over $30,000 in today's money. And of course I'm going to pay taxes on the whole million when I withdraw it.

So Where *Do* You Put an IRA?

No longer can you simply keep putting money aside and bank on its taking care of your retirement. You have to manage your money. That means putting your IRA someplace where you can make the decisions about it—not necessarily all of them, not the ones about day-to-day nitty-gritty affairs, but the major decisions affecting the long-term course of your hard-earned investment in the future.

The place that lends the most flexibility to your IRA planning, at the same time meeting the SLYC system requirements of providing for safety, liquidity, and yield for your investment, is one of the new no-load mutual fund families.

These fund groups offer, within their network, a variety of investment possibilities, among which you can switch, in most cases, without a fee and by means of a simple phone call. Their members include stock funds, bond funds, and money funds—usually several of each—and the investment objectives of the various individual funds range from high growth to conservative income.

The minimum initial investment for an IRA account in

one of these fund groups ranges from $240 to $500, except where certain of the member funds retain a separate minimum of their own. Minimums for subsequent investments vary, as do the minimum amounts which can be switched from one fund to another within the group. In some cases, the number of switches allowed per year may also be regulated. See Table 16 for a brief comparative summary of the services and requirements these fund groups offer.

Table 16 Mutual Fund Families Offering IRA Plan Services

Fund Families	Funds Available/ Objective*	IRA Investment Minimums: Initial/ Subsequent	Fees?	IRA Switching Restrictions
The Dreyfus Corp. (800) 223-5525 (212) 223-0303	Liquid Assets/MF Money Market Instruments/MF A Bond Plus/B Fund/G Leveraged/G No. 9/G Special Income/I Tax Exempt Bond/I Dreyfus Third Century/G	$750/none	$5 initial $2.50 annual	No switching fee, unlimited switches per year, a minimum of $500 must be switched between existing accounts or $750 for a new account
Fidelity Management Research (800) 223-6190 (617) 523-1919	Fidelity High Income/Fund B Fidelity Limited Term Municipals/B Fidelity Thrift Trust/B Fidelity Trend Fund/G Fidelity Fund/G/I Fidelity Cash Reserves/MF Fidelity Daily Income Trust/MF Fidelity U.S. Government Reserves/MF Fidelity Corporate Bond Fund/I Fidelity Equity Income Fund/I Fidelity Government Securities Fund/I	$500/$250	$10 annual	No switching fee, four switches per year, minimum must meet requirements of each fund

Table 16   (continued)

Fund Families	Funds Available/ Objective*	IRA Investment Minimums: Initial/ Subsequent	Fees?	IRA Switching Restrictions
Fidelity Management Research (cont.)	Fidelity High Yield Municipals /I Fidelity Puritan Fund			
Scudder Funds Distributors Corp. (800) 453-9500	Cash Investment Trust MF Common Stock/G Government Money Fund/MF Muni Bond/B International/G Development/G	$240/none	None	No switching fee, unlimited switches per year, no limit on amount exchanged. If maintaining more than one account, a minimum of $500 must be switched.
Stein Roe & Farnham (312) 368-7825 (800) 621-0302	Cash Reserves/MF Bond/B Special/G Balanced/B Tax Exempt Bond/B Capital Opportunities/G	$500/$50	$6 annual	No switching fee, unlimited switches, $500 minimum needed to exchange, but has a 30-day holding period
T. Rowe Price, Associates (800) 638-5660 (301) 547-2308	Prime Reserves /MF Growth Stock/G New Era/G New Income/I International/G Tax Exempt Money Fund/MF New Horizons/G	$500/$500	$3 initial only	No switching fee, unlimited switches, amount exchanged must be a minimum of $500, after that $50
Value Line Securities, Inc. (800) 223-0818 (212) 687-3965	Value Line Cash /MF Value Line Income/I Value Line Lev. Growth/G Value Line Special Situations/G Value Line Fund/G	Money fund, $1,000/$100 Bond fund $1,000/$250 All others, $250/none	$5.25 setup $6 initial $6 annual	No switching fee, unlimited switches. Minimum of $1,000 must be switched for money fund and bond fund, $250 for all other funds

Table 16   (continued)

Fund Families	Funds Available/ Objective*	IRA Investment Minimums: Initial/ Subsequent	Fees?	IRA Switching Restrictions
Vanguard Group of Investment Companies (800) 362-0530 (800) 523-7025	Vanguard Fixed Income High Yield/B	$500/$50	$10 annual	No switching fee, unlimited switches per year, minimum must meet requirements of each fund
	Vanguard Fixed Income Investment/Grade B			
	Vanguard Fixed Income GNMA/ Portfolio B			
	Vanguard Municipal High Yield/B			
	Vanguard Municipal Long-term/B			
	Vanguard Municipal Short-term/B			
	Vanguard Municipal Money Market/B			
	Vanguard Money Market Trust Prime/MF			
	Vanguard Money Market Trust Federal 1/MF			
	Wellesley Income Fund/I			
	Wellington Fund Bal.			
	Windsor Fund/G			

*B—Bond fund   G—Growth fund   MF—Money fund
 I—Income fund   G/I—Growth and income fund

If the savings pool you can earmark for your IRA doesn't meet the minimum requirements to open an account in a fund family, don't wait to get started. There are twenty-five money funds which have no minimum initial investment requirements for their IRA plans (see Table 17). So you can open a retirement account with one of these funds for as little as that $11.79 a week the IRS makes available through its withholding provisions. Later on, when you've accumulated more retirement income in your account, you can transfer to another IRA plan if that first money fund does not meet your new investment goals.

Table 17   Money Funds Offering No Minimum Deposit IRA Plans

Fund	Minimum Investment	Maintenance fee Initial/ Subsequent
Alliance Capital Reserves	None	$5/10
Alliance Government Reserves	None	5/10
American Liquid Trust	None	None/10
Capital Preservation Fund	None	5/12
Chancellor Government Securities	None	5/10
Composite Cash Management	None	10/15
Current Interest	None	5/5
Eaton & Howard Cash Mgmt. Fund	None	Depends on amount invested
IDS Cash Management Fund, Inc.	None	10/yr.
IDS Government Securities Money Fund	None	10/None
Money Mart Assets	None	5/10
Pennsylvania Money Fund	None	10/10
Quaker Cash Reserves	None	5/10
Seligman Cash Mgmt. Fund	None	5/5
Sigma Money Market Fund	None	10/10
Sigma Government Securities Fund	None	10/10
Transamerica Cash Reserve	None	None/6
US Treasury Securities Fund	None	1
Vanguard Money Market Trust/Prime Portfolio	None	10/10
Vanguard Money Market Trust/Federal Portfolio	None	10/10

Opening an IRA account with a fund doesn't mean your money is married to that fund until you retire. Transferring your money from one IRA plan to another IRA plan requires only the filling out of a simple form. The only current exception to this rule is bank IRAs using time deposits, where a penalty for early withdrawal will apply.

Choosing a home for your IRA may be one of the most important choices you make about the savings you set aside for the golden years. So whether you invest in a fund group or a money fund, read the prospectus before you put your money down.

Score One for Safety

On one point of safety I can put your mind at rest. A letter from W. H., of Bridgeport, Connecticut, brought up a matter which reminded me of that bank ad warning about the mutual funds not being insured. W.H. asked me:

If one invests in an IRA account administered by a mutual fund, what happens to the IRA account should the mutual fund fail and perhaps go into bankruptcy?

First of all, mutual funds don't fail and go into bankruptcy. The only way that could happen would be if all the securities in which the mutual fund invested went bad. This would involve the failure of dozens of corporations and/or banks. And where would the mutual fund investors be during this? Nothing's holding them in the mutual fund. If its performance were that bad, the press would be writing long articles about it. Secrets are hard to keep in today's economy.

A mutual fund's sponsor, on the other hand, could go bankrupt. But as far as you're concerned, so what? It had problems, but you wouldn't. The mutual fund's custodian bank merely holds the fund's securities. They are not available to the sponsor's creditors. Faced with the prospect of the sponsor's bankruptcy, the fund's board of directors would simply fire the sponsor and hire another, protecting your rights. In fact, the fund would likely fire the sponsor long before its problems became publicly known.

The SEC, which regulates mutual funds, was set up to protect the rights of investors. It's on your side!

But What about All the Bookkeeping?

Almost every IRA program has administrative fees, including a no-load mutual fund group. The no-load feature simply means that there are no initial *sales* fees for investing in the fund.

Most no-load mutual fund groups charge about $10 annually in administrative fees. That's not a great deal to pay for a whole lot of bookkeeping that would otherwise fall on your shoulders. In fact, it's a real bargain.

Sometimes It Pays to Be Self-Employed

The government is doing everything it can to eliminate, over the course of time, the self-employed in this country. The various administrators' platitudes aside, the bookkeeping requirements and special taxes applied to the relatively small number of self-employed individuals left in the United States are so onerous as to put these people on the endangered species list.

People who work for someone else often dream about the freedom of self-employment. Less often do they actually break loose and set out on their own.

When they do, they are suddenly faced with the stark reality of having none of the fringe benefits they'd like and paying for some they might not want. Consider social security, for instance. If you're employed and paying 6.3 percent of your income for social security alone, you have every right to scream that the take is too much. But look at the bright side of your predicament. If you were self-employed, you'd be paying over 10 percent—right off the top. No deductions, nothing.

Still, let's keep trying to look on the bright side, even if we happen to be self-employed. The bright side of self-employment these days is the new improved Keogh plan. Previously, if you were a self-employed individual you were allowed to put $7,500 a year or 15 percent of your salary, whichever was less, into a Keogh plan. The limit for a tax-deductible Keogh contribution has now been raised to $15,000 a year, which means that those who are self-employed and earning over $50,000 annually can at least put away more tax savings money than they ever could before. In 1984, as a result of the Tax Equity and Fiscal Responsibility Act of 1982, you will be able to contribute 25 percent of your income or $30,000 into your Keogh plan, whichever is less.

You are also allowed to have an IRA account in addition to your Keogh plan. So any individual earning $100,000 or more annually can put away up to $17,000 a year tax free. Since most lawyers, doctors, and dentists—who constitute the majority of the high-earning self-employed—are already incorporated and thus unable to have a Keogh plan, I'm not sure how many people will actually be able to take advantage of these new expanded benefits. But there they are.

Come to think of it, my plumber has a Keogh plan.

You cannot borrow from a Keogh plan without incurring an early-distribution penalty more severe than the one for an IRA. Not only do you have to pay a 10 percent penalty plus the regular income tax due, but by your withdrawal you are *disqualified from making tax-deductible contributions to a Keogh plan for the next five years*.

A Pay Cut Beats Having an IRA

Do you suppose your boss would mind giving you a pay cut? If not, try to get one. It will be very profitable—for you. If this sounds contradictory, not to mention absurd, well, blame it on the tax laws, because that's the way they are these days.

Consider for a moment the modern executive office. The latest rage is to have it looking like a living room. The higher the executive's rank, the less it should look like he's working. Gone are the overflowing files, the in and out boxes, the memo pads, in some cases even the desk. Everything in the old office except the telephone (with perhaps an adjunct computer terminal discreetly hidden in a walnut cabinet), and the pictures (the family ones being replaced by works of art) has been removed. The office now resembles a comfortable sitting room replete with couch, easy chairs, and a coffee table displaying *Forbes* and *Architectural Digest,* beneath which a corporate report might inadvertently show a timid, dogeared corner.

Does the American executive not work any more? Hardly the case. The fact is that decor, like the company car and the expense account, is tax deductible. It's cheaper for the firm to come across with grandeur than with a raise. It's cheaper for the executive as well. He doesn't have to pay taxes on the perks.

Wages are a deductible expense as well, of course. But while they're deductible, they also lead to further company costs in the form of taxation. The company has to pay the social security tax, payroll taxes, unemployment insurance, and workmen's compensation on your salary. Reduce your salary, and the company has to pay less all around. Theodora Benna, a vice-president of the benefits consulting firm of Johnson Cos. Companies, estimates that a company saves ten cents on the dollar in payroll taxes alone with employee pay cuts.

SARA—a Tax Cut and Savings, Too

Fine, you say, I love my boss and wish him well, but what do I get out of all this besides a pay cut? The answer is, *more money*. And the reason is a little-known shelter created by a tax law change made in 1978. It goes by the name of Section 401K. The actual regulations governing this shelter, known as the salary reduction plan, were not issued by the Internal Revenue Service until November of 1981, so even your boss may not be aware of its benefits yet. Here's how it works.

Under Section 401K, you were allowed to sock away up to about 6 percent of your earned income a year tax free in a company-sponsored account. The company takes this money out of your pay in the form of a salary reduction. The money never shows up on your paycheck.

Since you haven't been paid that money, you're not liable for any taxes on it. The fact that you might already have an IRA or some other tax shelter makes no difference. You can still take advantage of the salary reduction provision. You don't get a tax deduction per se as you do in the case of an IRA plan. But if you're making, say, $25,000 a year and you take a pay cut of $1,500 a year, why, then your income is only $23,500 a year. This is your new tax base, and of course it lowers your taxes considerably.

There is no dollar-amount limit (like the $2,000 limit on IRA deposits, for instance) on Section 401K salary reduction. There's only the 6 percent maximum. So should you be fortunate enough to make $35,000 a year, why, then you can take a $2,100 pay cut.

Not only is your federally taxable income reduced, but you, like your employer, escape the social security tax on the amount by which your pay is reduced—and the social security tax is up to 6.55 percent for the first $32,400 earned in 1982. Furthermore, while IRA contributions may be subject to state and city income taxes, you can't be asked to pay any taxes at all on a pay cut, can you?

(Your boss may even match your contribution to a salary reduction account.) This is an excellent way to take tax-free raises. Additionally, the payout benefits for a salary reduction plan are much more liberal than those of an IRA plan. At normal retirement age, or as specified in your employer's contract (usually age 65), *you must with-draw this deferred compensation in a lump sum and use special ten-year forward-averaging tax laws to reduce your tax liabilities. By comparison, when you finally collect on your IRA, you can only use general income-averaging adjustments and your money is taxed as ordinary income.*

Finally, there's the matter of penalties for early withdrawal. These are unavoidable, and rightly so. After all, this is retirement money we're talking about. You shouldn't spend it. But what if disaster strikes? A real emergency? For instance, your house burns down, and the insurance, for any number of possible reasons known only to the insurance company's legal department, covers only a small part of the loss.

Obviously current shelter takes precedence over the exigencies of a more distant future. Yet if you withdraw money from an IRA plan to meet such an emergency, a 10 percent penalty is immediately slapped onto the amount—on top of the taxes owed. With a salary reduction plan, you can withdraw part of your money in a true emergency without paying any penalty at all. What actually constitutes true emergency has not yet been defined by the IRS, but some people feel the classification will be liberal enough to cover even withdrawals for your children's college education.

So new that few companies have offered it yet, the salary reduction plan has met with an enthusiastic response wherever it has been implemented. Employees seem to love taking a pay cut if it means a tax cut plus more savings.

Honeywell, Inc., of Minneapolis set up a salary reduction plan in 1981, offering its employees the choice of a 4 percent salary reduction plan and/or a company-operated IRA. The salary reduction won by a margin of two to one, with 25 percent of the employees choosing both. Well, why not both?

The repositories provided for the employee savings in the Honeywell plan include a high-interest fund, a stock and bond mutual fund, and a straight stock mutual fund. A built-in option allows the employees to switch savings from one fund to another quarterly.

Two additional tax-avoidance angles—one for individuals and the other for corporations—are variable annuity programs and new twists on the corporate tax exclusion of dividends. Let's consider the corporate angle first, since it is the simplest and the least touched by the hands of the IRS (so far, anyway).

Recent innovations provide corporate (but not individual) investors with partially tax-sheltered yields and relatively stable principal values; these are floating-rate preferred stocks and specific qualified dividend portfolios. Both types of investments pay dividends which qualify for the 85 percent dividend exclusions available to corporations on their federal tax returns. That means that the first 85 percent of the dividends received is free of all federal taxes. The next 15 percent is taxed at the corporate tax rate (no more than 46 percent of 15 percent, or 6.9 percent). That's a pretty good deal!

The floating-rate preferred stocks are new, and to date have been issued only by a few New York City banks. The rates so far have been attractive—near money market levels—and float with money market rates to be readjusted each quarter. This feature ensures that the principal value of these stocks returns to par at the beginning of each quarter. In a falling interest-rate market, these stocks will actually appreciate. However, these stocks must be held until the end of each quarter to earn the dividends qualifying for the tax exclusion.

As of this writing, Fidelity and Vanguard both offer qualified dividend portfolios. The advantages of a mutual fund enabling corporations to earn qualified dividends is that daily dividends of a *diversified* portfolio mean a safer investment both in terms of liquidity (you can sell before quarter-end) and risk (you are automatically diversified).

The second tax-avoidance angle, this one for individuals, is the use of variable annuities. By investing in a mutual fund through a variable annuity program run by an insurance company, you can tax-defer your mutual fund earnings until you decide to withdraw the money. This means that you can tax-shelter monies over and above your IRA and SARA investments (although you cannot deduct variable annuity contributions from your taxes). Variable annuities, while attractive to many investors, do have some drawbacks. The IRS has already intervened and forced insurance companies to restructure their variable annuity programs. While variable annuity programs may well be a terrific investment opportunity in the eighties, the jury is still out on some of the specific legal issues involved as we go to press. For an update on these intriguing investments, write to us and we'll send you a free report ("Variable Annuities," Box 411, Holliston, MA 01746).

So there's your retirement tax team—IRA, Keogh, and SARA. Invest among them wisely for tax-deferred dollars.

And now, for all you've read about retirement plans, in this book and elsewhere, do you know, come to think about it, how to get your money out of them once the right time comes?

Probably not. Everybody seems to be telling you how to put your money into tax-deferred retirement accounts. But nobody seems to be telling you how to collect on them. Well, I'm going to tell you that. After all, getting the money out when you need it is what investing is all about.

8

Reaping Your Rewards Right—
for Even More Profits

> A man who both spends and saves
> money is the happiest man, because
> he has both enjoyments.
> —*Samuel Johnson*

Will the Golden Years Be Made of Lead?

Retirement without poverty became an almost universal goal in the Cinderella, Sleeping Beauty, and-they-lived-happily-ever-after post-World-War-II environment. It was quite a change from the past, when people worked until they died or were no longer capable of working, at which point they lingered on in abject poverty or on charity.

Today the goal is to enjoy our days of retirement without financial worries. Why else do the promoters call them the golden years? And why did the politicians set up the social security system if not to ease our way (and assure their reelection)?

Social Insecurity

Unfortunately, the people's golden dream of social security is rapidly turning into a nightmare of deficits for the government. Mismanaged from the start—the social security program was never properly funded, and it spends today what it hopes to earn tomorrow—this grand scheme is about to collapse. Not completely, mind you, and not for people already collecting from the program—that would be politically unacceptable. But bit by bit the benefits will be cut down to size. They will be taxed—again. The age at which you will be eligible to collect will rise to sixty-eight, then sixty-nine, then seventy. If you're in your forties now, retirement for you will probably come at seventy-five—if it comes at all. For the government's desperate hope is that most of us will be collecting our pension from that big payout window up in the sky by then. It's the only way social security is going to survive.

Even corporate pension plans, a lot of them anyway, are vastly underfunded. Like social security, they'll worry about tomorrow when it comes. That's why you need your retirement team of IRA, Keogh, and SARA—and then some—*plus the know-how to cash in on your various retirement plans in a cost-effective and profitable way.*

The Mechanics of Withdrawing

When all is said and done, your savings and investments are geared toward one thing in the end, namely, spending the money. Now, spending is something we probably all know enough about to be considered experts. And when it comes to getting money out of a bank or a money fund account, the mechanics are simple enough. You merely write a check for the amount you need. But what about withdrawing cash from a stock fund or a bond fund?

Cashing in Your Chips

The no-load mutual fund families make your withdrawal from stock or bond investments a whole lot easier by the simple means of transferring funds into your home-base money fund account. From there you simply write a check against your account.

In the old days, the procedure for cashing in on a similar investment could be tedious indeed, as witness the following letter from J. B., of Green Bay, Wisconsin:

A month ago we decided to cash in a Nuveen Municipal Account, 74 Series, that was suffering a Chinese water-torture death, and it took them about ten days to get the funds transferred. You must sign the certificate, get it guaranteed, send it in by U.S. Postal Service. They look it over and cash it in. Then with a holiday weekend (the return mail problem we avoided by asking for a wire transfer, which they agreed to only after our broker pleaded with them)—at long last the money was transferred. This whole procedure reminds one of banking and trading in the days of the pony express. Another name for it could be, "Hang onto the sucker's money as long as we can."

Well, J. B., now you understand the value of the telephone switch feature offered by the SLYC mutual funds. With these mutual funds, you don't have to worry about long settlement dates, redemptions by mail and—wait a minute—did you say broker? Why are you paying for services you should be getting free?

In the case of a nonaffiliated no-load stock or bond fund, you collect by means of a simple letter of request. However, if you've been keeping the certificates for your shares at home, you must still sign and forward them to the fund by registered mail before you can receive your investment proceeds.

Alternately, some funds have a provision whereby you can cash in your shares by means of a telephone request. They keep a voice recording of your speech patterns for purposes of verification and fraud prevention. Of course, if you're planning to use this telephone feature, your share certificates must be kept with the fund at all times.

IRAs and Keoghs—Out It Comes, Ready or Not

Retrieving your money from an IRA or a Keogh plan seems to be a very neglected area of information. Sure, the ads all say that at such and such an age you'll have so much money. But most banks and other IRA managers stop there. One almost has the feeling they think of it as their money somehow, and, like social security administrators, they'd rather you didn't draw it out at all.

By now we all know that we can start withdrawing money from our IRA and Keogh plans when we're 59½, and we have to begin withdrawing by the time we're 70½. Now why the half year is tucked in there is beyond me. Sometimes I think regulators simply aren't happy unless they can make things at least *look* more complex than they are. Then too, a precise number like 59½ is somehow more intimidating than a plain old round number like sixty. It lends authority to its user. In any case, the limits are there to stay, intimidating to you personally or not.

Having to draw your money out on the basis of actuarial tables might seem even more intimidating to some people. But you have no choice. At the age of 70½, a man must start drawing money out of his IRA or Keogh as if he were going to live a little longer than twelve years more, and a woman must start drawing out as if she were going to live for fifteen more years. Perish the thought that you should live two or three years beyond that. However, joint life expectancy figures can extend the payout period considerably for couples. (See Tables 18 through 20 for typical life expectancies according to the IRS).

Table 18 The Life Expectancy of Single Individuals as Calculated by the IRS

	Life Expectancy, Years	
Age	Male	Female
59½	18.9	22.4
60	18.2	21.7
61	17.5	21.0
62	16.9	20.3
63	16.2	19.6
64	15.6	18.9
65	15.0	18.2
66	14.4	17.5
67	13.8	16.9
68	13.2	16.2
69	12.6	15.6
70½	12.1	15.0

Source: Internal Revenue Service

Table 19 The Life Expectancy of Married Couples and Last Survivors Where Both Parties Are the Same Age

Age	Life Expectancy, Years	
	Husband	Wife
59	23.8	26.2
60*	23.4	25.7
61	23.0	25.2
62	22.6	24.7
63	22.2	24.3
64	21.9	23.8
65	21.6	23.4
66	21.3	23.0
67	21.0	22.6
68	20.7	22.2
69	20.4	21.9
70*	20.2	21.6

* At age 59½, may begin withdrawals from IRA; at age 70½, must begin withdrawals from IRA.
Source: Internal Revenue Service

Table 20 The Life Expectancy of Married Couples and Last Survivors Where the Wife Is Younger by Five Years

Age		Life Expectancy,
Male	Female	Years*
59	54	29.6
60†	55	28.8
61	56	27.9
62	57	27.1
63	58	26.2
64	59	25.4
65	60	24.6
66	61	23.8
67	62	23.0
68	63	22.2
69	64	21.5
70†	65	20.7
71	66	20.0

* Based on husband's age, assuming the IRA plan is in his name
† At age 59½, may begin withdrawals from IRA; at age 70½ must begin withdrawals from IRA.
Source: Internal Revenue Service

Withdraw or Else

If withdrawal plans are rarely discussed when IRAs and Keoghs are being sold, such things as penalties for failing to withdraw usually aren't even mentioned at all. <u>Yet *failure to withdraw from your IRA or Keogh at least the amount specified for your age by the IRS actuarial tables can lead to a penalty of up to 50 percent*</u>. In actuality the so-called penalty is an excise tax forfeiture. But fancy nomenclature aside, what it means is simply a lot more money for the tax man and a lot less for you.

Consider a hypothetical example in which the actuarial tables dictate that you must withdraw $4,000 during a given year. Suppose your house is paid for, and with your social security income and other savings you really don't need more than $1,000 from your IRA account. So that's all you withdraw from it. Well, the revenue agents aren't going to accept that.

You should have withdrawn $4,000—and paid the taxes due on it, however minimal they might be at that point in your life. So they're going to want a tax penalty: The $4,000 you were supposed to withdraw less the $1,000 you actually did withdraw equals $3,000; 50 percent of $3,000 is $1,500. That's the IRS's legitimate retaliatory take. You lose, taxpayer.

But nothing says you have to spend that $4,000 you have to withdraw. You can put it right back into savings in the form of a mutual fund or any other savings plan you choose. The only stipulation is that you can't put it—or leave it—in a tax-sheltered IRA plan. When it's time to collect, one way or another the government intends to claim its due.

When Three Minus Two Equals Four

Even with forced withdrawal, your retirement nest egg will actually continue to swell if you do things right. You have the option of withdrawing everything on retirement—all at once, in a lump sum distribution—and then use general income-averaging adjustments. But if you do that, your capital loses its tax-free growth potential.

An alternative option open to you is to withdraw money

Figure 15
The Withdrawal Effect

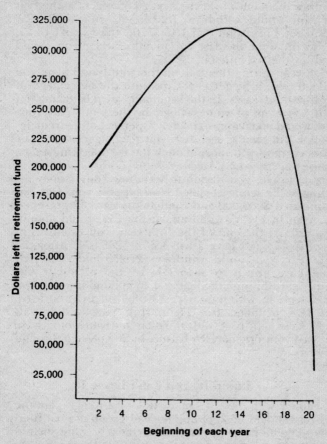

Withdrawing $200,000 out of an IRA over 20 years. assuming it is paying 12%.
What you will have left in retirement each year.

on a schedule based on your life expectancy according to the IRS actuarial tables.

For example, suppose you're a man 70½ years old married to a woman five years younger. You've socked away $200,000 in your IRA. The actuarial tables say you must withdraw the money over the next 20.35 years. So the first year you would withdraw 1/20.35 of your total IRA investment, the second year 1/19.35, the third year 1/18.35, and so on until the last 3½ months, when you would withdraw the last little bit.

Each year during the span on this withdrawal plan, you would receive a bigger check, because the percentage of withdrawal increases. In the beginning you'd be taking out about 5 percent of your savings; by the tenth year your check would equal approximately 9 percent of the remaining total. But even as each year you get a bigger take, your IRA is earning you more money for the following years, because *your remaining balance is earning compound interest.*

For example, you decide to withdraw your money according to the actuarial tables. Now suppose your IRA has accumulated $200,000 and continues to earn 12 percent a year. Your first year's withdrawal in that case would amount to $9,820. At the end of the fifth year, you would withdraw $15,475 and have a balance of $265,871. After the tenth year, you would withdraw $27,253 and your IRA would have grown to $315,937. By the twentieth and a third year, through the magic of compound interest, you would have to withdraw over $30,000 in order to leave your IRA penniless (see Figure 15). Your withdrawals would have kept pace with inflation and you would have increased your original IRA balance by 269 percent through the years.

Lump It, You Can't Leave It

The money withdrawn from an IRA or a Keogh plan the final year should be kept in a no-load group mutual fund account, an all-purpose cash management account such as the ones now being offered by many of the brokerage houses (discussed on page 39), or someplace else where you can reach it quickly and conveniently.

For a very few investors, those who find themselves still in the 40 to 50 percent income tax bracket even after they've retired, there is the alternative of putting that last lump sum payout in a tax-free fund. It will mean a lower yield, but, of course, that will be more than made up for by the fact that you're paying less in taxes. (See the taxable-funds/tax-free-funds ratio on page 135.)

For the rest of us, a more balanced investment is in order. This is not the time to be speculating in the stock market, nor is it the time to be cowering in a corner of the bank, holding thirty-month bank savings certificates. As one of my favorite senior citzens puts it, "For some of us, thirty months is forever." What you need at this point is liquidity.

Because you also want safety and yield, the SLYC system is still your best investment friend. When I was first thinking of writing this book, a *Moneyletter* subscriber wrote to me:

> I think the older subscribers would appreciate a chapter of your book on the things to watch out for in the way of security. I am sixty-six. I have money in a money fund that just handles government securities. I feel safe there, but I have money in a mutual fund, too. Now what kind of mutual fund—growth, income, bond—is for me? Is it wise to take the dividends quarterly in case I might need the money and find by not doing this that the stocks had dropped at a time when I needed my money? I'll be anxiously waiting for your next book on mutual funds. Bravo!

Here's my answer to V.N., of Fort Wayne, Indiana. The beauty of non-load mutual funds with telephone exchange privileges is that any time you need money, you can simply transfer it into a money fund (if it isn't already there), write a check on your fund account or order a wire redemption in the amount you need, and the money is instantly available. There is no need to keep a savings account for emergency money. With your luck, if it's like mine, you'll likely need the money on a weekend and the bank will be closed. But you can write a money fund check any time.

As to the right mutual fund for you, that depends entirely on the markets at the time of your investment, and the 12 Percent Solution keeps you on top of the markets at all times. <u>You see, there is no single type of mutual fund that will be right all of the time.</u> That all changed when inflation completely upset the financial world, creating both problems and opportunities for investors who understand what is going on in the economy. If you've read this far in the book, you have the tools to win most of the time.

You Should Live So Long

If you are worried about your retirement savings running out, an insurance annuity may be the solution for you. On the whole, a well-managed withdrawal plan, as I'll show you, keeps your savings growing and is better than an annuity because it avoids the relatively expensive premium you must pay in order to acquire the annuity. Still, psychologically, some people feel more comfortable with an annuity. If you are one of those people, consider putting part of your retirement nest egg into an annuity and leaving the rest available for regular withdrawal from your IRA plan.

Annuities come in four basic forms, tailored to different personal and family needs. The most basic type is the _life-only_ annuity. It pays you a specified amount for the duration of your life, whether that be a month or a hundred years from the time you buy the annuity. Once you die, there is no further payment, nothing left over for heirs or charity.

A _life-and-period-certainty_ annuity pays you or your heirs for a specific period of time, typically ten years, no matter how long you actually live. An _installment-refund_ annuity guarantees to pay out to you or your heirs a minimum equal to your original investment. If you live longer, the annuity keeps right on paying, although when you die there are no further payments to your heirs. Last, there are _joint-life_ annuities, which, as the name implies, cover two people. Typically, the payments are based on both life expectancies and made first to both parties, then to the survivor.

Procedurally, all these annuity plans have one thing in common, namely, that <u>you must transfer funds from an IRA into such an annuity before you reach the age of 70½. After that age, the tax laws no longer allow the transaction.</u>

A Check a Month May Not Be Best

The usual recommendation for withdrawing funds from a non-annuity treatment account is the check-a-month plan. To implement this plan, first you deposit your stock fund certificates with the fund, or more accurately, with its transfer agent. If the certificates have been left with the stock fund or if they are shares in a money fund, you skip this step.

Next you fill out a withdrawal application, stating how much you wish a month. This isn't a permanent commitment. You may increase or decrease the amount of the checks any time you wish. You may even stop them altogether if you wish. Every time a check does arrive, however, you will also receive a statement indicating the balance and status of your account.

For instance, if you determine that you're going to need $100 a month above and beyond your social security and your pension benefits to cover your living expenses, you can instruct the fund to send you a monthly check for that amount drawn on your account. The fund will arrange for this to be done automatically until such time as it's told to stop—or until you run out of money, something which careful planning, we hope, will prevent. Such an automatic withdrawal plan can utilize money earned in either dividends or capital gains or both. Or the plan can draw down the capital itself. It's your money, and when retirement comes you can decide how much you need and can afford to withdraw, regularly or otherwise.

The reason a check-a-month withdrawal plan is often recommended is that it adds regularity to your budgeting and spending. It's like getting the old familiar paycheck.

The reason I personally don't recommend it is that you can keep your money earning more money if you withdraw it only as you need it. Letting the money ride is the quickest way to increase your holdings.

The outflow of money is never really regular, even in retirement years. For instance, heating bills (or air-conditioning bills if you're in the Sun Belt) add seasonal bulges to your spending. Insurance bills may arrive once a year or quarterly. Capital expenses such as for a car or a vacation trip to see the grandchildren would normally be met separately. But when it comes to cashing in on your retirement plan, it's much better to leave the money earning more tax-free money in its shelter for as long as possible.

So withdraw the money as you need it instead of on a regular basis. And try to bunch most of your large expenses together in January and February whenever possible. Remember that you're going to have to pay income tax on your withdrawals. But the tax becomes due only on the money you withdraw in a given year. And taxes due on what you take out at the beginning of the year aren't payable until April of the following year, which means even this amount due can be earning you more tax-free income for up to fifteen months.

Simplifying Your Life

One of the complications in withdrawing your money from an investment is keeping track of the whens, wheres, and hows of it all, in order both to keep your own financial planning under control and to keep the IRS happy and off your back. If you have a lot of diversified investments, record keeping and organizing your reinvestments of capital gains and dividends could be enough to drive you up the wall.

Here's where mutual funds can really simplify your life. For instance, you can request the fund to reinvest all your distributions, both capital gains and dividends. Or you can ask it to reinvest only the dividends and send you the capital gains, which are taxed at a lower rate than dividends are. And the capital gains distribution, in the case of most funds, comes at the end of the year—just in time for the Christmas bills, if that's what you want the money for.

You can also have the fund send you the dividends quarterly and reinvest just the capital gains. Quarterly payments might make your particular budget easier to live with, while plowing back the capital gains would meanwhile keep your fund growing.

A mutual fund's year-end statement will detail the payouts for you. The fund will also send you a 1099 form showing your total dividends and capital gains for the year (with a copy going to the IRS). This is all the paperwork you'll need for making out your tax return on those earnings.

Incidentally, even if you reinvest the dividends and/or capital gains except in the case of IRA and Keogh plans, you will still be liable for the taxes on these gains in the year in which they are declared. However, when you follow a reinvestment schedule, you are allowed to subtract the cost of these dividends and capital gains from your profit for tax purposes once you sell the shares.

It works like this. Say you invested $10,000 initially ten years ago. All dividends and capital gains were reinvested. The $10,000 by itself grew to $26,872. The divdends over the years amounted to $3,048 and bought enough shares to now be worth $5,720. The capital gains reinvested over the years equaled $4,052 and bought enough shares to now be worth $5,100. The total value of all the shares if you sell them now is $37,692. Your initial $10,000 grew by $27,692.

However, since you paid the taxes on the dividends and capital gains as they were declared, you now owe taxes on only $20,592 [that's $37,692 − ($10,000 + $3,048 + $4,052).] And all of that $20,592 is taxed at the lower capital gains rate.

Here, too, the fund will lay out all the figures and do the paperwork for you. About the only thing it won't do is pay the taxes. Unfortunately that's something you have to do yourself.

Capital Isn't Sacred Anymore

Something else you have to do yourself is spend the money. Now this isn't much of a problem for most people. But for the recently retired it can be. There's always that last nagging doubt—*will the money I've saved last for all the years ahead?* A good question, particularly at the point at which you're forced to draw all the money out of your tax-deferred retirement plan. By the IRS actuarial tables you're supposed to have gone to that happy tax-free hunting ground in the sky by then. Yet here you are with a lump sum and an unknown number of years ahead. So often, in this predicament, people stint on themselves, figuring that they can't touch the capital but must live off the income alone. Well, there's nothing sacred about capital at this stage of the game. What is crucial is not running out of money yourself. To this end, the magic triangle in Figure 16 will show you how long your capital will last if you choose to draw out at a rate greater than your investment is earning at current interest rates.

No matter how you spend it, it's always possible that you'll end up with more money than you need. If that's what happens to you after reading this book and putting its plans into effect, I can only hope that too much money is the worst problem you have to face in the future.

Figure 16
The Magic Triangle

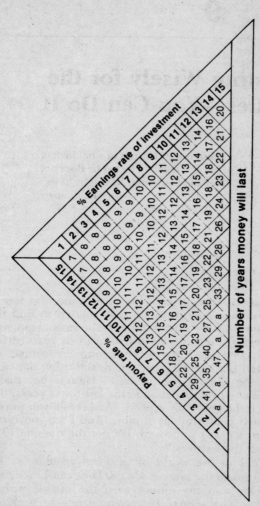

Years represent an approximation: In reality your payment would expire at different times during the year.

a > 50 years

Earnings rate compounded monthly

9

Investing Wisely for the Eighties—You Can Do It

> Man is not the sum of what he has but the totality of what he does not yet have, of what he might have.
> —*Jean-Paul Sartre*

Visiting his son at college, a friend of mine who was an alumnus of the same institution was amazed to find that the questions on his son's final exam in economics were identical with the ones on his own some thirty years earlier. Since the same professor was teaching the course, my friend asked him, "How come you're still using the exam you gave me when I studied here? Hasn't your dismal field made any progress at all in the last thirty years?"

To which the professor replied, "As I recall, you weren't a particularly good student of mine. And I see your grasp of economics hasn't improved. It's not the questions that change, but the answers."

So it goes in the world of personal economics. The questions remain the same as always. How can I save more money? How can my money earn the utmost without undue risks? What's the best way to prepare for retirement? But the answers—those have changed a lot.

The days of carefully putting so much a month in the bank and leaving it there to grow and grow over the years are gone. Gone too are the days when the stock market was the place to make a real profit—in the go-go years of low commissions—and the bond market was where the rich invested wealth for safety and security. Today, in search of safe yields we can count on for our inflation- and tax-battered savings, we move among many different types of investments, following the pointer of elusive interest rates.

Buy, hold, and pray is dead. Today you must be prepared to make changes in your financial game plan to match changing circumctances. This doesn't mean becoming a trader, as Wall Street puts it, someone who is constantly jumping in and out of investments, trying to make an extra dollar here and there. Far from it. Amateur traders only make other people rich. And there are very few traders around who are not amateurs.

No, what you must be is a helmsman for your investments, directing them through treacherous new market shoals. And to do this, you must be, above all, flexible. For in today's highly volatile investment climate, it's the changes you have to keep your eye on.

The unveiling of the money market was a revelation for millions of small savers and investors. The thought of making 16, 17, even 18 percent yields on safe investments certainly hadn't crossed our minds a few years ago. In fact, the retail money market barely existed five years ago. Today it's almost a trillion-dollar market.

While most once-in-a-lifetime investment opportunities seem to fade after a while, the money market is probably with us for the duration. But while it is unlikely ever to disappear entirely, new opportunities are overtaking it.

This book is designed to help you recognize those opportunities, and also, just as important, to recognize when they disappear. Of course, sometimes, it's still best to sit out the economic storms invested in your favorite money fund. But, increasingly, it pays to cross over market boundaries. That's why I've given you the 12 Percent Solution—*so you'll know when to cross over*. And the fact that it's an *automatic* switching system is what can make it work for you consistently through all the variations in the up and down motion of today's rapidly fluctuating market scene.

Always remember, however, that a solution may not be the same tomorrow as it is today. That's one more change you have to keep your eye on. *Caveat emptor.*

What Are Your Goals?

Why are you investing? A surprising number of people can't answer this most basic question. They'll say, "To make money," as if the answer were obvious. Fine. That part of it is. But money for *what*, exactly? And how important is that goal to you? So-so? Or important enough to make sacrifices in order to reach it?

Retirement, a college education for the kids, a fishing boat, a skiing vacation in the Alps—certainly such goals are ranked differently on a scale of values by different people. How about your goals? Can you rank them? Right now? If not, maybe what you need to do is dream a bit.

Organizing Your Dreams

If people would dream more, they'd be a lot better off. The fact is, dreaming is frowned upon as being somehow unproductive. It brings to mind the stereotype image of little John or Jane staring out the school window, and the teacher's stern reprimand, "Stop dreaming and get to work."

Work for what? The stereotype usually leaves out the sequel, the fact that dreaming little John and Jane are the only ones in the class who eventually get somewhere. They do that because they have a dream, a goal.

So pick a nice day, a comfortable chair, a cool drink, a pad and pen—and dream. Invite the family, if you have one, to join you. Talk about the things you like to do and what you'd like to be doing in the future. Make a list of those things. Then try to evaluate them. *It's much easier to save for concrete, measurable goals than for an undefined future.*

Even inexperienced dreamers will come up with far more targets to shoot for than there are arrows in their quiver, so the next step is to sort through your dreams. Separate the long-term ones from those you might be able to achieve within a year or two. Than rank the dreams in each group by importance. If you could only have one dream, which one would it be? Which is the least important? Are there any that to all intents and purposes are unobtainable—owning the Chase Manhattan Bank, for instance?

There are your goals, ranked and ready to be reached. Now how are you going to reach them?

First you have to determine the costs. Not the costs today, but the costs current at the time you plan to reach the goals. If, for instance, you have a child who will be heading for college in ten years, and you'd like to provide the wherewithal for his or her college education, then setting your savings target at today's college costs will leave you severely disappointed at the end of those ten years. _Count on inflation when you count the cost of your dreams_. And keep your investment arrow aimed at the target. Adjustments may have to be made. You're aiming at a moving target, and you must compensate for the wildly swinging economic changes ahead in this country.

You're going to have to learn to be very flexible. If you make the mistake of falling in love with your investments, you will die of a broken heart. So be prepared to match your goals with the right investment strategies.

For a retirement account, under the current tax law it makes sense to earn as much as possible in dividends and interest, and not worry too much about capital appreciation. A fishing boat or some other relatively short-term savings target, in the two- to three-year range, calls instead for a definite focus on the lower-taxed capital gains.

Financial Housecleaning

The first thing you'll probably notice about your goals, once you have pinned them down, is that your current finances simply won't do. You might have to cut back on the number of goals you have set, or at least change the size of those goals. But to a larger extent the change you have to make lies in putting your financial house in order—rearranging the furniture, holding a garage sale, so to speak. When it comes to financial matters, most of us are weighed down by a lot of excess baggage in the form of outdated ideas, inappropriate or underutilized investments, or simply unawareness of what is actually happening to our money now that inflation has cut so sharply into our daily lives.

Your Personal Inflation Index

Inflation has probably been the leading topic of financial conversation for several years. One of its factors, however, seems to have been consistently overlooked, and that's the way it affects your personal expectations.

There's a lot to be said for developing your own personal inflation index (PII, I'm going to dub it). After all, you aren't the typical consumer on which the consumer price index is based, and your financial goals aren't typical either. Typical is mythical. Having your own index will do your financial plans a world of good.

Rare is the individual who keeps a complete set of financial records year by year. And I'm not going to suggest you need do so. No doubt many a rich man keeps a daily log of every cent he spends. But many more of the wealthy hire accountants to do it for them, and personally have no idea of what they spend except on an overall basis. There are stories of millionaires making their fortunes through private cost accounting, but my personal feeling is that that's not the key you need. You do need to establish your operating costs, just as a business does; you don't need to track it in such detail.

But if you have a complete set of canceled checks and bills from last year, so much the better. Pick two months, one from wintertime and one from the summer, say February and July, to help even out seasonal variations. Gather up all the expenditure information you have for these two months and classify it by categories—mortgage, food, entertainment, clothes, and so on. Do the same for this year.

Now how much more are you spending this year for utilities, medical expenses, eating out, and the rest of the categories? The difference is your personal inflation rate. Keep track of it on an annual basis, and you'll have a much more focused picture of how inflation is actually affecting you.

The other facet of personal inflation, the inflation of expectations, is much less readily formulated. As their financial situation improves, most people upgrade their standard of living over the years. They expect to live better because they earn more. In fact, they expect to live so much better that their increase in living costs actually exceeds their increase in earning power. This is what I call the inflation of expectations.

In part it's due to the tax structure. As you earn more, an ever-increasing percentage of your pay goes to the tax man. You think in terms of a $100 a month raise, and of spending $100 more a month, but taxes let you keep only a fraction of that $100. So you end up feeling richer than you really are.

Over the years you upgrade the kind of car you drive, you go to better restaurants, you buy some fancy new gadgets—video recorders or food processors—things you wouldn't have considered before. Well, perhaps it's time to take a hard look at what you're doing and see if you shouldn't call a halt to some of it. This you can do by zero-based budgeting.

Zero-Based Budgeting

One of those great ideas that ended up being buried in bureaucracy, zero-based budgeting was a much talked about financial idea early in President Carter's term, before he started floundering in the morass of Washington.

The essence of the idea is to start a new budget each year. Weigh every allocation anew. The mortgage, for instance—if it was $611.33 a month last year, should you continue to spend that much on it this year? Most people don't have a choice. It's a fixed payment they have to make. Short of such drastic measures as selling the house and moving to a less expensive one, this figure will not change.

Almost every other spending category, however, can be altered to save money—money that can be invested to help you build up capital for your dreams. In a country where 11 percent of the entire potato crop goes to making potato chips, and where the consumption of soft drinks alone has reached an average of over 400 cans per person a year, saving a little here and a little there is far from impossible.

You can start your zero-based budgeting and long-term savings planning today. Fiscally, budgets are usually thought of as running for a year—starting in January. However, some companies begin their fiscal year in July, others in April. Start yours this month. Don't stall by saying you have to wait until the beginning of next year.

✕ Strategies to Start Out With

With your goals defined and your budget pared down (provided your goals make that worthwhile), you're ready to start investing your savings. As you map out your investments, there are four basic strategies to keep in mind.

Strategy #1. *Play it safe.* Don't risk your capital. The risks of a particular investment should always be assessed in relation to protection of capital as well as return. You will have to take some risks sometime with at least part of your capital if you want above-average growth. But those risks must be weighed carefully. Remember that if you lose 50 percent of your money, you'll have to make 100 percent on what's left simply in order to get even again.

Strategy #2. *For your retirement savings, you can afford to concentrate on yield.* This emphasis is a product of the recent tax changes—and may last only until the next tax changes (the major ones will probably be around 1985). Money put aside for retirement in IRAs or Keoghs should be invested primarily to take advantage of the opportunity to tax-shelter dividends, interest, and short-term capital gains. These retirement accounts pay no current taxes, so you don't have to worry about the fact that normally such earned income and short-term gains are taxed at the highest rate applying to you. In your tax shelter, the taxes are deferred until you retire.

Strategy #3. *For short-term goals, seek capital gains.* Capital for short-term goals, those only two or three years away, should be invested to emphasize capital gains rather than yield. Under the new ERTA law, even if you're in the 50 percent tax bracket, the maximum tax on capital gains is 20 percent. So here you get to keep a lot more of what you earn than you would in the case of dividend or interest income. Once again, the emphasis derives from the current tax structure.

Strategy #4. *For really short-term goals and for ready cash, stay liquid.* You can't claim a long-term capital gain on anything held for under a year, and on the whole it usually takes two years or so for an investment to offer reasonably significant capital gain. So for goals of two years or less, keep your cash in a high-yielding, liquid money fund. Stay away from certificates of deposit and other bank instruments that lock up your money timewise. Even the stock and bond funds usually part of your investment strategy are not suitable for really short-term goals. Because of the brief time span involved, you can't afford to sit out the market if it goes temporarily against you.

Variations on the SLYC Theme

Overall, investing through a no-load mutual fund family, switching between a growth stock and a money fund as the 12 Percent Solution shows you which way the profits lie, is the most prudent way for the small investor to keep his savings safe, liquid, and high-yielding. *The opposite of a diversified investment is a gamble.*

But there are many times when you'll want to consider varying your risk strategy. For instance, when it comes to getting those car payments off your back, you might be willing to take more of a gamble than you'd take on your retirement investment or on savings you're setting aside for your child's college expenses. If so, for your car pool you might choose a professional fund. Just remember to open separate accounts for your targets so that risks taken for one don't jeopardize the safety of the others.

You might even consider different funds or fund families for two goals, even if the investment objectives of your two targets are quite similar. For if one fund happened to do spectacularly well, you could transfer any excess profit from your supersuccessful account to the other if it happened to be floundering. Such a situation is the only time you should ever consider a switch of this kind, however. It's all too easy to transfer money from a distant-goal account to a near-goal one in order to achieve a sense of accomplishment or satisfy an immediate urge. While this does mean achieving one goal more quickly, it also lessens the chances of success for your long-term goal greatly.

Again, depending on your own monetary personality, you might decide that a goal such as a sailboat or a vacation hideaway is more in the dream category than it is in the realm of the essential. You could afford a four-years-

or-nothing gamble on it, as opposed to waiting for ten years and certitude. You'd be able to enjoy it more if you had it sooner, and if you didn't have it at all, well, then you could live without it.

If you were willing to gamble even more, you might forgo the 12 Percent Solution altogether. Instead of opting for the minimum acceptable return, the normal investment philosophy of the SLYC system, you might decide to go all out for this particular target, investing its allotted capital in high-beta performance funds and switching among them as your investment instinct—or one of the fund-switching newsletters—dictates. (See Appendix A for a listing of the newsletters that might help you switch.)

How to Be SLYC When You Don't Have Enough Money Yet

To fully implement the SLYC system, you probably need a minimum of about $10,000. You can certainly start with less, but then you must make a decision before you start. You must decide how likely you feel the chance of economic chaos is—total economic chaos, that is, which in many ways could be worse than even the Great Depression.

Some people feel that economic disaster is right around the corner. Others, while not denying the possibility, consider its chances remote. If you feel they are remote enough so that you don't need to worry about them, then you might decide you can safely put off your catastrophe-proofing and just be SLY until you have accumulated $10,000.

If, on the other hand, you feel there's a pretty good chance of disaster being only a year or two away, then be SLYC. Catastrophe-proof your savings even if it means putting more than the suggested 10 percent of your portfolio into your insurance plan. For instance, if the savings you start out with amount to $2,000, then the minimum $500 or $600 you would need for a deep-discount Treasury bond and the $200 to $400 required to buy gold coins would represent almost 50 percent of your total capital, 50 percent that would not grow the way your investments will. You'd be spending as much on the insurance for your SLYC plan as you'd be spending on the investments themselves. On the other hand, of course, should disaster strike, this 50 percent would be your life ring.

The Uneven Steps of Every Climb

From the very outset of your investing career, you must remember that you are not going to be dealing with straight-line events. For any one of your given savings targets, you can say that today you and your money are at the starting point, and ten years from now, say, you want both you and your money to have arrived at the goal post. But it would be difficult indeed to arrive exactly on schedule, to the very day and by the precise path you are mapping out years, perhaps even decades, before the projected event.

Then too, you may well find that you are not approaching your financial goals evenly. You may sprint ahead, then fall behind on some of them, maybe even on all of them. With your eye steadfastly on your targets, you may have to remind yourself that your actual path in realizing each and every one of them is bound to follow what stock chartists call a mountain graph (see Figure 17). *It's not as neat as a straight line, but it gets you there.*

Building Up Momentum

If you study those lines in Figure 17 for a minute, you're probably going to notice that they start up in a rather shallow fashion. The ascent to your goal becomes steeper and steeper.

In this case, the ever steeper climb does not mean that the task is becoming increasingly difficult. Quite to the contrary, the accelerating curve is due to the force of past savings. A savings investment is very like a rocket. Starting out slowly, it gathers momentum more and more rapidly. The more money you add to your savings, the more money that money earns.

At some point between a quarter of the way and halfway to your goal, your savings earnings begin to contribute more money than you do on a regular basis. Now there's real velocity working for you.

The accumulated earnings on your money keep increasing all the time. And on an overall, idealized curve, each

Figure 17

A Typical Savings Pattern

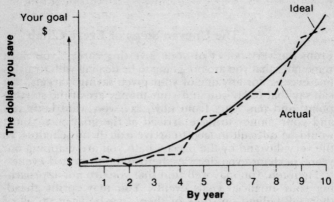

increase is larger than the last. But in actuality, at times the trend is momentarily down, as we have seen. These downswings are compensated for by the times the upward trend is sharper than that of the ideal. Life's that way.

But what do these curves mean to you in terms of how to project each of your various goals on the investment grid? Well, first of all, they tell you that it will always be easier to save for a long-term goal (say a goal ten years or further away) than for a medium-term goal (two to ten years in the future) or a short-term objective (less than two years away).

Also, because you have less time to work with in reaching your short-term targets, you'll have to be more cautious in mapping out your route to them. If you don't watch out, that downdraft in the mountain graph may hit just when you're ready to cash in your chips and spend the money on its allotted goal.

The likelihood of your being caught short this way on a long-term goal, even if you've chosen a more volatile mutual fund to attain it, is reduced both because by the time its due date approaches you'll be higher up the ascending curve, and so the downswings will not be as large in comparison to the cumulative amount of the savings, and because the time scale is longer. If you need to postpone realizing the gain on a long-term goal for six months or a year in order to let the accumulation curve smooth itself out, you'll be waiting a relatively short time to cash in on your objective. One year out of ten is, after all, only 10 percent. One year out of two, on the other hand, would mean a 50 percent delay in reaching your goal.

So your game plan calls for not only matching each investment you make to the goal for which it is targeted, but matching it to the exigencies of time as well. Do that, and you can reach any reasonable target you choose using the 12 Percent Solution and the SLYC system. So map out where you want your money to take you—and then go to it.

When you started reading this book you were a saver becoming an investor. Now follow the 12 Percent Solution, develop some tricks of your own, and don't become a slave to a mechanical rule. The 12 Percent Solution can get you started but you've got to develop your own investing style and continue to learn.

A Final Note

Don't be afraid to reread parts of this book. Smart investing is hard work. Luck is part of it, I admit—but, the harder I work, the luckier I get.

Glossary

ABA (American Bankers' Association)   The national trade association for bankers. The purpose of the ABA is to keep members aware of developments which affect the banking industry.

Accumulation Plan   An arrangement by which an investor can purchase mutual fund shares periodically in large or small amounts, usually with provisions for the reinvestment of income dividends and the acceptance of capital gains distributions in additional shares. Plans are of two types, voluntary and contractual.

Adviser, or Investment Adviser   The organization which is employed by a fund's management to give professional advice and to supervise and administer its assets.

Asked Price   The asked price of a fund share refers to the net asset value per share plus sales charge, if any. For no-load funds, bid and asked prices are the same.

B.P. (basis point)   The movement of interest rates, or yields, expressed in hundredths of a percent. Example: 100 b.p. = 1 percent. 12.50 percent is 50 b.p. more than 12.00 percent.

Balanced Fund   A mutual fund which has an investment policy of "balancing" its portfolio, generally by including bonds, preferred stocks, and common stocks.

BAs (bankers' acceptances)   Short-term non-interest-bearing notes sold at a discount and redeemed at maturity for full face value. Primarily used to finance foreign trade. BAs represent a future claim on a U.S. bank that provides lines of credit to U.S. importers. BAs are collateralized by the goods to be sold and are guaranteed by the importer's U.S. bank.

Blue Chip The common stock of a large, well-known corporation with a relatively stable record of earnings and dividend payments over a period of many years.

Blue Sky Laws Laws of the various states governing the sale of securities, including mutual fund shares, and the activities of brokers and dealers within the particular state.

Bond A security representing debt—a loan from the bond-holder of the corporation.

Bond Fund A mutual fund whose portfolio consists primarily of bonds. The emphasis is normally on income rather than growth.

Book Shares A modern share-recording system which eliminates the need for mutual fund share certificates but gives the fund shareowner a record of his holdings. Also called uncertificated shares.

Breakpoint Dollar-value level of a purchase of mutual fund shares at the precise point where the percentage of the sales charge decreases. A typical sales-charge schedule includes five or six breakpoints.

Broker A person in the business of effecting securities transactions for others. He receives a commission for his services. Closed-end investment company shares are usually bought and sold through brokers.

Call An option contract that gives the holder the right to purchase a particular security from another party at a prespecified price during the term of the option.

Capital Gains *Long-term* capital gains are profits realized from the sale of securities held for more than one year and are taxed at a maximum rate of 20 percent; *short-term* capital gains are profits from such sales when the security is held one year or less and are taxed as ordinary income.

Capital Gains Distribution Payments to mutual fund shareholders of gains realized on the sale of the fund's portfolio securities. These amounts usually are paid once a year. Many funds offer their shareholders a choice of accepting these dividends in cash or in fund shares of equal value.

Capital Growth An increase in market value of securities. This is a long-term objective of many investors and investment companies.

Cash Equivalent Includes receivables, U.S. government securities, short-term commercial paper, and short-term municipal and corporate bonds and notes.

Certificates of Deposit (CDs) Generally short-term, interest-bearing negotiable certificates issued by commercial banks or savings and loan associations against funds deposited in the issuing institution.

CMA Merrill Lynch's Cash Management Account. A "central assets account" which consists of a margin brokerage account tied, by computer, to a money fund. All earnings from securities are automatically transferred to the money fund so earnings never sit idle.

CIF (Corporate Income Fund) A unit investment trust (created by Merrill Lynch). There are usually short-term (six months), intermediate-term (three years) and long term (30 years). Each unit usually equals about $1,000.

Check-Writing Privilege A service offered mainly by money market funds, permitting shareholders of such funds to write checks against their fund holdings. Salient point is that holdings will continue to earn dividends until checks are cleared.

Cash Position Term denoting cash plus cash equivalent minus current liabilities.

CDs *See* Certificates of Deposit.

Closed-End Fund or Investment Company Closed-end companies issue only a limited number of shares and do not redeem them; their shares are traded in the securities market as operating business corporations, with supply and demand determining the price. Also called "publicly traded" funds.

Closed-up Fund An open-end mutual fund which has discontinued the sale of its shares to the general public, but still will accept redemptions.

Commercial Paper Short-term, unsecured promissory notes issued by corporations to finance short-term credit needs. Commercial paper is usually sold on a discount basis and has a maturity at the time of issuance not exceeding nine months.

Common Stock A security representing ownership of a corporation's assets. The payment of common stock dividends and assets follows payments on bonds, debentures, and preferred stocks. Voting rights are normally accorded holders of common stock.

Common Stock Fund A mutual fund whose portfolio consists primarily of common stocks. The emphasis of such funds is generally on growth.

Conduit Tax Treatment Term used to describe the method by which regulated investment companies and their shareholders are taxed. The company is considered simply a "conduit," or channel, which serves to pass investment income and realized capital gains through to the tax-paying shareholders and, therefore, is not itself also taxed on such income and gains.

Contractual Plan An accumulation plan under which the total intended investment is stated, with a specified payment period and provision for regular monthly or quarterly investments. A substantial portion of the total sales charge is deducted from the first year's payments.

Conversion Privilege *See* Exchange Privilege.

Custodian The organization—a bank or a trust company—which holds in custody and safekeeping the securities and other assets of a mutual fund. *See also* IRA.

Dealer A person or firm who regularly buys and sells securities for others from his or her own account of securities. In contrast, a broker acts as an agent for others. Frequently, broker and dealer functions are synonymous. Mutual fund shares are usually purchased through dealers.

Debenture A bond secured only by the general credit of the corporation.

DIDC (Depository Institutions Deregulation Committee) The regulatory committee charged by Congress with phasing out interest rate restrictions on bank deposits.

Direct Purchase Fund A no-load or low-load mutual fund. Investors purchase shares directly from the fund, rather than through an investment dealer or broker.

Distributions Dividends paid from net investment income and payments made from realized capital gains.

Distributor The principal underwriter—either a person or company—that purchases open-end investment company shares directly from the issuer for resale to others.

Diversification The mutual fund policy of spreading investments among a number of different securities to reduce the risk inherent in investing. Diversification may be among types of securities, different companies, different industries, or geographical locations.

Diversified Investment Company To be so classified, the Investment Company Act requires that 75 percent of a fund's assets be allocated so that not more than 5 percent of its total assets are invested in one company. In addition, it can hold no more than 10 percent of the outstanding voting securities of another company.

Dividend A payment from income on a share of common or preferred stock.

Dollar-Cost Averaging A policy of investing equal amounts of money at regular intervals regardless of whether the stock market is moving up or down. The investor acquires more shares in periods of lower securities prices and fewer shares in periods of higher prices.

Dual-Purpose Fund A type of investment company, introduced to the United States from England in early 1967, which is designed to serve the needs of two distinct types of investors: (1) those interested only in come and (2) those interested solely in possible capital growth. Has two separate classes of shares.

Equity Fund A mutual fund that invests in stocks.

Eurodollar CDs Deposits in foreign branches of American banks, denominated in dollars.

Exchange Fund An investment company organized to permit persons holding individual securities with large unrealized capital appreciation to exchange these securities, without payment of capital gains tax, for fund shares in order to achieve diversification and to obtain professional investment management.

Exchange Privilege The right to exchange the shares of one open-end fund for those of another under the same sponsorship at nominal cost or at a reduced sales charge. This is considered a sale and new purchase for tax purposes. (Same as conversion privilege.)

Ex Dividend When a dividend is declared by a corporation, it is payable on a designated date to stockholders of record as of a certain date. NYSE rules that if a stock is sold three business days prior or subsequent to stated date and prior to the date of payment, *the dividend belongs to the seller and not to the buyer.*

Expense Ratio The proportion that annual operating costs—excluding income taxes and interest paid—bear to average net assets for the year.

Fair Value Under the Investment Company Act, value determined in good faith by the board of directors for those securities and assets for which there is no market quotation readily available.

FDIC (Federal Deposit Insurance Corporation) The federal agency which guarantees funds up to $100,000 at member banks. FDIC also makes loans to buy assets from member banks to facilitate mergers or help prevent bank failures.

Fiduciary An individual who is granted legal rights and powers to be exercised for the benefit of another.

Forward Pricing The policy by which mutual fund shares are priced for sale or redemption at the price next computed after the receipt of an order. Pricing is usually done once a day at the close of the New York Stock Exchange.

FSLIC (Federal Savings and Loan Insurance Corporation) The federal agency established to insure funds on deposit at member S&Ls.

Fully Managed Fund While this term can be applied to most investment companies, it is sometimes used in a more restricted context to describe a fund lacking any restrictions on its securities portfolio or the extent of cash and equivalents it may hold.

Growth Fund A mutual fund with growth of capital a primary objective, to be obtained principally through investments in common stocks with growth potential.

Growth-Income Fund A mutual fund with the objective of providing both income and long-term growth.

Hedge To offset. One attempts to hedge against inflation by purchasing securities whose values should respond to inflationary developments. Securities having these qualities are "inflation hedges."

Hedge Fund A mutual fund or investment company which regularly hedges its market commitments by holding securities it believes are likely to increase in value and "shorting" other securities it believes are likely to decrease in value.

Incentive Compensation A fee based on management performance in relation to specified market indexes. It is paid to the fund's adviser.

Income Fund A mutual fund investing in stocks and bonds paying high dividends and interest; current income is the primary objective.

Index Fund A mutual fund whose investment objective is to match the composite investment performance of a large group of publicly traded common stocks, generally those represented by the Standard & Poor's 500 Composite Stock Price Index.

Individual Retirement Account (IRA) A retirement program for individuals with employment income. An individual may contribute up to $2,000 per year to an IRA investment account and defer taxes until the money is withdrawn.

IRA Glossary

Collectibles: an investment in a physical object which has value by virtue of its rarity or intrinsic or artistic value. Collectibles receive very special tax treatment since they do not generate capital gains or taxable income when they are traded for new collectible assets.

Custodian: the institution which retains *physical control* of IRA assets, usually a commercial bank or trust company.

Distribution of IRA Assets: under Federal law a distribution is a withdrawal from IRA assets for more than 60 days. Penalties are levied on all "early" withdrawals before the age of 59½ except for disabled persons, who may withdraw their money at any time without penalty (but with the usual taxes).

IRA Rollover: the transfer of IRA assets of investments from one trustee to another. This can be done only once a year and the rollover must be completed within 60 calendar days. If the rollover is not completed within this time period, penalties are assessed at 10 percent of the assets withdrawn, plus ordinary income taxes on the distribution (withdrawal) for the current year, at present, a maximum of 50 percent.

Ordinary Income: income taxed at the maximum rate schedule, such as employment income, income from a business, etc.

Tax-deferred: income on which tax is levied only when it is distributed.

Tax-exempt: income on which no federal tax is levied.

Trustee: the institution which maintains *administrative control* over IRA assets; a commercial bank, savings and loan association, mutual savings bank, trust company, or stockbroker.

Investment Company Generic term including mutual funds and other types of companies principally engaged in the business of investing the funds of their shareholders.

Investment Income Dividends Payments to mutual fund shareholders or dividends and interest earned on portfolio securities after deduction of operating expenses. These usually are made quarterly.

Investment Objective The specific goal, such as long-term capital growth or current income, which the investor or mutual fund pursues.

IRA *See* Individual Retirement Account.

Keogh Plan A retirement program, similar to an IRA, for self-employed individuals and their employees based on tax-saving provisions. A Keogh plan may be funded with mutual fund shares. (Also known as an H.R. 10 Plan.)

Legal List List published by a state government that sets standards or specifically enumerates those securities that are proper investments for trust funds.

Letter of Intention A pledge to purchase a sufficient amount of shares of a load fund within a limited period (usually 13 months) to qualify for the reduced selling charge that would apply to a comparable lump-sum purchase.

Leverage The effect of the use of borrowed money or other senior securities, magnifying the changes in the assets or earnings available for junior issues.

Liquid Easily convertible into cash or exchangeable for other values.

Liquid Asset Fund A money market or cash management fund invested in short-term securities.

Management Fee The amount paid to the investment adviser for his services.

Money Market Certificate (MMC) A six-month bank certificate of deposit with a $10,000 minimum deposit.

The interest rate is tied to the six-month U.S. Treasury bill.

Money Market Fund Mutual funds investing in short-term money market instruments—bank certificates of deposit, bankers' acceptances, commercial paper, and government securities.

Municipal Bond Fund Unit investment trust or open-end company whose shares represent diversified holdings of tax-exempt securities, the income from which is exempt from federal taxes.

Mutual Fund An open-end investment company which combines the money of many people whose investment goals are similar and invests this money in a wide variety of securities.

National Association of Securities Dealers (NASD) An organization of brokers and dealers in the over-the-counter securities market which administers rules of fair practice and rules to prevent fraudulent acts, for the protection of the investing public.

Net Asset Value per Share The market worth of an investment company's total resources—securities, cash, and any accrued earnings—after deduction of liabilities divided by the number of shares outstanding.

Net Realized Capital Gain per Share The amount of capital gains realized on the sale of portfolio securities of a fund during an accounting period after deducting losses realized, divided by the number of shares outstanding.

No-Load Fund A mutual fund that requires no fee to open an account. See Direct Purchase Fund.

NOW Account Negotiable Order of Withdrawal. An interest-bearing checking account.

Offering Price The asked price.

Open-End Investment Company The more formal name for a mutual fund. The words open-end indicate that it continuously offers new shares to investors and redeems them on demand.

Ordinary Income *See* IRA Glossary.

Payroll Deduction Plan An arrangement whereby an employee may accumulate shares in a mutual fund by authorizing his or her employer to deduct and transfer to a fund a specified amount from salary at stated times.

Periodic Payment Plan An accumulation plan.

Performance Fund A term generally applied to open-end investment companies which appear to emphasize short-term results and which have usually had rapid turnover of portfolio holdings. May also refer to funds with outstanding records of capital growth, regardless of policies by which results were achieved.

Portfolio The securities owned by an investment company.

Prospectus The official booklet which describes a mutual fund and offers its shares for sale. It contains information as required by the Securities and Exchange Commission on such subjects as the fund's investment objectives and policies, services, investment restrictions, officers and directors, how shares can be bought and redeemed, its charges, and its financial statements.

Publicly Traded Fund A closed-end investment company.

Put An option contract that gives the holder the right to sell a particular security to another party at a pre-specified price during the term of the option.

Qualified Retirement Plan A private retirement plan that meets the rules and regulations of the Internal Revenue Service. Contributions to a qualified retirement plan are in almost all cases tax deductible and earnings on such contributions are always tax-sheltered until retirement.

Redemption Price The amount per share the mutual fund shareholder receives when he cashes in his shares (also known as "liquidating price" or "bid price"). The value of the shares depends on the market value of the company's portfolio securities at the time.

Reinvestment Privilege A service provided by most mutual funds for the automatic reinvestment of a shareholder's income dividends and capital gains distributions in additional shares.

Repo or Repurchase Agreement A contract between a seller and a buyer of federal government or other securities whereby the seller agrees to buy back the securities at an agreed upon price after a stated period.

Retail Repo An agreement with a bank or thrift institution whereby the customer lends a certain amount of money for a set period of time (less than 90 days) at a certain interest rate. The agreement is collateralized by U.S. government securities only.

Rollover   *See* IRA Glossary.

Round Lot   A fixed unit of trading (usually 100 shares) to which prevailing commission rates on a securities exchange will apply.

Sales Charge   The amount charged in connection with public distribution of fund shares. It is added to the net asset value per share in computing the offering price and is paid to the dealer and underwriter.

Savings and Loan Association (S&L)   A financial institution that accepts time deposits and uses this money primarily for financing home mortgages. Some S&Ls are stock corporations. These are usually chartered and regulated on the state level. Many S&Ls are mutually owned by their depositors, who receive dividends from the association's profits.

Securities and Exchange Commission (SEC)   An independent agency of the U.S. government which administers the various federal securities laws for the protection of the shareholder.

Short Sale   The sale of a security which is now owned, in the hope that the price will go down so that it can be repurchased at a profit. The person making a short sale borrows stock in order to make delivery to the buyer and must eventually purchase the stock for return to the lender.

Small Savers' Certificate (SSC)   A 30-month bank certificate of deposit. The interest rate is tied to 30-month Treasury security rates. There is no set minimum deposit.

Specialty Fund   A mutual fund specializing in the securities of certain industries, special types of securities, or in regional investments.

Split Funding   A program which combines the purchase of mutual fund shares with the purchase of life insurance contracts or other products.

Tax-exempt   *See* IRA Glossary.

Tax-deferred   *See* IRA Glossary.

Treasury Bill (T-bill)   A certificate showing a short-term obligation of the U.S. government. Treasury bills bear no interest, but are sold at discount. They are sold to the public at weekly auctions and mature in less than one year.

Tax-Free Fund A mutual fund which invests in fixed-income securities issued by state and local governments. Interest payments on such securities qualify for exemption from federal income taxes.

Transfer Agent The organization which is employed by a mutual fund to prepare and maintain records relating to the accounts of its shareholders.

Trustee *See* IRA Glossary.

Turnover Ratio The extent to which an investment company's portfolio is turned over during the course of a year. For a closed-end company, total purchases and sales of securities (other than U.S. government obligations and short-term notes) are divided by two and then divided by average assets. For a mutual fund, a rough calculation can be made by dividing the lesser of portfolio purchase or sales (to eliminate the effects of net sales or redemptions of fund shares) by average assets.

Uncertificated Shares Ownership of fund shares credited to a shareholder's account without the issuance of stock certificates.

Unit Investment Trust (UIT) A type of mutual fund offered by brokerage houses investing primarily in certificates of deposit. UITs are sold in $1,000 units.

Underwriter or Principal Underwriter The organization which acts as chief distributor of a mutual fund's shares; it is often the same as or affiliated with the adviser.

Unrealized Appreciation or Depreciation The amount by which the market value of portfolio holdings on a given date exceeds or falls short of their cost.

Variable Annuity An insurance annuity contract under which the dollar payments received are not fixed but fluctuate more or less in line with average common stock prices.

Voluntary Plan An accumulation plan without any stated duration or specific requirements other than an initial specified minimum investment. Sales charges are applied to each purchase as it is made.

Withdrawal Plan An arrangement many open-end companies have which enables investors to receive fixed payments—usually monthly or quarterly. The actual payout is to be determined by the investor.

Yield Income received from investments, usually expressed as a percentage of market price; also referred to as return.

Appendix A

Newsletters That Help You Invest

Donoghue's FUNDLETTER™ (published by William E. Donoghue), included in MONEYLETTER®
Box 411
Holliston, MA 01746
   Features investment advice monthly according to the SLYC System, news and developments in the markets, and ranks the top-performing no-load funds. Free Sample Upon Request!
Donoghue's MONEY FUND DIRECTORY (published by William E. Donoghue)
Box 540
Holliston, MA 01746
   Annual publication that lists money fund addresses, telephone numbers, investment requirements. Price $24.
Donoghue's MONEYLETTER® (published by William E. Donoghue)
Box 411
Holliston, MA 01746
   Consumer investment newsletter (twice-monthly). Features investment advice, updates on IRA and Keogh,

Donoghue's MONEY MARKET RATINGS, and new money market developments. Price $87. Free Sample Upon Request!

Donoghue's MUTUAL FUNDS ALMANAC (published by William E. Donoghue)
Box 540
Holliston, MA 01746

Reports on over 605 mutual and money market funds. Provides a ten-year performance record and narrative on mutual fund investing. Price $25. Published annually.

Current Performance and Dividend Record
Wiesenberger Investment Companies Service
210 South Street
Boston, MA 02111

Report of performance and dividends on over 400 mutual funds.

Fundline
The Menashe Timing Service
David H. Menashe & Company
P.O. Box 663
Woodland Hills, CA 91365

Ranks no-load mutual funds by performance. Features market timing recommendations for no-load top performers using the Menashe Cycle Theory.

Growth Fund Guide and *Growth Fund Research* Newsletters
Growth Fund Research Bldg.
Yreka, CA 96097

Rates the top performing aggressive and middle-of-the-road no-load growth funds. Features market timing and investment advice.

Handbook for No-Load Investors
P.O. Box 283
Hastings-on-Hudson, NY 10706

Narrative and ten-year statistical reports on no-load mutual funds.

Johnson's Company Charts
246 Homewood Avenue
Buffalo, NY 14217

Presents charts and data on mutual funds. Annual.

Mutual Funds Forum
Investment Company Institute
1775 K Street NW
Washington, DC 20006

Not an investment newsletter, but a professional journal. Features commentary by experts on important issues and developments in the mutual funds industry.

Newsletter Digest
2335 Pansy Street
Huntsville, AL 35801

Bimonthly newsletter featuring opinions of numerous investment newsletter publishers covering a wide variety of investment outlooks from hard money to equities and the money market.

No-Load Fund X
DAL Investment Company
235 Montgomery Street
San Francisco, CA 94104

Ranks top performing no-load funds by class. Features news and market commentary.

The No-Load Fund Investor
P.O. Box 283
Hastings-on-Hudson
NY 10706

Features top performing no-load funds by class, investment advice, and stock market commentary related to mutual funds.

Performance Guide Publications
P.O. Box 2604
Palos Verdes Peninsula, CA 90274

Reports on no-load and load fund performance by class. Features important economic indicators, market timing, and commentary.

Personal Finance
901 N. Washington Street
Alexandria, VA 22314

This monthly newsletter features in-depth articles by leading authorities in the investment world covering a wide range of topics.

Prime Investment Alert: An Advisory for No-Load Investors
Prime Financial Associates
P.O. Box 8308
Portland, Maine 04104

Features investment advice based on market timing indicators. Reports mutual funds news and performance of leading no-load funds by class.

Switch Fund Advisory
Schabacker Investment Management
Chestnut Oak Drive
Gaithersberg, MD 20706

> Market timing advice for mutual fund switching families. Features charts and fund performance of load and no-load mutual fund families.

Telephone Switch Newsletter
Box 2101
Huntington Beach, CA 92647

> Market timing advice for low load and no-load telephone switching funds. Reports on performance of funds by class.

U.S. Financial Data
Federal Reserve Bank of St. Louis
P.O. Box 442
St. Louis, MO 63166

> Free publication published weekly. Features charts and graphs on money market data.

United Mutual Fund Selector
United Business Services
210 Newbury Street
Boston, MA 02116

> Reports on load and no-load fund preformance by class. Features specific reports on mutual funds, techniques, and news.

Appendix B

The 12 Percent Solution: Mutual Funds Switching Based on Money Market Mutual Fund Yields as a Market Timing Indicator

ABSTRACT

The quarterly earnings on the 12 Percent Solution, a mutual funds switching system based on the changes in the average monthly money fund yields between 13 and 10 percent, was compared to a random series of switch indicators. The average monthly rate of all taxable money funds and the monthly percent gain on an aggressive growth fund index were used to represent switches between an investor's money fund and a performance stock fund for the period of September 30, 1975, through June 30, 1982.

The results of the study revealed that the 12 Percent Solution significantly outperformed the random switches at the .10 level of significance. Using the 12 Percent Solution, an initial $10,000 investment grew to $32,544, or at an annual compound rate of 19.1 percent. The $10,000 investment switched at random grew to $21,901 or at an annual compound rate of 12.16 percent. The mean quarterly earnings on the 12 Percent Solution were $835.33 versus the $440.78 using the random switch.

INTRODUCTION

The average monthly yield for all taxable money market mutual funds can be used as an effective mutual fund switching indicator. By using Donoghue's 12 Percent Solution (as described in Chapter 7), a money fund investment is switched into an aggressive growth equity fund when the average annual money fund yield breaks through the ranges of 13 to 10 percent. Investors increase their equity fund holdings when money fund rates decline and increase their money fund holdings when rates rise. It is expected that by using this system, investors can considerably enhance their earnings.

Because high interest rates pressure corporate earnings and future growth, the demand for stock wanes. Profit margins are squeezed as businesses borrow in the short-term because of higher than expected long-term interest rates. In addition, the high yields in the money market, with relatively minor risk, are more attractive to investors than the uncertainties of the stock market. As a result, the higher yields in the wholesale and retail money markets have further dampened the demand for stocks. As the demand for equities subsides, stock prices recede. For example, the average yield on money funds in 1981 was 16.8 percent. During this time the Dow Jones Industrial Average lost 9.2 percent and the S&P 500 declined 7.26 percent. Only fifteen mutual funds out of over 600 outperformed the average money fund.

To prove the validity of a switching system based on money fund yields, it must be shown that Donoghue's 12 Percent Solution significantly outperforms random exchanges between money funds and stock funds. It was hypothesized that by switching according to the barriers of the 12 Percent Solution, the earnings on a $10,000 investment would grow at a greater rate of return than by switching randomly between the two types of funds.

METHOD

The quarterly earnings on the 12 Percent Solution from October 1, 1975 (when money fund yields were first reported by *Donoghue's Money Fund Report*), to June 30, 1982, were compared to switches based on random chance. A Mann-Whitney Analysis was used to determine if there were significant differences between the median quarterly earnings to each system. A nondirectional *t*-test for two independent means was used to compare the mean quarterly earnings.

PROCEDURE

Switches were made based on the average monthly annualized yield on all taxable money funds. A switch was signaled when the money fund yield met the criterion of the 12 Percent Solution. The actual switches occurred at the beginning of the following month.

The calculation of earnings was based on the following: The hypothetical investment (indicated by the 12 Percent Solution) in a money fund was multiplied by the average monthly money fund yield, assuming dividends reinvested every month. The percentage of monthly gain on the aggressive growth fund index was multiplied by the amount assumed invested in an aggressive growth fund, assuming that all earnings were reinvested. The growth fund index, a composite of 20 growth funds, was priced at 1970 = 100 and assumed that all dividends and capital gains were reinvested.

The 12 Percent Solution barriers and the percent of assets invested in each type of fund are as follows: *Barrier I,* when money fund yields are above the 13 percent barrier, 100 percent is invested in money funds; *Barrier II,* between 13 and 12 percent, 75 percent is invested in money funds and 25 percent in aggressive growth funds; *Barrier III,* as rates decline through 12 percent into the 12 and 11 percent range, the investment would be equally divided between a money fund and an aggressive growth fund; *Barrier IV,* when rates are between 11 and 10 percent, 25 percent would be invested in a money fund and 75 percent invested in an aggressive growth fund; *Barrier V,* as money fund rates break below 10 percent, 100 percent is invested in an aggressive growth fund.

RESULTS

A Mann-Whitney Analysis revealed a statistically significant difference between the median quarterly earnings (z = 1.471, $p < .10$). In addition the mean quarterly rank of earnings in the 12 Percent Solution (31) was significantly greater than the mean quarterly rank due to random chance (24).

A t-test for two independent means revealed a significant difference in mean quarterly earnings (t = 1.643, df = 52, $p < .10$). The mean quarterly earnings on the 12 Percent Solution ($835.33) was significantly greater than that of random chance ($440.78) (see Table B-1).

Table B-1

	Earnings	Annual Compound Rate	Mean Quarterly Earnings	Mean Quarterly Rank
12 Percent Solution	$22,544	19.10%	$835.33*	31
Random Chance	11,901	12.16	440.78	24

*$p < .10$

DISCUSSION

The results of the 12 Percent Solution clearly demonstrate that the system is operating on a greater than chance basis. By taking advantage of a monthly decline in interest rates through active switching between money funds and aggressive growth funds, an investor can increase his or her earnings. As money fund rates broke the barriers of the 12 Percent Solution, monthly investments in the aggressive growth fund index would have grown at a monthly rate of 7.29 percent in March, 1979; 4.24 percent in June, 1979; 6.54 percent in August, 1979; 8.23 percent in November, 1979; 4.41 percent in August, 1980; 4.54 percent in September, 1980; and 10.52 percent in November, 1980, to cite some examples.

Prior to the first switch into a money fund in February, 1979, when assets were 100 percent invested in the aggressive growth fund index, earnings grew at a 7.3 percent annual compound rate while money funds averaged 5.82 percent. From January, 1979, through June, 1982, during the switching period there were no quarterly losses on the 12 Percent Solution. Assets would have been 100 percent invested in money funds the entire year of 1981. As a result, earnings would have increased 16.8 percent while the aggressive growth fund index declined 7 percent.

Based on the past 6¾ years, using the 12 Percent Solution considerably enhanced earnings. During that time a $10,000 investment in money funds would have grown to $18,697, while being 100 percent invested in the aggressive growth fund index would have resulted in a total of $24,773. The 12 Percent Solution far outpaced both of these investments as well as the unsystematic switching system.

Appendix C Donoghue's Mutual Funds Directory

I. MONEY FUNDS

Fund	Year Organized	Total Assets*	Number of Shareholders	Annual Rate of Return 1 Yr.	5 Yrs.	10 Yrs.	Services Offered† T	C	X	K	I	Minimum Initial Investment
Active Assets Money Trust 5 World Trade Center New York, NY 10048 (800) 221-3778	81	$ 1,272.3	81,206	9.85	—	—	Y	Y	N	N	N	$20,000
Alliance Capital Reserves 140 Broadway New York, NY 10005 (800) 221-5672	78	862.2	127,614	9.27	—	—	Y	Y	Y	Y	Y	none
Alpha Cash Management Two Piedmont Center, Ste 500 Atlanta, GA 30063 (800) 241-1662	81	2.2	397	8.75	—	—	Y	Y	Y	Y	Y	1,000

*Assets in $millions as of June 30, 1983. Source: Donoghue's MONEY FUND REPORT® of Holliston, MA 01746.
†T = Wire Transfer X = Intra-Group Exchange I = IRA Plan Available Y = Available
C = Check Writing K = Keogh Plan Available N = Not available

American Express Money Fund P.O. Box 1335 Boston, MA 02205 (800) 343-1300	82	27.4	6,157	9.69	—	—	Y	Y	Y	N	Y	1,000
American General Reserve Fund 2777 Allen Parkway P.O. Box 1411 Houston, TX 77251 (800) 231-7166	74	270.5	32,698	9.95	—	—	Y	Y	Y	Y	Y	1,000
Keystone Liquid Trust 99 High St. Boston, MA 02110 (800) 225-2618	75	235.6	28,766	9.30	—	—	Y	Y	Y	Y	Y	1000
American Nat'l. Money Mkt. 2 Moody Plaza Galveston, TX 77550 (215) 786-6016 (800) 231-4646	81	15.6	1,385	10.19	—	—	Y	Y	Y	Y	Y	2,000
Axe-Houghton M M 400 Benedict Ave. Tarrytown, NY 10591 (914) 631-8131 (800) 431-1030	81	34.4	1,326	9.08	—	—	Y	Y	Y	Y	Y	1,000

I. MONEY FUNDS (continued)

Fund	Year Organized	Total Assets*	Number of Shareholders	Annual Rate of Return 1 Yr.	5 Yrs.	10 Yrs.	Services Offered† T C X K I					Minimum Initial Investment
Babson Money Market Three Crown Center 2440 Pershing Rd. Kansas City, MO 64108 (800) 821-5591	80	70.4	4,150	9.71	—	—	Y	Y	Y	Y	Y	1,000
Birr Wilson Money Fund 155 Sansome St. San Francisco, CA 94104 (415) 983-7700	81	76.0	16,466	9.67	—	—	Y	Y	N	Y	Y	3,000
Boston Co. Cash Mgmt. One Boston Place Boston, MA 02106 (800) 343-6324	79	267.9	15,037	9.99	—	—	Y	Y	Y	Y	Y	1,000
Capital Cash Mgmt. Trust 200 Park Ave. Suite 2530 New York, NY 10017 (212) 697-6666 (800) 952-6666	76	134.1	6,009	9.51	—	—	Y	Y	N	N	Y	1,000

Cash Equivalent Fund 120 South La Salle St. Chicago, IL 60603 (800) 621-1048	79	4,117.5	358,108	10.30	—	Y Y Y Y			1,000
Cash Mgmt. Trust America 333 South Hope St. Los Angeles, CA 90071 (800) 421-8791	76	535.5	25,811	9.67	—	Y Y Y Y			5,000
Cash Reserve Management One Battery Park Plaza New York, NY 10004 (212) 742-6003	76	4,783.4	386,604	9.87	—	Y Y N N			10,000
Centennial Money Mkt. Tr. 3600 South Yosemite St. Denver, CO 80237 (303) 770-2345 (800) 525-9310	81	148.8	9,831	9.41	—	N N Y N			500
CMA Money Fund 633 Third Ave. 29th fl. New York, NY (800) 221-4146	77	11,995.2	—	9.87	—	Y Y N N			20,000 relationship required
Colonial M M Trust 75 Federal St. Boston, MA 02110 (800) 225-2365	80	10.5	973	9.33	—	Y Y Y Y			3,000

I. MONEY FUNDS (continued)

Fund	Year Organized	Total Assets*	Number of Shareholders	Annual Rate of Return 1 Yr.	5 Yrs.	10 Yrs.	Services Offered† T C X K I	Minimum Initial Investment
Columbia Daily Income 621 S.W. Morrison St. Portland, OR 97205 (800) 547-1037	74	451.3	43,762	9.12	—	—	Y Y Y Y Y	1,000
Composite Cash Management Seafirst Financial Ctr. 9th fl. Spokane, WA 99201 (509) 624-4101 (800) 541-0830	79	165.1	23,767	9.53	—	—	Y Y Y Y Y	1,000
Connecticut Mut. Liq. Acc't. 140 Garden Street Hartford, CT 06115 (800) 243-0064	82	49.8	3,666	9.45	—	—	Y Y N Y Y	1,000
Current Interest 333 Clay St., Suite 4300 Houston, TX 77002 (713) 751-2400 (collect)	74	1,158.5	105,788	9.60	—	—	Y Y Y Y Y	1,000
Daily Cash Accumulation 3600 S. Yosemite St. Denver, CO 80237 (800) 525-9310	72	3,297.4	342,072	9.50	—	—	Y Y Y Y Y	500

Daily Income 100 Park Avenue New York, NY 10017 (212) 370-1240	74	496.5	23,010	9.44	—	—	Y	Y	Y	N	Y	5,000
DBL Cash Fund 60 Broad St. New York, NY 10004 (212) 480-6385	81	907.9	75,472	9.91	—	—	Y	Y	N	Y	Y	1,000
Delaware Cash Reserve 10 Penn Center Plaza Philadelphia, PA 19103 (800) 523-4640	78	1,380.2	226,659	9.95	—	—	Y	Y	Y	Y	Y	1,000
Bull & Bear Dollar Reserves 11 Hanover Square, 11th fl. New York, NY 10005 (800) 431-6060	80	103.2	18,582	9.61	—	—	Y	Y	Y	Y	Y	1,000
Dreyfus Liquid Assets 600 Madison Avenue New York, NY 10022 (800) 645-6561	74	8,213.8	735,664	10.26	—	—	Y	Y	Y	Y	Y	2,500
Eaton & Vance Cash Mgmt. 24 Federal Street Boston, MA 02110 (800) 225-6265	75	177.9	14,507	9.46	—	—	Y	Y	Y	Y	Y	1,000

I. MONEY FUNDS (continued)

Fund	Year Organized	Total Assets*	Number of Shareholders	Annual Rate of Return 1 Yr.	5 Yrs.	10 Yrs.	Services Offered† T C X K I	Minimum Initial Investment
E.D. Jones Daily Passport Trust 201 Progress Parkway Maryland Heights, MO 63043 (314) 576-0100	80	542.3	82,978	9.45	—	—	Y Y N Y Y	5,000
EGT Money Market Trust 421 Seventh Ave. Pittsburgh, PA 15219 (412) 288-1561	81	92.4	9,041	9.47	—	—	Y Y N Y Y	5,000
Equitable Money Market 100 West 52nd St. New York, NY 10019 (800) 223-0970	80	278.1	39,316	9.73	—	—	Y Y N N N	1,000
Fahnestock Daily Income 110 Wall St. New York, NY 10005 (800) 221-2990	80	137.6	11,599	9.53	—	—	Y Y Y Y N	1,000
FBL Money Market 5400 University Ave. West Des Moines, IA 50265 (800) 247-4170	81	38.5	5,809	9.10	—	—	Y Y Y Y Y	1,500

Fidelity Cash Reserves 82 Devonshire St. Boston, MA 02109 (800) 225-6190	79	3,331.4	493,984	10.05	—	Y Y Y Y	1,000
Fidelity Daily Income 82 Devonshire St. Boston, MA 02109 (800) 225-6190	74	2,616.6	56,229	10.01	—	Y Y Y Y	10,000
Financial Daily Income P.O. Box 2040 Denver, CO 80201 (800) 525-9831	76	196.8	21,803	9.74	—	Y Y Y Y	1,000
First American Money Fund 3033 Excelsior Blvd. Minneapolis, MN 55391 (800) 328-6020	81	37.6	74	9.86	—	Y Y N N	1,000
First Investors Cash Mgmt. 120 Wall St. New York, NY 10005 (800) 221-3790	78	377.7	51,594	9.47	—	Y Y Y Y	1,000
Franklin Money Fund 155 Bovet Rd. San Mateo, CA 94402 (800) 227-6781	76	802.4	177,399	9.54	—	Y Y Y Y	500

I. MONEY FUNDS (continued)

Fund	Year Organized	Total Assets*	Number of Shareholders	Annual Rate of Return 1 Yr.	5 Yrs.	10 Yrs.	Services Offered† T	C	X	K	I	Minimum Initial Investment
Gradison Cash Reserves The 580 Bldg. 580 Walnut St. Cincinnati, OH 45202 (800) 543-1818	76	455.8	46,866	9.47	—	—	Y	Y	Y	Y	N	1,000
Great Lakes Money Fund 400 Renaissance Center, Suite 265 Detroit, MI 48243 (313) 259-9900	82	4.7	1,073	8.84	—	—	Y	Y	N	Y	Y	1,000
Home Life Money Mgmt. 253 Broadway New York, NY 10007 (800) 221-5733	82	10.0	751	9.56	—	—	Y	Y	N	N	Y	1,000
Hutton AMA Cash Fund One Battery Park Plaza New York, NY 10004 (800) 221-9459	81	173.8	9,309	9.91	—	—	N	Y	N	N	N	1,000
IDS Cash Management 1000 Roanoke Bldg. Minneapolis, MN 55402 (800) 328-8300	75	903.0	119,604	10.07	—	—	Y	Y	Y	Y	Y	2,000

Sears Liquid Asset 5 World Trade Center New York, NY 10048 (212) 938-4554 (800) 221-2685	75	6063.8	702,739	9.94	—	Y Y Y Y	5,000
John Hancock Cash Mgmt. Hancock Place P.O. Box 111 Boston, MA 02117 (617) 421-6043 (800) 225-5291	79	441.1	89,282	9.11	—	Y Y Y Y	1,000
Kemper Money Market 120 South La Salle St. Chicago, IL 60603 (800) 621-1048	74	3,435.0	326,687	10.46	—	Y Y Y Y	1,000
L. F. Rothschild Earn. & Liq. 55 Water Street New York, NY 10041 (212) 425-3300	82	360.2	29,811	9.64	—	N Y N Y	2,500
Legg Mason Cash Res. Trust 7 E. Redwood St. Baltimore, MD 21203 (800) 245-4270	79	213.0	21,886	9.31	—	Y Y N Y	5,000

I. MONEY FUNDS (continued)

Fund	Year Organized	Total Assets*	Number of Shareholders	Annual Rate of Return 1 Yr.	5 Yrs.	10 Yrs.	Services Offered† T	C	X	K	I	Minimum Initial Investment
Lehman Cash Management Fund, Inc. 55 Water St. New York, NY 10041 (212) 558-3288 (800) 221-5350	81	660.0	23,192	9.68	—	—	Y	Y	Y	Y	Y	2,500
Lexington Money Market 580 Sylvan Avenue Englewood Cliffs, NJ 07632 (800) 526-4791	76	236.5	29,517	9.88	—	—	Y	Y	Y	Y	Y	1,000
Liquid Capital Income 1331 Euclid Avenue Cleveland, OH 44115 (800) 321-2322	74	1,408.2	132,427	9.64	—	—	Y	Y	Y	N	N	1,000
Liquid Green Trust 600 Guaranty Bldg. 20 N. Meridian St. Indianapolis, IN 46204 (800) 428-4492	80	125.3	16,625	9.88	—	—	Y	Y	Y	Y	Y	1,000

Lord Abbett Cash Reserve 63 Wall Street New York, NY 10005 (800) 221-9995	79	228.1	36,431	9.19	—	Y	Y	Y	Y	1,000
Mass. Cash Management 200 Berkeley Street Boston, MA 02116 (617) 956-1200	75	702.2	51,403	9.84	—	Y	Y	Y	Y	1,000
McDonald Money Market 767 Fifth Ave. New York, NY 10153 (216) 623-2000	81	142.2	9,258	9.22	—	Y	Y	N	N	5,000
Merrill Lynch Ready Asset 633 Third Ave. 29th fl. New York, NY 10017 (800) 221-7210	75	13,798.3	1,171,505	9.95	—	Y	Y	Y	Y	5,000
MFS Managed Cash Acc't. 200 Berkeley Street Boston, MA 02116 (617) 423-3500	82	30.6	10,465	9.43	—	Y	Y	Y	Y	1,000
Midwest Inc. Tr. Cash Mgmt. 522 Dixie Terminal Bldg. Cincinnati, OH 45202 (800) 543-0407	82	43.2	3,953	9.53	—	Y	Y	Y	N	1,000

I. MONEY FUNDS (continued)

Fund	Year Organized	Total Assets*	Number of Shareholders	Annual Rate of Return 1 Yr.	5 Yrs.	10 Yrs.	Services Offered† T C X K I	Minimum Initial Investment
Money Market Management 421 Seventh Avenue Pittsburgh, PA 15219 (800) 245-2423	74	292.4	37,083	9.49	—	—	Y Y Y Y Y	1,000
Money Mkt. Instruments Tr. 421 Seventh Ave. Federated Inv. Bldg. Pittsburgh, PA 15219 (800) 245-4270	82	147.1	11,091	9.34	—	—	Y Y N Y Y	1,000
Money Shares One Wall Street New York, NY 10005 (800) 221-5757	78	8.9	890	8.66	—	—	Y Y Y Y Y	1,000
Moneymart Assets 100 Gold St. New York, NY 10038 (800) 221-7984	76	2,628.8	242,567	9.89	—	—	Y Y Y Y Y	1,000
Morgan Keegan Daily Cash One Commerce Square Memphis, TN 38103 (901) 523-1501	80	63.3	4,352	9.33	—	—	Y Y N Y Y	5,000

Mutual of Omaha Cash 10235 Regency Circle Omaha, NB 68114 (402) 397-8555	81	20.7	2,382	8.97	—	Y Y N Y	set by brokers
Mutual of Omaha MM Acc't. 10235 Regency Circle Omaha, NB 68114 (800) 228-9661	79	312.6	36,451	9.42	—	Y Y Y Y	1,000
National Cash Reserves 605 Third Avenue New York, NY 10158 (800) 223-7757	82	31.0	2,064	9.69	—	Y Y Y Y	1,000
National Liquid Reserves 1345 Ave. of the Americas New York, NY 10105 (800) 221-2990	74	1,537.8	148,544	10.03	—	Y Y Y Y	1,000
NEL Cash Management Tr. 501 Boylston St. Boston, MA 02117 (800) 225-7670	78	688.2	72,171	9.95	—	Y Y Y Y	1,000
Newton Money Fund 733 North Van Buren St. Milwaukee, WI 53202 (414) 347-1141	81	11.1	865	9.36	—	Y Y Y Y	1,000

I. MONEY FUNDS (continued)

Fund	Year Organized	Total Assets*	Number of Shareholders	Annual Rate of Return 1 Yr.	5 Yrs.	10 Yrs.	Services Offered† T	C	X	K	I	Minimum Initial Investment
Offerman Money Market 5100 Gamble Dr. Minneapolis, MN 55481 (612) 541-8999	81	8.5	1,303	9.10	—	—	Y	Y	N	N	N	2,000
Oppenheimer Money Market Two Broadway, 26th Floor New York, NY 10004 (800) 525-7040	74	1,064.8	122,252	9.70	—	—	Y	Y	Y	Y	Y	1,000
Paine Webber Cash Fund 1120 20th St., NW Washington, DC 20036 (212) 437-5306	78	4,386.7	398,515	9.65	—	—	Y	Y	N	Y	Y	5,000
Parkway Cash Fund 3411 Silverside Rd. Wilmington, DE 19810 (800) 441-7786	79	442.7	53,055	9.63	—	—	Y	Y	Y	Y	Y	1,000
CAM Fund, Inc. Box 1981 Valley Forge, PA 19481 (215) 783-6789	81	11.8	2,050	9.09	—	—	Y	Y	N	N	Y	500

Phoenix M M Series One American Row Hartford, CT 06115 (203) 278-8050	80	39.4	4,659	9.60	—	Y	Y	Y	Y	Y	1,000
Plimoney Fund 777 Walker Suite 2000 Houston, TX 77002 (215) 629-9800	80	45.2	5,182	9.20	—	Y	Y	Y	Y	Y	1,000
Putnam Daily Dividend One Post Office Square Boston, MA 02109 (800) 225-1581	76	300.4	34,462	10.00	—	Y	Y	Y	Y	Y	1,000
Reserve 810 Seventh Ave. New York, NY 10019 (800) 223-5547	71	2,010.8	(estimate) 80,427	9.94	—	Y	Y	Y	N	Y	1,000
Safeco Money Mkt. Mutual Safeco Plaza, T-15 Seattle, WA 98185 (800) 426-6730	82	16.6	1,671	10.05	—	Y	Y	Y	Y	Y	1,000
Scudder Cash Invest. Trust 175 Federal St. Boston, MA 02110 (800) 453-9500	75	896.5	84,387	9.25	—	Y	Y	Y	Y	Y	1,000

I. MONEY FUNDS (continued)

Fund	Year Organized	Total Assets*	Number of Shareholders	Annual Rate of Return 1 Yr.	5 Yrs.	10 Yrs.	Services Offered† T	C	X	K	I	Minimum Initial Investment
Securities Group Money 500 Park Ave. New York, NY 10022 (800) 221-1230	81	.4	57	9.24	—	—	Y	Y	Y	N	N	10,000
Security CASH FUND 700 Harrison St. Topeka, KS 66636 (800) 255-3509	80	57.0	8,390	9.01	—	—	Y	Y	Y	Y	Y	1,000
Selected Money Market 105 W. Adams St. Chicago, IL 60603 (800) 621-7321	77	37.1	4,758	9.16	—	—	Y	Y	Y	Y	Y	1,000
Seligman Cash Management One Bankers Trust Plaza New York, NY 10006 (800) 221-2450	77	408.3	48,097	9.47	—	—	Y	Y	Y	Y	Y	1,000
Sentinel Cash Mgmt. Fund National Life Drive Montpelier, VT 05602 (800) 526-3032	81	29.5	2,085	9.43	—	—	Y	Y	Y	Y	Y	1,000

Sentry Cash Management 1800 North Point Dr. Stevens Point, WI 54481 (800) 826-0266	81	33.1	3,588	9.45	—	Y	Y	Y	Y	1,000
Shearson Daily Dividend Two World Trade Center New York, NY 10048 (212) 321-6554	79	4,209.9	372,959	9.82	—	Y	N	Y	Y	5,000
Shearson FMA Cash Two World Trade Center New York, NY 10048 (800) 221-3636	82	450.0	20,781	9.63	—	N	Y	Y	N	$25,000 relationship required
Short Term Income 100 Park Avenue New York, NY 10017 (800) 221-2990	80	199.4	8,926	9.46	—	Y	N	N	N	1,000
Short Term Yield Sec. 11 Greenway Plaza, Suite 1919 Houston, TX 77046 (713) 626-1919	77	22.4	2,086	9.08	—	Y	Y	Y	Y	1,250
Sigma Money Market 3801 Kennett Pike, C-200 Wilmington, DE 19807 (800) 441-9490	80	8.4	874	8.73	—	Y	Y	Y	Y	500

I. MONEY FUNDS (continued)

Fund	Year Organized	Total Assets*	Number of Shareholders	Annual Rate of Return 1 Yr.	5 Yrs.	10 Yrs.	Services Offered† T	C	X	K	I	Minimum Initial Investment
St. Paul Money Fund P.O. Box 43284 St. Paul, MN 55164 (800) 328-1064	79	96.4	9,588	9.34	—	—	Y	Y	Y	Y	Y	3,000
Standby Reserve Fund One Battery Park Plaza New York, NY 10004 (212) 460-0682	81	204.8	16,290	9.65	—	—	Y	N	N	Y	Y	2,000
Stein Roe Cash Reserves 150 S. Wacker Dr. Chicago, IL 60606 (800) 621-0320	76	714.6	29,288	9.68	—	—	Y	Y	Y	Y	Y	2,500
Sutro Money Market 421 Seventh Ave. Federated Inv. Bldg. Pittsburgh, PA 15219 (415) 445-8500	82	100.5	12,551	9.45	—	—	Y	N	N	Y	Y	5,000
T. Rowe Price Prime Res. 100 E. Pratt Street Baltimore, MD 21202 (800) 638-5660	76	2,530.6	299,690	10.01	—	—	Y	Y	Y	Y	Y	2,000

Transamerica Cash Reserve 1150 S. Olive St. Los Angeles, CA 90015 (800) 527-0727	80	266.0	13,300	9.84	—	Y	Y	Y	Y	1,000
Trust for Cash Reserves 421 Seventh Ave. Pittsburgh, PA 15219 (800) 245-2423	79	165.3	13,990	9.33	—	Y	Y	N	Y	5,000
Tucker Anthony Cash 3 Center Plaza Boston, MA 02108 (800) 225-6258	81	334.8	37,797	9.36	—	Y	Y	Y	N	2,500
United Cash Management One Crown Center, P.O. Box 1343 Kansas City, MO 64141 (800) 821-5664	79	347.3	74,050	9.70	—	Y	Y	Y	Y	1,000
USAA Mutual Fund Inc., MM 9800 Fredericksburg Rd. San Antonio, TX 78288 (800) 531-8181	81	114.2	21,765	9.45	—	Y	Y	Y	Y	1,000
Value Line Cash 711 Third Ave. New York, NY 10017 (800) 223-0818	79	468.9	66,335	10.07	—	Y	Y	Y	Y	1,000

I. MONEY FUNDS (continued)

Fund	Year Organized	Total Assets*	Number of Shareholders	Annual Rate of Return 1 Yr.	5 Yrs.	10 Yrs.	Services Offered† T	C	X	K	I	Minimum Initial Investment
Vanguard Money Market P.O. Box 2600 Valley Forge, PA 19460 (800) 523-7025	75	935.4	89,902	9.92	—	—	Y	Y	Y	Y	Y	1,000
Wayne Hummer Mon. Tr. M M 175 West Jackson Blvd., Suite 1700 Chicago, IL 60604 (312) 431-1700	82	56.8	3,933	9.13	—	—	N	Y	N	N	Y	3,000
Webster Cash Reserve 20 Exchange Place New York, NY 10005 (212) 635-5055	79	1,151.4	79,044	9.71	—	—	Y	N	N	N	N	1,500

A. Government-Only Money Funds

Fund	Year Organized	Total Assets*	Number of Shareholders	Annual Rate of Return 1 Yr.	5 Yrs.	10 Yrs.	Services Offered† T	C	X	K	I	Minimum Initial Investment
AARP U.S. Gov't. M M 421 Seventh Ave. Pittsburgh, PA 15219 (800) 245-4770	79	$3,134.9	534,055	9.02	—	—	Y	Y	N	Y	Y	$ 500

Fund								Minimum
Active Assets Gov't. Sec. 5 World Trade Center New York, NY 10048 (800) 221-3778	81	112.0	5,279	8.49	—	—	Y Y N N N	20,000 relationship required
Alex Brown Gov't. P.O. Box 17250 Baltimore, MD 21203 (800) 638-4276	82	63.4	1,290	8.96	—	—	Y Y Y N Y	1,500
Alliance Gov't. Reserves 140 Broadway New York, NY 10005 (800) 221-5672.	79	158.8	9,019	8.57	—	—	Y Y Y Y Y	None
Alpha Cash Mgmt. Gov't. Sec. Two Piedmont Center, Suite 500 Atlanta, GA 30063 (800) 241-1662	81	2.6	211	9.09	—	—	Y Y Y Y Y	1,000
American Express Gov't. P.O. Box 1335 Boston, MA 02205 (800) 343-1300	82	15.7	2,132	8.80	—	—	Y Y Y N Y	1,000

*Assets in $millions as of June 30, 1983. Source: Donoghue's MONEY FUND REPORT® of Holliston, MA 01746.

†T = Wire Transfer   X = Intra-Group Exchange   I = IRA Plan Available   Y = Available
C = Check Writing   K = Keogh Plan Available   N = Not available

A. Government-Only Money Funds (continued)

Fund	Year Organized	Total Assets*	Number of Shareholders	Annual Rate of Return 1 Yr.	5 Yrs.	10 Yrs.	Services Offered† T	C	X	K	I	Minimum Initial Investment
Boston Co. Gov't. Money One Boston Place Boston, MA 02106 (800) 343-6324	82	29.9	1,099	8.59	—	—	Y	Y	Y	Y	Y	1,000
Capital Preservation 755 Page Mill Rd. Palo Alto, CA 94304 (800) 482-3389	72	1,677.5	142,490	8.22	—	—	Y	Y	Y	Y	Y	1,000
Capital Preservation II 755 Page Mill Rd. Palo Alto, CA 94304 (800) 227-8380	80	624.9	40,650	8.62	—	—	Y	Y	Y	N	N	5,000
Cardinal Gov't. Sec. Trust 155 East Broad St. Columbus, OH 43215 (800) 848-7734	80	302.1	26,973	9.30	—	—	Y	Y	N	N	N	1,000
Carnegie Gov't. Securities 1331 Euclid Avenue Cleveland, OH 44115 (800) 321-2322	80	169.0	7,585	8.79	—	—	Y	Y	Y	N	Y	1,000

Cash Eq. Fund Gov't. Sec. 120 S. LaSalle St. Chicago, IL 60603 (800) 621-1048	81	405.5	23,568	8.90	—	Y	Y	Y	Y		1,000
Centennial Gov't. Trust 3600 South Yosemite St. Denver, CO 80237 (303) 770-2345 (800) 525-9310	81	9.1	477	7.89	—	N	N	Y	N		500
Daily Cash Government 3600 South Yosemite St. Denver, CO 80237 (303) 770-2345 (800) 525-9310	82	58.9	2,453	8.16	—	Y	Y	Y	Y		500
DBL Cash Gov't. Sec. 60 Broad Street New York, NY 10004 (212) 480-2975	81	174.1	5,567	9.10	—	Y	N	Y	N		1,000
Delaware Treasury Reserve 10 Penn Center Plaza Philadelphia, PA 19103 (800) 523-4640	82	65.9	6,252	8.95	—	Y	Y	Y	Y		1,000

A. Government-Only Money Funds (continued)

Fund	Year Organized	Total Assets*	Number of Shareholders	Annual Rate of Return 1 Yr.	5 Yrs.	10 Yrs.	Services Offered† T C X K I					Minimum Initial Investment
Fidelity U.S. Gov't. Res. 82 Devonshire St. Boston, MA 02109 (800) 225-6190	81	291.5	25,719	8.85	—	—	Y	Y	Y	Y	Y	1,000
Financial Plnrs. Fed. Sec. 1730 K St., NW Suite 915 Washington, DC 20006 (800) 424-8570	80	11.9	1,607	8.45	—	—	Y	Y	Y	Y	Y	500
First Trust M.M.F. Gov't. 110 N. Franklin Chicago, IL 60606 (800) 621-4770	80	3.5	507	8.00	—	—	Y	Y	N	Y	Y	none
First Variable Rate Gov't. 1700 Pennsylvania Ave., NW, Ste. 270 Washington, DC 20006 (800) 368-2748	76	815.7	80,798	9.24	—	—	Y	Y	Y	Y	Y	2,000
Florida Mutual U.S. Gov't. One Financial Plaza, Suite 1507 Ft. Lauderdale, FL 33394 (305) 522-0200 (800) 432-1592	80	5.3	1,001	8.10	—	—	Y	Y	N	N	N	1,000

Founders Money Market 655 Broadway, Suite 700 Denver, CO 80203 (800) 525-2440	81	16.3	1,599	8.39	—	Y	Y	Y	Y		1,000
Franklin Federal Money 155 Bovet Rd. San Mateo, CA 94402 (800) 227-6781	80	110.4	21,356	8.55	—	Y	Y	Y	Y		500
Fund for Gov't. Investors 1735 K St., NW, Suite 1200 Washington, DC 20006 (202) 861-1800 (collect)	75	922.1	34,770	8.89	—	Y	Y	N	Y		2,500
Fund for Ready Income 2100 M St., NW Suite 316 Washington, DC 20063 (800) 424-2881	80	.7	303	8.58	—	Y	Y	N	Y		500
Government Investors Tr. 1800 North Kent St. Arlington, VA 22209 (800) 336-3063	79	403.4	37,797	9.16	—	Y	Y	N	Y		2,000
Gradison U.S. Gov't. Trust The 580 Building 580 Walnut St. Cincinnati, OH 45202 (800) 543-1818	82	21.4	1,470	8.52	—	Y	Y	Y	N	Y	1,000

A. Government-Only Money Funds (continued)

Fund	Year Organized	Total Assets*	Number of Shareholders	Annual Rate of Return 1 Yr.	5 Yrs.	10 Yrs.	Services Offered† T	C	X	K	I	Minimum Initial Investment
Hilliard Lyons Cash Mgmt. 545 South Third St. Louisville, KY 40202 (502) 583-8400	80	130.2	10,742	8.58	—	—	Y	Y	N	N	Y	3,000
Hutton Government Fund One Battery Park Plaza New York, NY 10004 (212) 742-6003	82	631.1	85,084	9.46	—	—	Y	Y	N	Y	Y	10,000
IDS Gov't. Sec. Money Fund 1000 Roanoke Bldg. Minneapolis, MN 55402 (800) 328-8300	82	17.9	2,564	8.86	—	—	N	Y	Y	Y	Y	2,000
Kemper Gov't. M M 120 S. LaSalle St. Chicago, IL 60603 (800) 621-1048	81	83.0	7,369	8.70	—	—	Y	Y	Y	Y	Y	1,000
Lehman Gov't. Fund 55 Water St. New York, NY 10041 (800) 221-5350	81	105.9	2,582	8.47	—	—	Y	Y	Y	Y	Y	2,500

Lexington Gov't. Securities M M 580 Sylvan Avenue Englewood Cliffs, NJ 07632 (800) 526-4791	81	20.7	2,291	8.42	—	Y	Y	N	Y	1,000
Merrill Lynch CMA Gov't. Sec. 633 Third Ave., 29th fl. New York, NY 10017 (800) 221-4146	81	1,237.4		9.04	—	Y	N	N	N	$20,000 relationship required
Merrill Lynch Gov't. 125 High Street Boston, MA 02110 (800) 225-1576	77	1,538.6	31,637	8.91	—	Y	Y	N	N	5,000
Midwest Inc. Tr. St. Gov't. 522 Dixie Terminal Bldg. Cincinnati, OH 45202 (800) 543-0407	74	162.9	13,157	8.70	—	Y	Y	Y	Y	1,000
Money Fund of U.S. Treas. Sec. 1107 Bethlehem Pike Floutown, PA 19031 (800) 523-0864	82	5.9	741	7.11	—	Y	Y	Y	Y	2,000
Prudential Bache Gov't. Sec. Tr. 100 Gold St. New York, NY 10038 (800) 221-7984	82	197.5	10,531	8.63	—	Y	Y	Y	Y	1,000

A. Government-Only Money Funds (continued)

Fund	Year Organized	Total Assets*	Number of Shareholders	Annual Rate of Return 1 Yr.	5 Yrs.	10 Yrs.	Services Offered† T C X K I	Minimum Initial Investment
Reserve Fund Gov't. 810 Seventh Avenue New York, NY 10019 (800) 223-5547	81	272.3		8.76	—	—	Y Y Y N Y	1,000
Scudder Gov't. Money 175 Federal St. Boston, MA 02110 (800) 453-9500	81	141.1	11,937	8.43	—	—	Y Y Y Y Y	1,000
Sears U.S. Gov't. M M Tr. 5 World Trade Center New York, NY 10048 (800) 621-2525	82	325.5	53,911	8.42	—	—	Y Y Y Y Y	1,000
Selected M M Gov't. Port. 105 W. Adams St. Chicago, IL 60603 (800) 621-7321	82	5.4	228	7.99	—	—	Y Y Y Y Y	1,000
Shearson FMA Gov't. Two World Trade Center New York, NY 10048 (800) 221-3636	82	66.3	1,914	8.68	—	—	N Y Y N N	$25,000 relationship required

Shearson Gov't. Agencies 2 World Trade Center, 106th Floor New York, NY 10048 (212) 321-6554	80	901.2	37,928	9.13	—	Y	N	Y	Y	5,000
Sigma Gov't. Securities 3801 Kennett Pike, C-200 Wilmington, DE 19807 (800) 441-9490	80	3.0	247	7.99	—	Y	Y	Y	Y	500
Strategic Treas. Positions 10110 Crestover Drive Dallas, TX 75229 (800) 527-5027	82	7.6	1,064	7.78	—	Y	Y	Y	Y	1,000
T. Rowe Price U.S. Treas. Money Fund 100 East Pratt Street Baltimore, MD 21202 (800) 638-5660	82	113.2	10,128	8.42	—	Y	Y	Y	Y	2,000
Tucker Anthony Gov't. Sec. 3 Center Plaza Boston, MA 02108 (800) 225-6258	82	81.5	3,632	8.64	—	Y	Y	N	N	2,500
U.S. Treasury Securities Fund P.O. Box 29467 San Antonio, TX 78229 (800) 531-5777	81	37.6	5,752	7.32	—	Y	Y	Y	Y	1,500

A. Government-Only Money Funds (continued)

Fund	Year Organized	Total Assets*	Number of Shareholders	Annual Rate of Return 1 Yr.	5 Yrs.	10 Yrs.	Services Offered† T C X K I	Minimum Initial Investment
Vanguard M M Trust Fed. P.O. Box 2600 Valley Forge, PA 19460 (800) 523-7025	81	356.2	27,199	8.98	—	—	Y Y Y Y Y	1,000
Wayne Hummer Mon. Tr. Gov't. 175 West Jackson Blvd. Suite 1700 Chicago, IL 60604 (312) 431-1700 (800) 621-4477	82	2.9	179	7.64	—	—	N Y N N Y	3,000

II. GROWTH FUNDS
A. No-Load Performance Funds

Fund	Year Organized	Total Assets*	Number of Shareholders	Annual Rate of Return 1 Yr.	5 Yrs.	10 Yrs.	Services Offered† T C X K I	Minimum Initial Investment
American Investors P.O. Box 2500 Greenwich, CT 06836 (800) 243-5353	57	$161.3	25,598	56.1	16.3	12.4	Y Y Y Y Y	$ 400

Bull & Bear Capital Growth 11 Hanover Square New York, NY 10005 (800) 431-6060	59	105.9	18,547	68.8	21.9	14.3	Y	N	Y Y	500
Columbia Growth P.O. Box 1350 Portland, OR 97207 (800) 547-1037	66	148.3	16,52T	94.8	28.1	20.1	Y	N	Y Y	500
Constellation Growth 331 Madison Ave. New York, NY 10017 (212) 557-8787	66	154.8	10,450	140.0	35.	22.6	Y	N	Y Y	1,000
Dreyfus Number Nine 767 Fifth Ave. New York, NY 10153 (800) 645-6561	69	358.1	50,638	66.4	21.2	19.1	N	N	Y N	500
Evergreen Fund 550 Mamaroneck Ave. Harrison, NY 10528 (914) 698-5711	71	208.5	11,172	84.0	29.8	27.4	Y	Y	N Y	1,500

*Assets in $millions as of June 30, 1983. Source: Monitored Assets Corp.

†T = Wire Transfer   X = Intra-Group Exchange   I = IRA Plan Available   Y = Available

C = Check Writing   K = Keogh Plan Available   N = Not available

A. No-Load Performance Funds (continued)

Fund	Year Organized	Total Assets*	Number of Shareholders	Annual Rate of Return 1 Yr.	5 Yrs.	10 Yrs.	Services Offered† T	C	X	K	I	Minimum Initial Investment
Explorer P.O. Box 1100 Valley Forge, PA 19482 (800) 523-7910	67	270.3	31,624	107.0	33.5	19.3	Y	Y	Y	Y	Y	500
Forty Four Wall Street 150 Broadway, Suite 814 New York, NY 10038 (800) 221-9522	68	250.0	24,000	100.8	23.7	25.3	Y	N	Y	Y	Y	1,000
Founders Special 655 Broadway, Suite 700 Denver, CO 80203 (800) 525-2400	60	100.2	11,104	111.2	30.3	16.1	Y	N	Y	Y	Y	250
Hartwell Growth 50 Rockefeller Plaza New York, NY 10020 (212) 247-8740	65	14.5	2,430	111.1	30.6	19.5	N	N	N	N	Y	300
Hartwell Leverage 50 Rockefeller Plaza New York, NY 10020 (212) 247-8740	68	71.9	3,163	129.5	36.2	26.0	N	N	N	N	Y	5,000

Janus 100 Fillmore St., Suite 300 Denver, CO 80206 (800) 525-3713	68	243.0	29,000	79.0	31.4	18.5	Y	N	N	Y	Y	1,000
Keystone S-3 Keystone Bldg. 99 High St. Boston MA 02110 (617) 338-3352	32	148.0	17,320	82.3	21.7	14.0	N	N	N	Y	Y	250
Keystone S-4 Keystone Bldg. 99 High St. Boston, MA 02104 (617) 338-3352	32	707.0	105,662	117.3	26.9	16.0	N	N	N	Y	Y	250
Leverage Fund of Boston 24 Federal Street Boston, MA 02110 (617) 482-8260	66	43.8	4,305	67.8	25.8	22.5	N	N	Y	Y	Y	1,000
Lexington Goldfund Inc. 580 Sylvan Ave. Englewood Cliffs, NJ 07632 (201) 567-2375	75	7.3	2,033	107.4	—	—	N	N	Y	Y	Y	1,000
Lexington Growth P.O. Box 1515 Englewood Cliffs, NJ 07632 (800) 526-4791	69	49.0	5,264	70.7	17.6	17.1	Y	N	Y	Y	Y	250

A. No-Load Performance Funds (continued)

Fund	Year Organized	Total Assets*	Number of Shareholders	Annual Rate of Return 1 Yr.	5 Yrs.	10 Yrs.	Services Offered† T	C	X	K	I	Minimum Initial Investment
Loomis-Sayles Capital Dev. P.O. Box 449, Back Bay Annex Boston, MA 02117 (617) 482-2450	61	162.4	5,847	113.6	35.5	17.9	N	N	Y	Y	Y	250
Medical Technology 1107 Bethlehem Pike Flourtown, PA 19031 (800) 523-0864	79	72.6	11,127	87.5	—	—	N	N	N	Y	Y	1,000
Neuwirth Fund 120 Broadway New York, NY 10005 (800) 221-5672	66	28.7	5,746	95.8	23.1	13.2	N	N	N	Y	Y	500
Newton Growth 733 N. Van Buren St. Milwaukee, WI 53202 (414) 347-1141	60	35.7	4,344	105.4	28.8	15.7	Y	N	Y	Y	Y	500
Omega 77 Franklin St. Boston, MA 02110 (617) 357-8480	68	32.7	11,500	50.7	17.1	13.6	N	N	N	N	N	5,000

One Hundred 899 Logan St., #211 Denver, CO 80203 (303) 837-1020	66	15.5	3,637	95.4	23.1	9.8	N	N	Y	Y	Y	250
Pennsylvania Mutual 1414 Ave. of the Americas New York, NY 10019 (800) 221-4268	62	78.5	13,600	99.2	24.0	22.7	N	N	N	Y	Y	500
Piltrend 111 N. Broad St. Philadelphia, PA 19107 (215) 563-6444	52	76.5	6,120	77.4	25.2	18.3	N	N	Y	Y	Y	None
Price New Horizons 100 E. Pratt St. Baltimore, MD 21202 (800) 638-1527	60	1,675.3	95,000	98.4	27.5	14.7	Y	Y	Y	Y	Y	1,000
Safeco Growth Safeco Plaza, T-15 Seattle, WA 98185 (800) 426-6730	67	66.8	5,900	78.2	22.0	18.8	N	N	Y	N	Y	200
Scudder Development 175 Federal St. Boston, MA 02110 (800) 225-2470	70	252.9	25,260	69.6	25.1	16.7	Y	N	N	Y	Y	2,000

A. No-Load Performance Funds (continued)

Fund	Year Organized	Total Assets*	Number of Shareholders	Annual Rate of Return 1 Yr.	5 Yrs.	10 Yrs.	Services Offered† T	C	X	K	I	Minimum Initial Investment
Sherman, Dean 120 Broadway New York, NY 10271 (212) 577-3850	67	5.1	1,500	60.6	14.9	15.7	N	N	N	Y	Y	1,000
St. Paul Special P.O. Box 43284 St. Paul, MN 55164 (612) 738-4265	79	19.5	1,316	87.2	33.4	17.4	N	N	Y	Y	Y	250
Stein R & F Capital Opp. 150 S. Wacker Dr. Chicago, IL 60606 (800) 621-0615	63	383.9	17,108	107.3	33.2	16.9	N	N	Y	Y	Y	2,500
Stein R & F Stock 150 S. Wacker Drive Chicago, IL 60606 (800) 621-0615	58	311.2	13,352	86.1	25.6	11.8	N	N	Y	Y	Y	2,500
Stein Roe Special 150 S. Wacker Dr. Chicago, IL 60606 (800) 621-0615	67	119.4	3,000	98.1	—	—	N	N	Y	Y	Y	2,500

Stratton Growth Wood/Butler/Skippack Pk. P.O. Box 550 Blue Bell, PA 19422 (215) 542-8025	72	12.9	1,593	75.0	19.4	16.6	N	N	Y	Y	1,000
Tudor Fund One New York Plaza New York, NY 10004 (212) 908-9582	68	81.2	3,612	113.8	34.5	22.2	N	N	Y	Y	1,000
Twentieth Century Growth P.O. Box 200 Kansas City, MO 64141 (816) 531-5575	57	689.0	not available	87.2	34.9	30.5	N	N	Y	Y	None
Twentieth Century Select P.O. Box 200 Kansas City, MO 64141 (816) 531-5575	57	531.0	not available	107.9	35.5	29.1	N	N	Y	Y	None
Twentieth Century Ultra 605 West 47th Street Kansas City, MO 64112 (816) 531-5575	57	539.0	not available	142.7	—	—	N	N	Y	Y	None
United Services Gold Shrs. P.O. Box 29467 San Antonio, TX 78229 (800) 531-5777	69	330.7	54,902	188.7	49.2	10.4	Y	N	Y	Y	500

A. No-Load Performance Funds (continued)

Fund	Year Organized	Total Assets*	Number of Shareholders	Annual Rate of Return			Services Offered†					Minimum Initial Investment
				1 Yr.	5 Yrs.	10 Yrs.	T	C	X	K	I	
USAA Sunbelt Era Fund 9800 Fredericksburg Rd. San Antonio, TX 78288 (512) 690-3392	not available	70.6	17,524	109.5	—	—	Y	N	Y	Y	Y	None
Value Line Spl. Situations 711 Third Ave. New York, NY 10017 (800) 223-0818	56	386.0	53,520	83.9	29.4	21.5	N	N	N	Y	Y	250
Weingarten Equity 331 Madison Ave. New York, NY 10017 (212) 557-8787	66	129,400	8,010	114.5	34.3	21.1	Y	N	Y	Y	Y	1,000

B. No-Load Straight Growth Funds

Fund	Year Organized	Total Assets*	Number of Shareholders	Annual Rate of Return			Services Offered†					Minimum Initial Investment
				1 Yr.	5 Yrs.	10 Yrs.	T	C	X	K	I	
Acorn 120 S. LaSalle St. Chicago, IL 60603 (313) 621-0630	69	$179.4	7,300	63.5	23.9	20.5	N	N	N	Y	Y	$1,000

							T	X	I	K	C	
Armstrong Associates 311 N. Market St., Suite 205 Dallas, TX 75202 (214) 744-5558	67	12.8	1,040	59.6	23.2	17.3	N	N	N	Y	Y	500
Babson Investment 2440 Pershing Rd. Kansas City, MO 64108 (800) 821-5591	59	249.3	14,292	55.6	14.7	7.0	N	N	Y	Y	Y	500
Devegh Mutual 120 Broadway New York, NY 10005 (800) 221-7780	50	71.0	5,746	54.6	19.1	11.4	N	N	N	Y	Y	250
Dreyfus Third Century 765 Fifth Ave. New York, NY 10153 (800) 645-6561	71	150.6	21,970	51.2	20.4	16.8	N	N	Y	Y	N	500
Elfun Trusts 112 Prospect St. P.O. Box 7900 Stamford, CT 06904 (203) 357-4141	35	355.8	14,557	69.3	21.1	12.3	N	N	N	N	N	None

*Assets in $ millions as of June 30, 1983. Source: Monitored Assets Corporation.
†T = Wire Transfer X = Intra-Group Exchange I = IRA Plan Available Y = Available
C = Check Writing K = Keogh Plan Available N = Not available

B. No-Load Straight Growth Funds (continued)

Fund	Year Organized	Total Assets*	Number of Shareholders	Annual Rate of Return 1 Yr.	5 Yrs.	10 Yrs.	Services Offered† T	C	X	K	I	Minimum Initial Investment
Fidelity Asset Inv. Trust 82 Devonshire St. Boston, MA 02109 (800) 225-6190	78	95.0	not available	91.3	—	—	Y	N	Y	Y	Y	1,000
Fidelity Fund 82 Devonshire St. Boston, MA 02109 (800) 225-6190	30	685.6	not available	68.3	21.3	13.5	Y	N	Y	Y	Y	500
Fidelity Trend 82 Devonshire St. Boston, MA 02109 (800) 225-6190	57	666.6	not available	62.5	16.7	9.3	Y	N	Y	Y	Y	1,000
Founders Growth 655 Broadway, Suite 700 Denver, CO 80203 (800) 525-2440	61	52.5	6,689	71.6	26.6	13.4	Y	N	Y	Y	Y	250
General Securities 133 S. Seventh Street Minneapolis, MN 55402 (612) 332-1212	51	13.4	5,913	59.8	17.0	15.0	N	N	N	Y	Y	100

Golconda Investors Ltd. 11 Hanover Square New York, NY 10005 (800) 847-4200	57	23.3	6,399	55.0	26.9	—	Y	N	Y	Y	Y	500
Growth Industry Shares 135 S. La Salle St. Chicago, IL 60603 (312) 346-4830	46	70.1	5,076	81.5	27.2	14.3	N	N	N	Y	Y	200
Ivest P.O. Box 1100 Valley Forge, PA 19482 (800) 523-7910	61	196.8	not available	72.9	20.3	10.1	Y	Y	Y	Y	Y	500
Keystone K-2 Keystone Bldg, 99 High St. Boston, MA 02110 (617) 338-3352	32	154.0	22,595	83.8	18.1	9.0	N	N	N	Y	Y	250
Legg Mason Value Trust 7 East Redwood Street Baltimore, MD 21203 (800) 368-2558	82	28.0	5,932	80.4	—	—	N	N	Y	Y	Y	1,000
Lexington Research P.O. Box 1515 Englewood Cliffs, NJ 07632 (800) 526-4791	39	131.7	5,859	67.6	20.7	12.8	Y	N	Y	Y	Y	250

B. No-Load Straight Growth Funds (continued)

Fund	Year Organized	Total Assets*	Number of Shareholders	Annual Rate of Return 1 Yr.	5 Yrs.	10 Yrs.	Services Offered† T	C	X	K	I	Minimum Initial Investment
Mairs & Power Growth W. 2062 First National Bank Bldg. St. Paul, MN 55101 (612) 222-8478	61	20.4	872	70.2	18.6	10.9	N	N	N	Y	Y	1,000
Manhattan 342 Madison Ave. New York, NY 10173 (212) 850-8300	65	79.9	not applicable	73.4	23.1	7.3	Y	N	Y	Y	Y	500
Mathers 120 S. Wacker Dr. Chicago, IL 60606 (312) 236-8215	65	224.3	9,986	63.4	21.2	17.0	Y	N	N	Y	Y	1,000
Morgan Growth P.O. Box 1100 Valley Forge, PA 19482 (800) 523-7910	68	417.2	71,725	81.3	22.1	14.5	Y	Y	Y	Y	Y	500
National Aviation & Tech. 50 Broad St. New York, NY 10004 (212) 482-8100	28	107.6	11,579	65.1	—	—	N	N	N	Y	Y	500

Nicholas 312 E. Wisconsin Av., Suite 601 Milwaukee, WI 53202 (414) 272-6133	68	160.6	14,529	85.1	28.9	18.2	Y	N	Y	Y	Y	500
One Hundred One 899 Logan St. Denver, CO 80203 (303) 837-1020	66	1.2	169	89.2	15.9	12.2	N	N	Y	Y	Y	250
Price Growth Stock 100 E. Pratt St. Baltimore, MD 21202 (800) 638-1527	50	1,114.5	102,115	53.3	12.2	5.6	Y	N	Y	Y	Y	500
Price New Era 100 E. Pratt St. Baltimore, MD 21202 (800) 638-1527	68	485.9	47,671	54.9	23.0	12.7	Y	N	Y	Y	Y	1,000
Pro Fund 1107 Bethlehem Pk. Flourtown, PA 19031 (800) 523-0864	66	42.4	3,239	62.1	13.5	6.8	N	N	Y	Y	Y	300
Rainbow Fund 60 Broad St. New York, NY 10004 (212) 964-7989	67	1.8	1,132	45.3	12.1	7.7	N	N	N	Y	Y	300

B. No-Load Straight Growth Funds (continued)

Fund	Year Organized	Total Assets*	Number of Shareholders	Annual Rate of Return 1 Yr.	5 Yrs.	10 Yrs.	Services Offered† T	C	X	K	I	Minimum Initial Investment
Safeco Equity Safeco Plaza Seattle, WA 98185 (800) 426-6730	32	35.9	2,754	49.7	15.9	13.2	N	N	N	Y	N	N	200
Scudder Capital Growth 175 Federal Street Boston, MA 02113 (800) 225-2470	56	230.8	21,698	78.8	21.3	12.3	Y	N	Y	Y	Y	1,000
Scudder International 175 Federal Street Boston, MA 02110 (800) 225-2470	53	108.6	5,550	42.7	14.5	6.4	Y	N	Y	Y	Y	1,000
Selected Special Shares 111 W. Washington St. Chicago, IL 60602 (800) 621-7321	39	38.2	not available	81.4	16.8	9.6	N	N	Y	Y	Y	200
Sierra Growth 1880 Century Park East Los Angeles, CA 90067 (213) 277-1450	56	7.2	843	58.8	—	—	N	N	N	N	N	100

Smith, Barney Equity 1345 Avenue of the Americas New York, NY 10105 (212) 399-6178	68	67.9	7,600	64.0	19.3	11.9	N	N	Y	Y	Y		100
State Farm Growth One State Farm Plaza Bloomington, IL 61701 (309) 766-2311	66	336.2	18,477	69.5	21.3	15.7	N	N	Y	Y	Y		50
Steadman American Ind. 1730 K St., NW Washington, DC 20006 (800) 424-8570	58	14.4	14,406	55.4	12.6	5.3	Y	N	Y	Y	Y		500
Stralem Fund 405 Park Ave. New York, NY 10022 (212) 888-8120	70	6.3	126	50.1	—	—	N	N	N	N	N		100
Unified Growth 20 N. Meridan St. 600 Guaranty Bldg. Indianapolis, IN 46204 (800) 428-4492	70	10.5	2,139	67.8	—	—	N	N	Y	Y	Y		200
USAA Growth 9800 Fredericksburg Rd. San Antonio, TX 78288 (512) 690-3392	70	109.3	32,310	77.4	20.6	8.0	Y	N	Y	Y	Y		250

B. No-Load Straight Growth Funds (continued)

Fund	Year Organized	Total Assets*	Number of Shareholders	Annual Rate of Return 1 Yr.	5 Yrs.	10 Yrs.	Services Offered† T	C	X	K	I	Minimum Initial Investment
Wade Fund Inc. 5100 Poplar Avenue-Suite 2224 Memphis, TN 38137 (901) 682-4613	61	576.3	82	53.4	16.7	10.2	N	N	N	N	N	None

C. No-Load Growth-Income Funds

Fund	Year Organized	Total Assets*	Number of Shareholders	Annual Rate of Return 1 Yr.	5 Yrs.	10 Yrs.	Services Offered† T	C	X	K	I	Minimum Initial Investment
Afuture 344 W. Front St. Media, PA 19063 (800) 523-7594	67	$47.8	8,450	60.5	28.0	16.2	Y	N	N	Y	Y	500
American Investors Income 88 Field Point Rd. Greenwich, CT 06830 (800) 243-5353	75	18.7	2,337	54.2	—	—	Y	N	Y	Y	Y	400

Babson Income Trust 2440 Pershing Rd. Kansas City, MO 64108 (800) 821-5591	44	36.3	4,000	29.0	8.8	7.0	N	N	N	Y	Y	500
Beacon Hill Mutual 75 Federal St. Boston, MA 02110 (617) 482-0795	64	2.6	1,850	39.1	13.1	7.8	N	N	N	Y	Y	None
Boston Co. Cap. Apprec. One Boston Place Boston, MA 02106 (800) 343-6324	47	245.0	22,828	52.6	15.2	7.8	Y	N	N	Y	N	250
Bridges Investment 8401 W. Dodge Rd. Omaha, NB 68114 (402) 397-4700	53	3.0	235	41.9	13.4	—	N	N	N	Y	Y	500
Bull & Bear Equity Income 11 Hanover Square New York, NY 10005 (800) 431-6060	61	5.0	1,304	35.2	11.4	11.6	Y	N	Y	Y	Y	500

*Assets in $millions as of June 30, 1983. Source: Monitored Assets Corporation.
†T = Wire Transfer   X = Intra-Group Exchange   I = IRA Plan Available   Y = Available
C = Check Writing   K = Keogh Plan Available   N = Not available

C. No-Load Growth-Income Funds (continued)

Fund	Year Organized	Total Assets*	Number of Shareholders	Annual Rate of Return 1 Yr.	5 Yrs.	10 Yrs.	Services Offered† T	C	X	K	I	Minimum Initial Investment
Directors Capital 30 Broad St. New York, NY 10004 (212) 635-0616	69	.417	1,440	-48.1	-22.2	-13.2	N	N	N	Y	Y	600
Dividend Growth Fund 11400 Rockville Pike Rockville, MD 20852 (301) 770-1600	80	3.7	716	13.1	—	—	N	N	N	Y	Y	50
Dodge & Cox Balanced One Post St., 35th Floor San Francisco, CA 94104 (415) 981-1710	31	19.4	476	44.2	15.0	10.4	N	N	N	Y	Y	250
Dodge & Cox Stock One Post St., 35th Floor San Francisco, CA 94104 (415) 981-1710	64	26.6	913	59.7	19.1	12.2	N	N	Y	Y	Y	250
Drexel Burnham 60 Broad St. New York, NY 10004 (212) 483-1436	60	77.0	not available	44.6	18.7	10.7	Y	N	N	N	Y	1,000

Dreyfus Special Income 600 Madison Ave. New York, NY 10022 (800) 223-5525	70	85.1	11,193	42.0	14.0	10.4	N	N	Y	Y	N	500
Evergreen Total Return 550 Mamaroneck Ave. Harrison, NY 10528 (914) 698-5711	78	38.4	1,388	57.4	—	—	Y	Y	Y	Y	Y	1,500
Fidelity Contrafund 82 Devonshire St. Boston, MA 02109 (800) 225-6190	63	86.8	13,523	60.8	19.4	15.4	Y	N	Y	Y	Y	1,000
Fidelity Equity Income 82 Devonshire St. Boston, MA 02109 (800) 225-6190	65	642.3	not available	67.5	25.3	20.6	Y	N	Y	Y	Y	1,000
Fidelity High Income 82 Devonshire St. Boston, MA 02109 (800) 225-6190	77	225.8	not available	44.9	12.0	—	Y	N	Y	Y	Y	2,500

C. No-Load Growth-Income Funds (continued)

Fund	Year Organized	Total Assets*	Number of Shareholders	Annual Rate of Return 1 Yr.	5 Yrs.	10 Yrs.	Services Offered† T	C	X	K	I	Minimum Initial Investment
Financial Dynamics 7503 Marin Dr., P.O. Box 2040 Denver, CO 80201 (800) 525-9831	67	101.3	20,234	70.5	23.7	16.2	Y	Y	Y	Y	Y	500
Financial Industrial Fund 7503 Marin Dr., P.O. Box 2040 Denver, CO 80201 (800) 525-9831	35	395.9	43,012	61.4	20.9	13.8	N	N	Y	Y	Y	500
Financial Industrial Inc. 7503 Marin Dr., P.O. Box 2040 Denver, CO 80201 (800) 525-9831	59	222.6	13,752	59.1	17.6	16.1	N	N	Y	Y	Y	500
Founders Income 655 Broadway, Suite 700 Denver, CO 80203 (800) 525-2440	62	6.6	936	33.2	17.0	11.3	Y	N	Y	Y	Y	250
Foursquare 24 Federal St. Boston, MA 02110 (800) 255-6131	61	5.8	3,575	45.6	13.2	8.2	N	N	N	Y	Y	50

G T Pacific 601 Montgomery St. San Francisco, CA 94111 (415) 392-6181	76	13.9	1,508	20.0	8.4	—	Y	N	N	N	Y	1,000
Gateway Option Income 1120 Carew Tower Cincinnati, OH 45202 (513) 621-7774	77	18.4	1,800	26.5	12.0	—	Y	N	N	Y	Y	1,500
General Electric S & S Prog. 112 Prospect St., P.O. Box 7900 Stamford, CT 06904 (203) 357-4104	67	655.1	84,673	55.2	15.3	5.5	N	N	N	N	N	None
Istel 345 Park Ave., 23rd Floor New York, NY 10154 (212) 644-3174	53	121.5	1,010	46.5	17.3	11.2	Y	N	N	N	Y	500
Ivy 201 Devonshire St. Boston, MA 02110 (617) 426-0636	60	103.2	24,968	65.7	25.1	12.2	Y	N	N	Y	Y	500

C. No-Load Growth-Income Funds (continued)

Fund	Year Organized	Total Assets*	Number of Shareholders	Annual Rate of Return			Services Offered†					Minimum Initial Investment
				1 Yr.	5 Yrs.	10 Yrs.	T	C	X	K	I	
Lexington GNMA Income 280 Sylvan Ave. Englewood Cliffs, NJ 07632 (800) 526-4791	73	19.1	3,698	22.5	5.8	—	Y	N	N	Y	Y	1,000
Liberty 342 Madison Ave. New York, NY 10173 (212) 850-8300	56	8.6	not available	33.6	9.4	4.5	Y	N	Y	Y	Y	500
Lindner Fund 200 S. Bemiston St. Louis, MO 63105 (314) 727-5305	54	270.8	29,902	50.4	28.9	25.5	Y	N	N	N	Y	1,000
Loomis-Sayles Mutual P.O. Box 449, Back Bay Annex Boston, MA 02117 (617) 267-6601	61	99.4	10,508	48.0	15.4	8.3	N	N	N	Y	Y	250
Mairs & Power Income W. 2062 First Nat'l. Bank Bldg. St. Paul, MN 55101 (612) 222-8478	61	2.8	126	41.7	—	—	N	N	N	Y	Y	1,000

Mutual of Omaha America 10235 Regency Circle Omaha, NB 68114 (800) 228-2499	72	20.7	5,549	9.8	8.3	—	Y	N	Y	Y	Y	250
Mutual Shares Corp. 26 Broadway New York, NY 10004 (800) 221-7864	49	215.3	16,347	51.0	19.6	22.9	N	N	N	Y	Y	1,000
National Industries 2130 S. Dahlia St. Denver, CO 80222 (303) 759-2400	58	31.9	28,593	34.4	13.7	10.1	N	N	N	N	N	250
Newton Income 733 N. Van Buren St. Milwaukee, WI 53202 (414) 347-1141	69	6.5	1,594	35.7	7.2	5.9	Y	N	Y	Y	Y	500
North Star Stock 1100 Dain Tower, P.O. Box 1160 Minneapolis, MN 55440 (612) 371-7780	77	39.5	770	59.7	18.2	11.8	N	N	Y	Y	Y	1,000

C. No-Load Growth-Income Funds (continued)

Fund	Year Organized	Total Assets*	Number of Shareholders	Annual Rate of Return 1 Yr.	5 Yrs.	10 Yrs.	Services Offered† T	C	X	K	I	Minimum Initial Investment
Northeast Investors Trust 50 Congress St. Boston, MA 02109 (800) 225-6704	50	175.2	12,064	40.3	9.5	7.6	N	N	Y	Y	Y	500
One William Street 55 Water St. New York, NY 10041 (800) 221-5350	58	393.8	30,418	69.1	22.8	12.0	N	N	Y	Y	Y	500
Partners Fund 342 Madison Ave., 16th Floor New York, NY 10173 (212) 850-8300	67	140.3	not available	44.4	25.3	18.9	Y	N	Y	Y	Y	250
Pax World Fund 224 State St. Portsmouth, NH 03801 (603) 431-8022	70	9.9	1,946	50.7	8.4	4.6	N	N	N	Y	Y	250
Penn Square Mutual 101 North Fifth St. Reading, PA 19603 (800) 523-8440	57	178.3	18,600	60.2	17.9	14.3	N	N	N	Y	Y	100

Pine Street 120 Broadway New York, NY 10005 (800) 221-7780	49	44.9	3,358	57.7	17.1	11.9	N N N Y Y	500
Price New Income 100 E. Pratt St. Baltimore, MD 21202 (800) 638-1527	73	687.2	58,512	24.4	10.2	—	Y Y Y Y Y	1,000
Pro Income 1107 Bethlehem Pk. Flourtown, PA 19031 (800) 523-0864	74	24.0	1,364	39.5	9.0	—	N N Y Y Y	300
Puritan 82 Devonshire St. Boston, MA 02109 (800) 225-6190	46	816.1	not available	51.4	18.1	14.1	Y Y Y Y Y	1,000
Qualified Div. Port 1 1250 Drummers Lane Valley Forge, PA 19482 (800) 523-7025	75	44.3	705	47.7	—	—	Y Y Y Y Y	3,000

C. No-Load Growth-Income Funds (continued)

Fund	Year Organized	Total Assets*	Number of Shareholders	Annual Rate of Return 1 Yr.	5 Yrs.	10 Yrs.	Services Offered† T	C	X	K	I	Minimum Initial Investment
Qualified Div. Port II 1250 Drummers Lane Valley Forge, PA 19482 (800) 523-7025	75	56.7	368	19.3	—	—	Y	Y	Y	Y	Y	3,000
Safeco Income Safeco Plaza, T-15 Seattle, WA 98185 (800) 426-6730	69	20.6	1,280	54.3	18.5	14.1	N	N	Y	N	Y	200
Scudder Common Stock 175 Federal St. Boston, MA 02110 (800) 225-2470	29	260.3	30,158	55.8	18.4	10.6	Y	N	Y	Y	Y	500
Scudder Income 175 Federal St. Boston, MA 02110 (800) 225-2470	28	107.0	14,694	35.6	8.7	5.5	Y	N	Y	Y	Y	500
Selected American Shares 111 W. Washington St. Chicago, IL 60602 (800) 621-7321	33	80.4	not available	42.0	13.3	7.6	N	N	Y	Y	Y	200

Sequoia 1290 Avenue of the Americas New York, NY 10104 (212) 245-4500	69	310.5	4,800	43.4	19.5	22.4	N	N	N	N	Y	1,000
Steadman Associated 1730 K St., NW Washington, DC 20006 (800) 424-8570	39	34.3	2,185	44.8	11.2	8.3	Y	N	Y	Y	Y	500
Steadman Investment 1730 K St., N.W. Washington, DC 20006 (800) 424-8570	56	15.8	15,885	37.2	11.9	7.0	Y	N	Y	Y	Y	500
Steadman Tech. & Growth 1730 K St., N.W. Washington, DC 20006 (800) 424-8570	67	9.8	not available	50.3	15.7	7.8	Y	N	Y	Y	Y	500
Stein R & F Balanced 150 S. Wacker Drive Chicago, IL 60606 (800) 621-0615	49	97.2	5,481	51.9	14.1	7.1	N	N	N	Y	Y	2,500

C. No-Load Growth-Income Funds (continued)

Fund	Year Organized	Total Assets*	Number of Shareholders	Annual Rate of Return 1 Yr.	5 Yrs.	10 Yrs.	Services Offered† T	C	X	K	I	Minimum Initial Investment
Transamerica New Income Box 2438 Los Angeles, CA 90051 (800) 631-0749	66	4.6	1,741	27.7	8.9	7.9	N	N	Y	Y	Y	100
Unified Accumulation 20 N. Meridan St. 600 Guaranty Bldg. Indianapolis, IN 46204 (800) 428-4492	77	7.1	2,632	40.8	—	—	N	N	Y	N	N	1,000
Unified Income 20 N. Meridan St. 600 Guaranty Bldg. Indianapolis, IN 46204 (800) 428-4492	77	7.2	1,079	53.0	—	—	N	N	Y	Y	Y	500
Unified Mutual 20 N. Meridan St. 600 Guaranty Bldg. Indianapolis, IN 46204 (800) 428-4492	63	9.8	1,700	54.5	14.8	9.4	N	N	Y	Y	Y	200

USAA Income 9800 Fredericksburg Rd. San Antonio, TX 78288 (512) 690-3390	73	37.8	10,435	24.0	8.6	—	Y	N	Y	Y	1,000
Value Line Fund 711 Third Ave. New York, NY 10017 (800) 223-0818	49	193.0	30,657	46.3	25.7	20.5	N	N	Y	Y	250
Value Line Income 711 Third Ave. New York, NY 10017 (800) 223-0818	52	131.0	22,053	40.2	23.1	17.0	N	N	Y	Y	250
Value Line Leveraged Grth. 711 Third Ave. New York, NY 10017 (212) 687-3965	72	228.0	37,265	50.1	24.4	23.5	N	N	Y	Y	250
Vanguard Fixed Inc. Hi. Yld. 1250 Drummers Lane Valley Forge, PA 19482 (800) 523-7025	72	72.1	7,766	33.0	—	—	Y	Y	Y	Y	3,000

C. No-Load Growth-Income Funds (continued)

Fund	Year Organized	Total Assets*	Number of Shareholders	Annual Rate of Return 1 Yr.	5 Yrs.	10 Yrs.	Services Offered† T	C	X	K	I	Minimum Initial Investment
Vanguard Fixed Inc. Inv. Gr. 1250 Drummers Lane Valley Forge, PA 19482 (800) 523-7025	72	65.1	7,047	28.5	9.2	7.7	Y	Y	Y	Y	Y	3,000
Vanguard GNMA 1250 Drummers Lane Valley Forge, PA 19482 (800) 523-7025	80	123.4	11,013	26.8	—	—	N	N	Y	Y	Y	3,000
Vanguard Index Trust 1250 Drummers Lane Valley Forge, PA 19482 (800) 523-7025	75	188.4	5,596	58.9	17.4	—	Y	Y	Y	Y	Y	3,000
Variable Stock 1250 State St. Springfield, MA 01133 (413) 785-5811	57	6.7	729	49.2	16.7	—	N	N	N	Y	Y	50
Wellesley Income 1250 Drummers Lane Valley Forge, PA 19482 (800) 523-7025	68	108.2	9,155	39.9	13.0	10.1	Y	Y	Y	Y	Y	500

Wellington 1250 Drummers Lane Valley Forge, PA 19482 (800) 523-7025	28	627.2		76.7	52.7	17.1	10.4	Y Y Y Y	500
Windsor 1250 Drummers Lane Valley Forge, PA 19482 (800) 523-7025	58	1,564.8	90,998	58.9	21.3	18.0	Y Y Y Y	500
Wisconsin Income 312 E. Wisconsin Ave., Suite 601 Milwaukee, WI 53202 (414) 272-6133	29	14.4	4,162	35.0	7.3	4.9	Y N Y Y Y	500

III. NO-LOAD BOND FUNDS

Fund	Year Organized	Total Assets*	Number of Shareholders	Annual Rate of Return 1 Yr.	5 Yrs.	10 Yrs.	Services Offered† T	C	X	K	I	Minimum Initial Investment
Dreyfus A Bonds Plus 600 Madison Ave. New York, NY 10022 (800) 223-5525	76	$109.4	not available	12.9	—	—	N	N	Y	Y	N	$2,500
Fidelity Corporate Bond 82 Devonshire St. Boson, MA 02109 (800) 225-6190	70	152.6	not available	28.8	8.1	7.1	Y	N	Y	Y	Y	2,500
Fidelity Gov't. Securities 82 Devonshire St. Boston, MA 02109 (800) 225-6190	79	82.3	5,525	11.5	—	—	Y	N	Y	Y	Y	1,000
Financial Bond Shares 7503 Marin Dr. P.O. Box 2040 Englewood, CO 80111 (800) 525-9831	77	8.1	1,093	26.0	9.0	—	Y	N	Y	Y	Y	1,000

Assets in $millions as of June 30, 1983. Source: Monitored Assets Corporation.
†T = Wire Transfer X = Intra-Group Exchange I = IRA Plan Available Y = Available
C = Check Writing K = Keogh Plan Available N = Not available

Fund for U.S. Gov't. Sec. 421 Seventh Ave. Pittsburgh, PA 15219 (800) 245-2423	69	52.0	6,839	35.2	8.9	6.9	Y N Y Y	250
North Star Bond 600 Dain Tower Minneapolis, MN 55402 (612) 371-7875	77	13.0	93	18.8	—	—	N N Y Y	1,000
Safeco Special Bond Safeco Plaza, T-15 Seattle, WA 98185 (800) 426-6730	69	2.1	276	22.3	9.5	8.5	N N Y N	200
Stein Roe Bond 150 S. Wacker Dr. Chicago, IL 60606 (800) 621-0615	78	84.1	3,300	13.6	—	—	N N Y Y	2,500

IV. TAX-FREE NO-LOAD FUNDS

A. Tax-Free Money Funds

Fund	Year Organized	Total Assets*	Number of Shareholders	Annual Rate of Return 1 Yr.	5 Yrs.	10 Yrs.	Services Offered† T	C	X	K	I	Minimum Initial Investment
Active Assets Tax-Free Tr. Five World Trade Center New York, NY 10048 (800) 221-3778	81	$ 138.4	5,499	5.41	—	—	Y	Y	N	N	N	$20,000
Babson Tax-Free Inc. Three Crown Ctr. 2440 Pershing Rd. Kansas City, MO 64108 (800) 821-5591	81	3.2	98	—	—	—	Y	Y	Y	N	N	1,000
Calvert Tax-Free Reserves 1700 Pennsylvania Ave., NW Washington, DC 20006 (800) 368-2748	81	125.8	4,096	5.82	—	—	Y	Y	Y	N	N	2,000
Centennial Tax-Exempt Tr. 3600 S. Yosemite St. Denver, CO 80237 (303) 770-2345	81	42.2	1,295	5.07	—	—	N	N	Y	N	N	500

Prud.-Bache Tax-Fr. MF 100 Gold St. New York, NY 10038 (800) 221-7984	79	143.9	6,633	5.44	—	Y	Y	Y	Y	2,500
CMA Tax-Exempt Fund 633 Third Ave. 29th Floor New York, NY 10017 (212) 221-7210	81	2535.6	N/A	5.47	—	N	Y	N	N	$20,000 relationship required
Delaware Tax-Free Money 10 Penn Center Plaza Philadelphia, PA 19103 (800) 523-1640	81	34.0	1426	5.40	—	Y	Y	Y	N	5,000
Dreyfus Tax-Ex. M. M. 600 Madison Ave. New York, NY 10022 (800) 645-6561	80	1512.2	30,278	5.70	—	Y	Y	Y	N	5,000

*All figures in $millions as of June 30, 1983. Source: Donoghue's MONEY FUND REPORTS ® of Holliston, MA 01746.

†T = Wire Transfer   X = Intra-Group Exchange   I = IRA Plan Available   Y = Available
C = Check Writing   K = Keogh Plan Available   N = Not available

A. Tax-Free Money Funds (continued)

Fund	Year Organized	Total Assets*	Number of Shareholders	Annual Rate of Return 1 Yr.	5 Yrs.	10 Yrs.	Services Offered† T	C	X	K	I	Minimum Initial Investment
Fidelity Tax-Ex. M. M. Tr. 82 Devonshire St. Boston, MA 02109 (800) 225-6190	80	1959.2	12,373	5.69	—	—	Y	Y	Y	N	N	10,000
Midwest Group Tax-Free Tr. M.M. 522 Dixie Terminal Bldg. Cincinnati, OH 45202 (800) 543-0407	81	21.7	637	5.37	—	—	Y	Y	Y	N	N	2,500
Franklin Tax-Free Inc. 155 Bovet Rd. San Mateo, CA 94402 (800) 227-6781	77	62.7	2,873	5.67	—	—	Y	N	Y	Y	Y	500
IDS Tax-Free Money 1000 Roanoke Bldg. Minneapolis, MN 55402 (800) 328-8300	80	61.6	2,531	5.67	—	—	Y	Y	Y	N	N	2,000
Parkway Tax-Free Reserve The Rodney Bldg. 3411 Silverside Rd. Wilmington, DE 19810 (800) 441-7786	81	29.6	797	5.11	—	—	Y	Y	Y	N	N	1,000

Sears Tax-Free Daily Five World Trade Center New York, NY 10048 (800) 221-2685	81	265.5	5,321	5.80	—	Y	Y	Y	N	5,000
Lehman Tax-Free M. M. 55 Water St. New York, NY 10041 (800) 221-5350	82	102.2	965	—	—	Y	Y	Y	N	2,500
Lexington Tax-Free Daily In. 580 Sylvan Ave. Englewood Cliffs, NJ 07632 (800) 526-4791	80	50.8	1,825	5.86	—	Y	Y	Y	N	1,000
Muni. Work. Cap. Tr. 200 Berkley St. Boston, MA 02116 (617) 423-3500	80	8.3	739	5.13	—	Y	Y	Y	N	1,000
Muni. Cash Reserve Mgmt. One Battery Park Plaza New York, NY 10004 (212) 742-6003	81	619.5	15,381	5.81	—	Y	Y	N	N	10,000

A. Tax-Free Money Funds (continued)

Fund	Year Organized	Total Assets*	Number of Shareholders	Annual Rate of Return 1 Yr.	5 Yrs.	10 Yrs.	Services Offered† T	C	X	K	I	Minimum Initial Investment
Nuveen Tax-Exempt M. M. 115 S. La Salle St. Chicago, IL 60603 (800) 621-2431	81	905.3	2,077	5.72	—	—	Y	N	N	N	N	25,000
Scudder Tax-Free Money 175 Federal St. Boston, MA 02110 (800) 453-9500	80	149.6	3,821	5.47	—	—	Y	Y	Y	N	N	1,000
Shearson FA Muni. Two World Trade Center New York, NY 10048 (800) 221-3636	82	128.9	2,464	5.07	—	—	N	Y	Y	N	N	5,000
T. Rowe Price Tax-Ex. Money Fund 100 E. Pratt St. Baltimore, MD 21202 (800) 638-5660	81	636.4	16,229	6.08	—	—	Y	Y	Y	N	N	2,000
Tax-Free Money Fund 1345 Ave. of the Americas New York, NY 10105 (800) 221-2990	80	225.1	2,608	5.29	—	—	Y	Y	Y	N	N	5,000

Fund	Year Organized	Total Assets*	Number of Shareholders	Annual Rate of Return 1 Yr.	5 Yrs.	10 Yrs.	Services Offered† T	C	X	K	I	Minimum Initial Investment
Vanguard Muni. Bd. M. M. P.O. Box 2600 Valley Forge, PA 19460 (800) 523-7025	80	281.9	6,194	5.70	—	—	Y	Y	Y	Y	Y	3,000

B. No-Load Tax-Free Bond Funds

Fund	Year Organized	Total Assets*	Number of Shareholders	Annual Rate of Return 1 Yr.	5 Yrs.	10 Yrs.	Services Offered† T	C	X	K	I	Minimum Initial Investment
Composite Tax-Exempt Bond Seafirst Financial Ctr., 9th Floor Spokane, WA 99201 (800) 541-0830	76	63.2	4,650	33.5	1.0	—	N	N	Y	Y	Y	1,000
Dreyfus Tax-Exempt Bond 600 Madison Ave. New York, NY 10022 (800) 223-5525	76	1,761.6	79,261	32.2	2.0	—	Y	N	Y	N	N	2,500

*Assets in $millions as of June 30, 1983. Source: Monitored Assets Corporation.
†T = Wire Transfer X = Intra-Group Exchange I = IRA Plan Available Y = Available
C = Check Writing K = Keogh Plan Available N = Not available
** "__" means not available.

B. No-Load Tax-Free Bond Funds (continued)

Fund	Year Organized	Total Assets*	Number of Shareholders	Annual Rate of Return 1 Yr.	5 Yrs.	10 Yrs.	Services Offered† T	C	X	K	I	Minimum Initial Investment
Elfun Tax-Exempt Income 112 Prospect St., P.O. Box 7900 Stamford, CT 06904 (203) 357-4141	77	188.6	17,122	40.6	—	—	N	N	N	N	N	1,000
Fidelity Muni. Bond 82 Devonshire St. Boston, MA 02109 (800) 225-6190	76	667.9	not available	31.6	1.4	—	Y	N	Y	N	N	2,500
Nuveen Municipal Bond 115 S. La Salle St. Chicago, IL 60603 (312) 782-2655	76	255.4	46,409	30.3	3.5	—	N	N	N	N	N	1,000
Rowe Price Tax-Free Income 100 E. Pratt St. Baltimore, MD 21202 (800) 638-1527	76	972.6	46,090	31.1	5.1	—	Y	Y	Y	Y	Y	1,000
Scudder Managed Muni. Bond 175 Federal St. Boston, MA 02110 (800) 225-2470	76	450.5	14,005	35.3	4.1	—	Y	N	Y	N	N	1,000

Selected Tax-Exempt Bond 111 W. Washington St. Chicago, IL 60602 (800) 621-7321	77	4.1	not available	26.9	0.4	—	Y N Y N N	1,000
Stein Roe Tax-Exempt Bond 150 S. Wacker Drive Chicago, IL 60606 (800) 621-0615	76	197.6	3,709	46.5	—	—	N N Y N N	2,500
Vanguard Muni. High Yield 1250 Drummers Lane Valley Forge, PA 19482 (800) 523-7025	76	150.1	6,603	30.6	—	—	Y Y Y N N	3,000
Vanguard Muni. Inter Term 1250 Drummers Lane Valley Forge, PA 19482 (800) 523-7025	76	139.9	5,732	23.5	2.3	—	Y Y Y N N	3,000
Vanguard Muni. Long Term 1250 Drummers Lane Valley Forge, PA 19482 (800) 523-7025	76	225.7	8,406	29.9	1.3	—	Y Y Y N N	3,000

Index

ABOUT THE AUTHORS

William E. Donoghue is an outspoken advocate of depositor's and investor's rights and a nationally recognized expert on corporate cash management, money market mutual funds and consumer money market instruments. Since 1968 he has trained cash management professionals from all of the top 50 banks, half of the Fortune 1000 corporations and thousands of smaller corporations, originally as moderator of Wharton Executive Seminars and later as Executive Director of Cash Management Institute, sponsor of the CMI National Forum, the premier spring cash management conference. Mr. Donoghue is a certified public accountant, registered investment advisor, nationally syndicated columnist, author of The Cash Managment Manual and publisher of three financial newsletters. He has had two bestselling books with Harper & Row, *William E. Donoghue's Complete Money Market Guide* and *William E. Donoghue's No-Load Mutual Fund Guide*. A popular and controversial speaker, he is a frequent guest on national radio and television programs including Wall $treet Week, The Today Show and PBS's Nightly Business Report.

Thomas Tilling is a private investor and financial writer. He lives with his wife and children in Connecticut.

MONEY TALKS!
How to get it and How to keep it!

BANTAM IS PLUGGED IN TO COMPUTERS

We Deliver!
And So Do These Bestsellers.